TABLE OF CONTENTS

SPECIAL BONUS

Want some free and deeply discounted coloring books and / or art supplies? Subscribe to our email list below and join our fanbase of creatives!

Scan QR Code Below

INTRODUCTION:

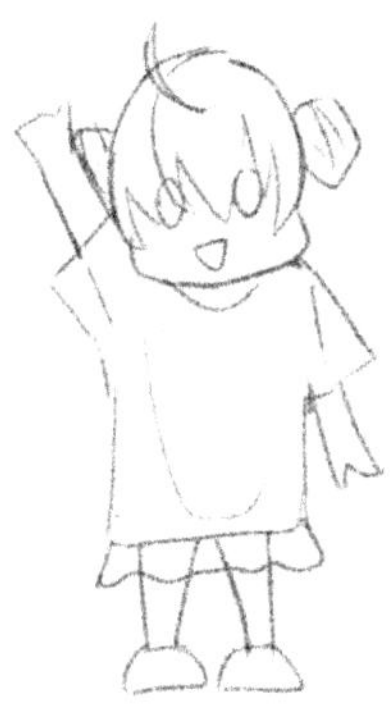

Hello future artists! I see you have an interest in drawing Kawaii Art!
Look no further, we shall dive into this world together and you'll come out as a pro
in all things cute, chibi, and frilly.

Before we get started, traveler, like any newcomer, we need context.

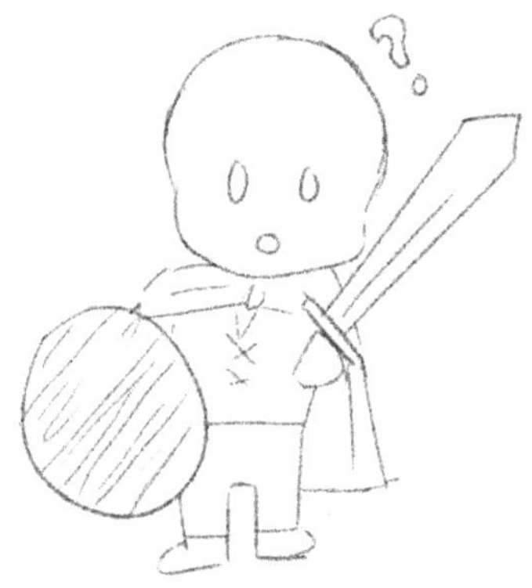

What is Anime?

A Japanese hand-drawn and computer-assisted animation.
In America we say anime to signify its origin, but in Japan anime just means any type of animation.

What do you mean by "Cute Stuff"?

Listen here. No, come closer as I whisper…"Have you ever watched *Sailor Moon*?"

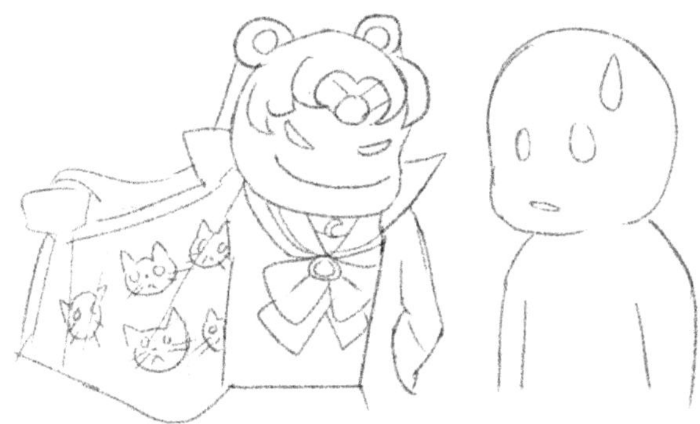

"YOU HAVEN'T? WHAT?!?!"
"Well, we mean things like cute animals, cute food designs, flowers, hearts, cute outfits
and accessories. You also CAN'T GO WITHOUT A CUTE POSE! That is a must.
There is a huge appreciation for all things cute, so it's important to know how to draw such things."

We will go over these art styles, so be prepared!

Anime: What you see in a normal anime. Even though the styles vary, we'll go over the most known style.
Manga: This will be a more Japanese comic book style that the anime is based on.
Chibi: Think big heads, and small bodies, to make it extra cute!
Kawaii: Cute patterns and styles, so very round and soft-looking drawings.

What you need:

Simple!
-Paper
-Pencil
-Eraser

…Remember, I will teach you the basic techniques. From there, don't forget to practice.
Even just doodling will help you to get better!

I would highly suggest drawing from references!

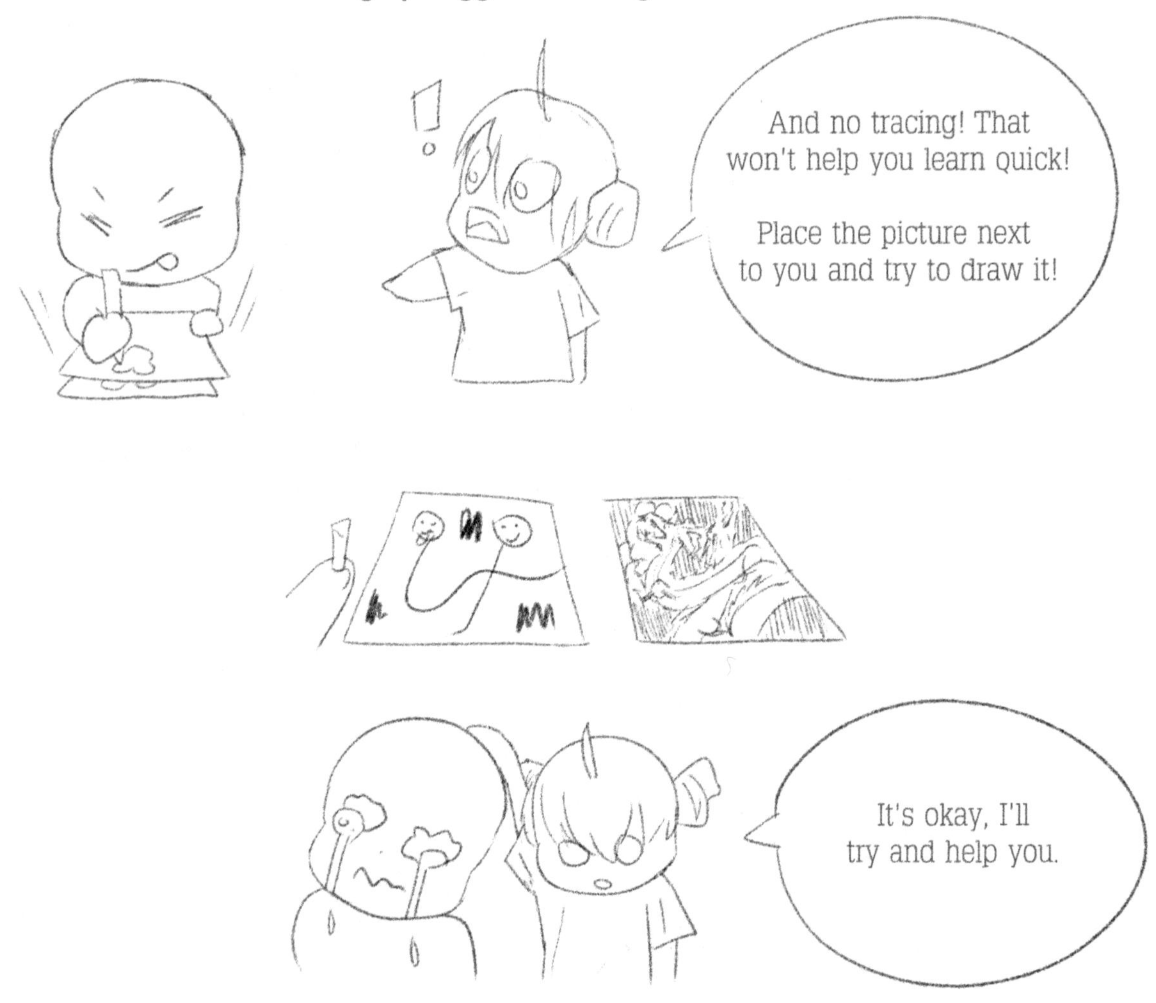

Well, I see there is a lot to do, so
Let's begin!

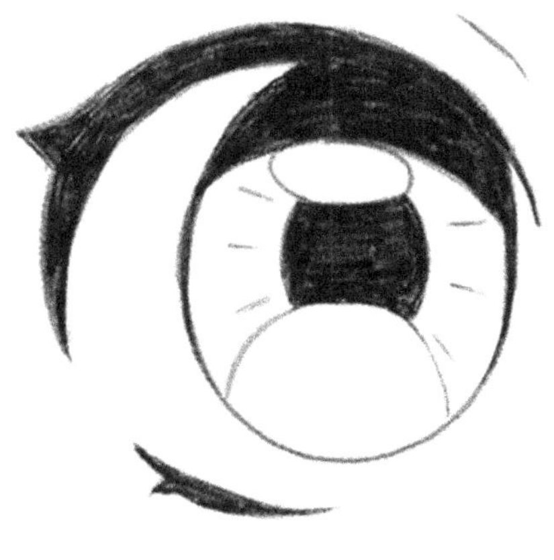 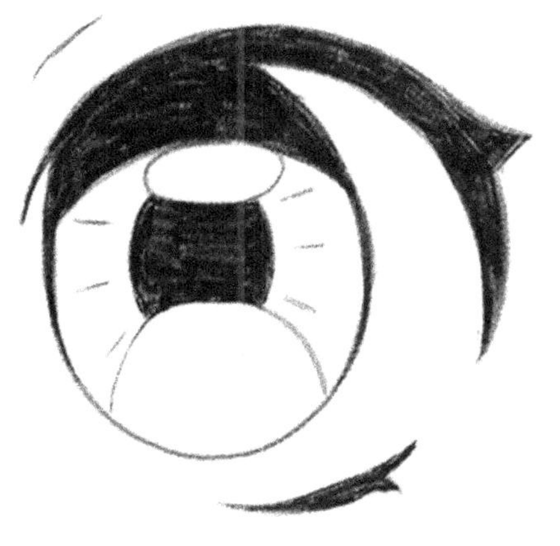

CHAPTER 1
Drawing Eyes

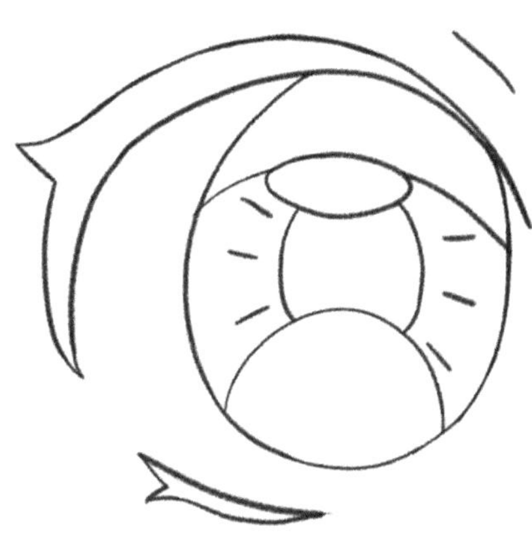 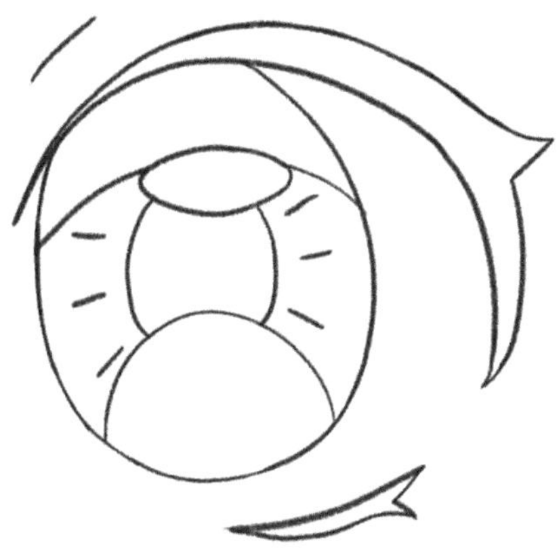

EYES

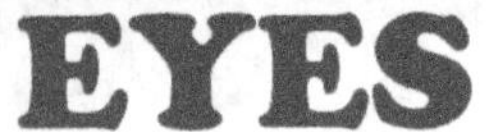

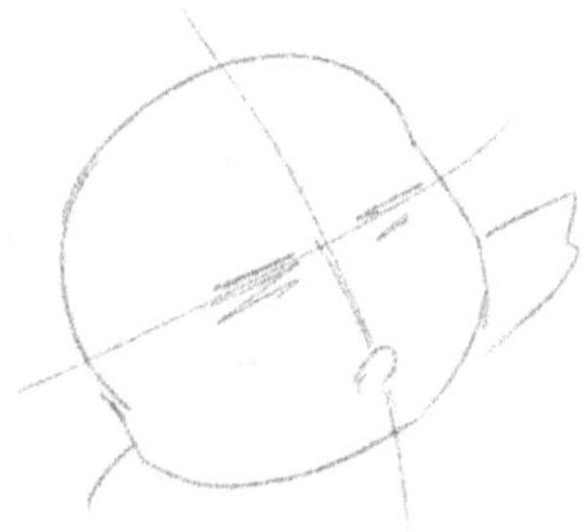

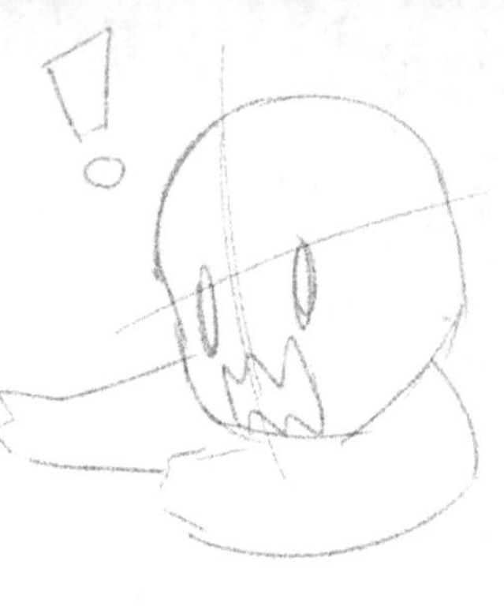

**Important tip: Please sketch lightly!!!
You might need to erase a few times
and no one wants noticable eraser marks!**

There are many different eyes, so you can be as creative as you want!
Remember that large expressive eyes are a common feature of cute
anime character design, as they can make characters appear more innocent and youthful.

Here are some trade secrets.

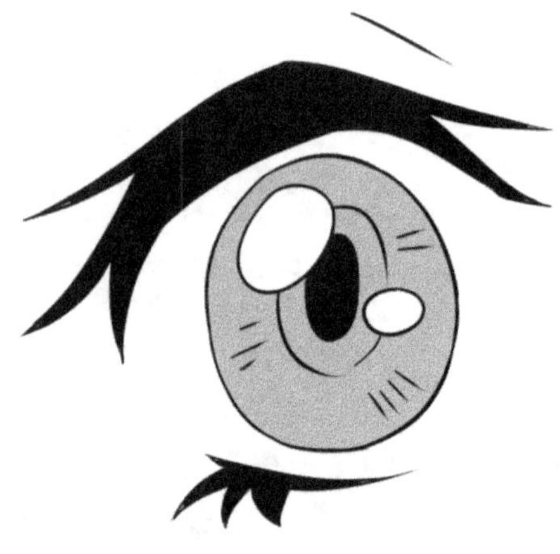

These eyes are for young people!
Please don't draw an old man with
these eyes.

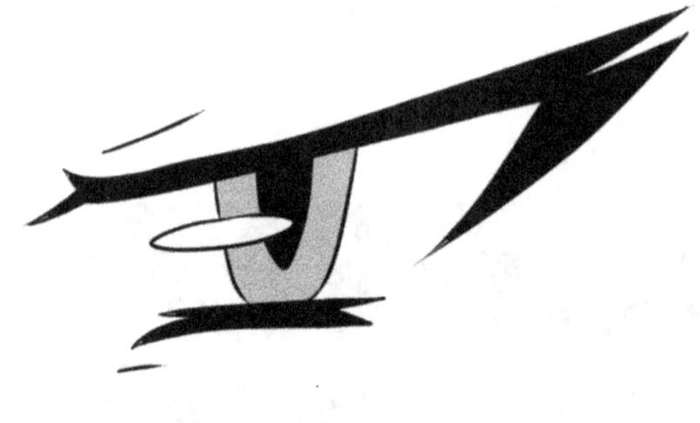

When people get older, their eyes
get thinner and smaller, like this.

Okay, we can continue...

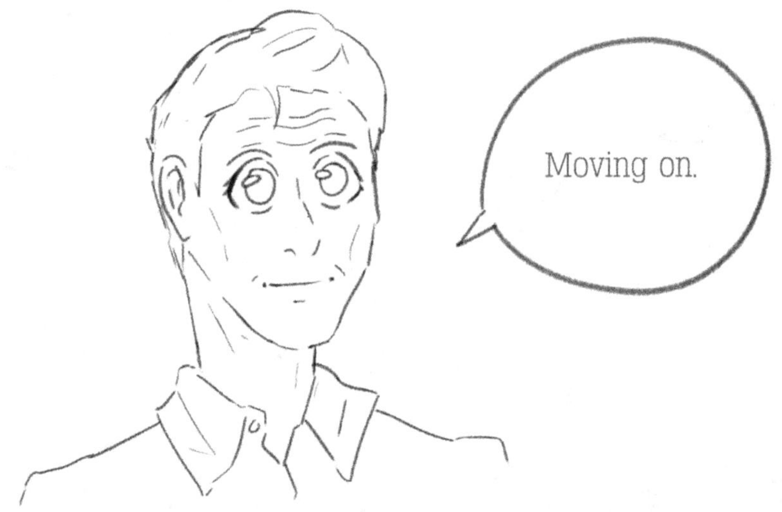

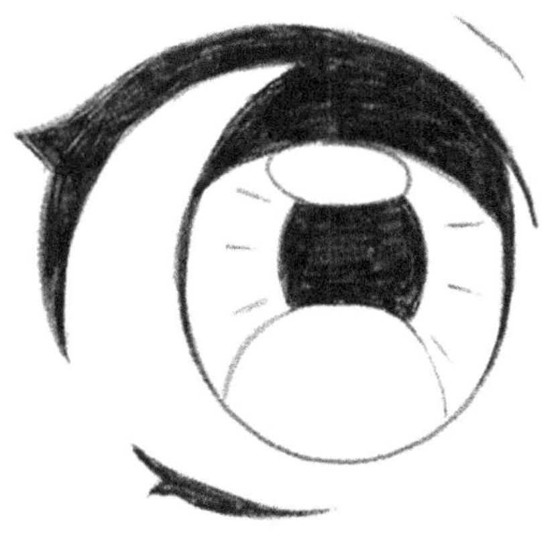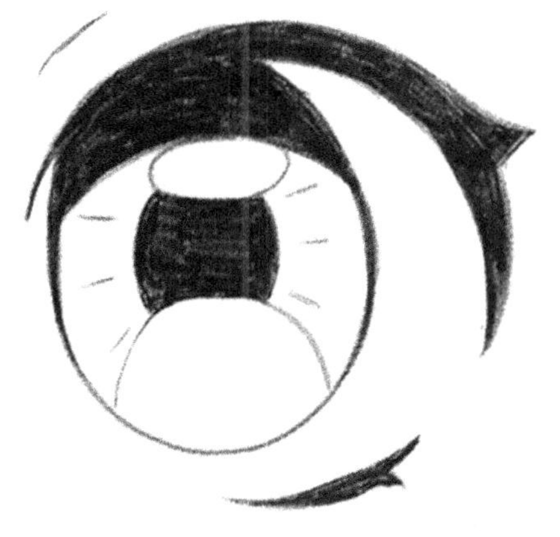

CHAPTER 1

Drawing Eyes

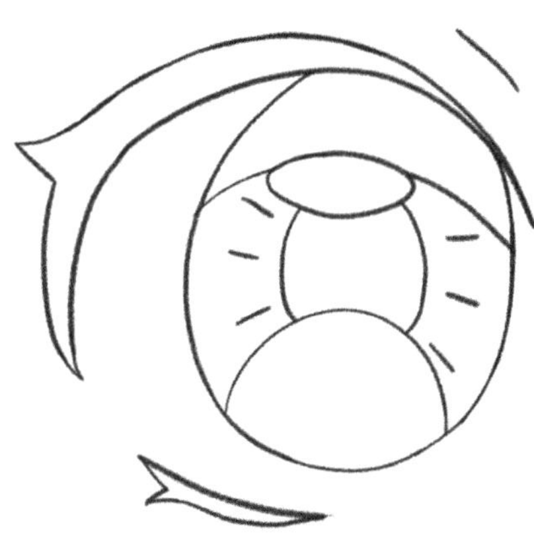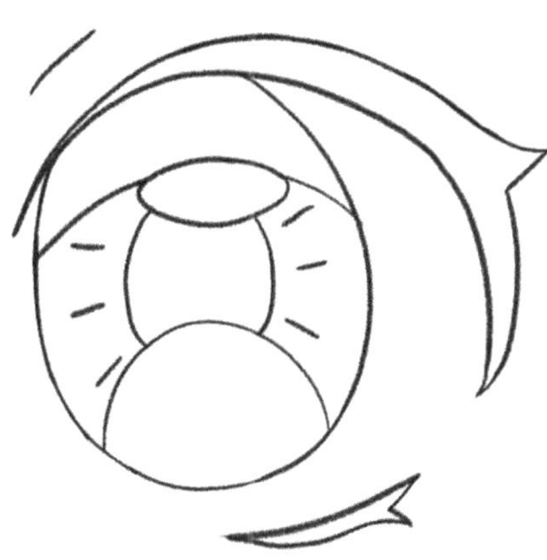

EYES

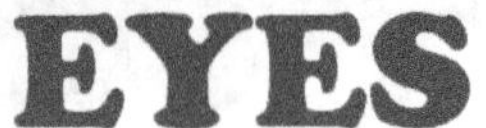

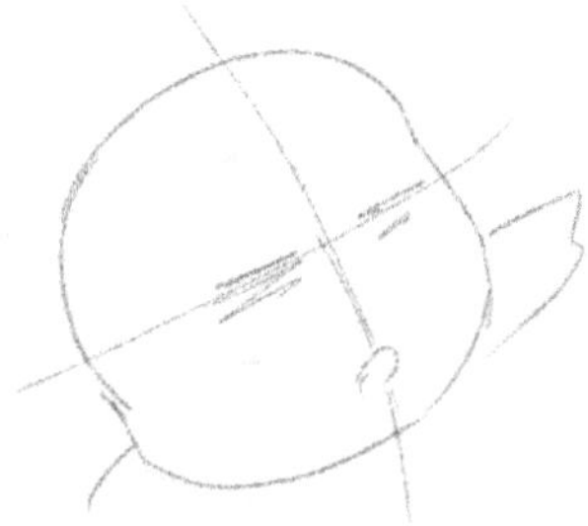

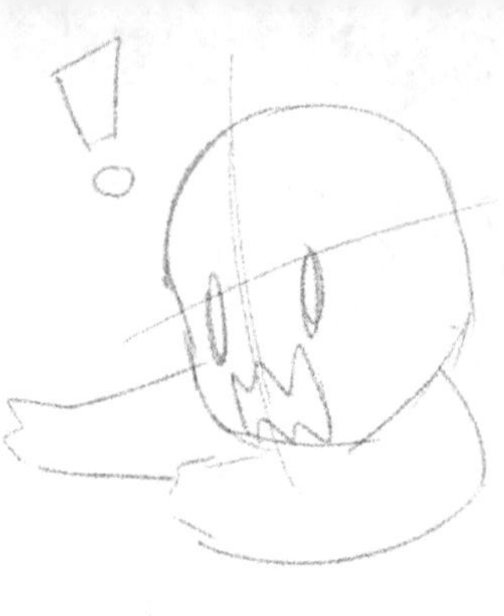

There are many different eyes, so you can be as creative as you want!
Remember that large expressive eyes are a common feature of cute
anime character design, as they can make characters appear more innocent and youthful.

Here are some trade secrets.

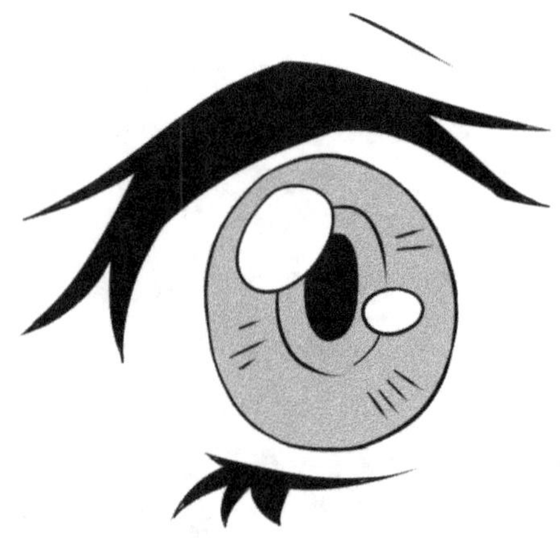

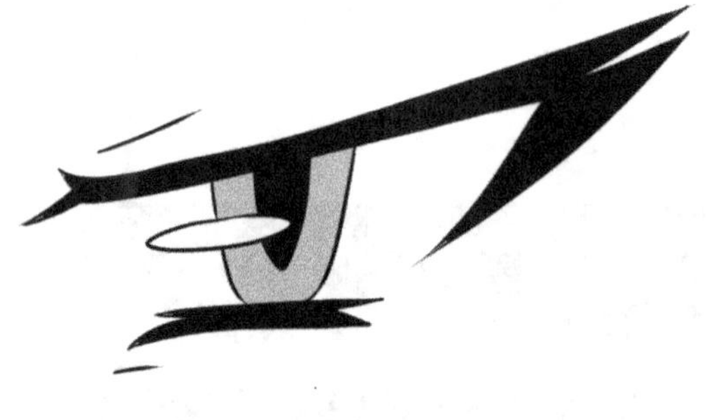

These eyes are for young people!
Please don't draw an old man with
these eyes.

When people get older, their eyes
get thinner and smaller, like this.

Okay, we can continue...

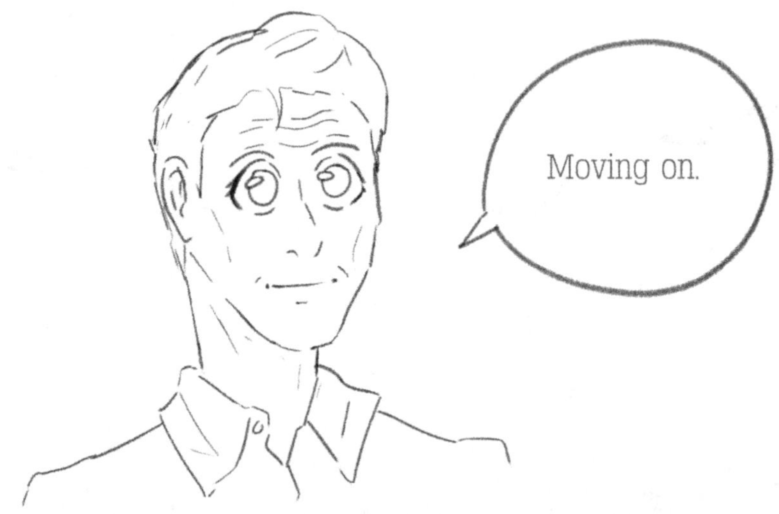

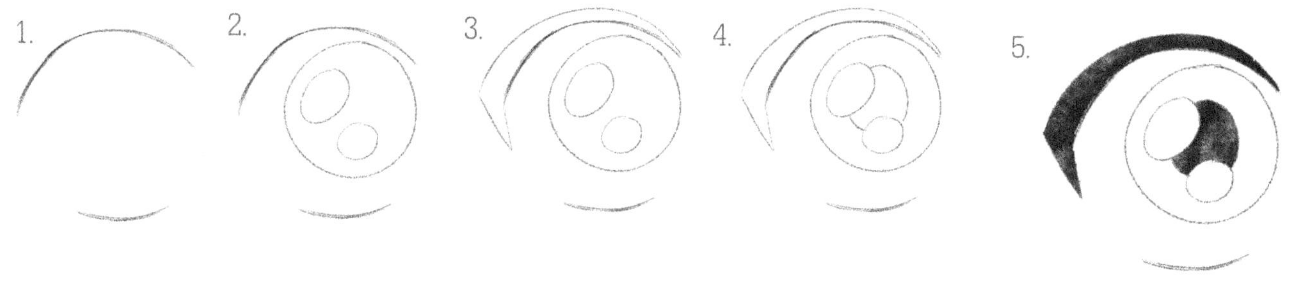

Mirrored version: Note that the eye highlights NEVER get mirrored!

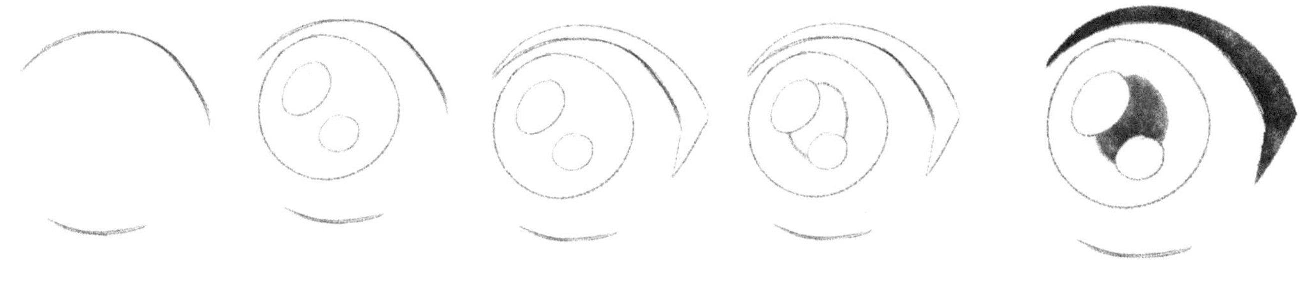

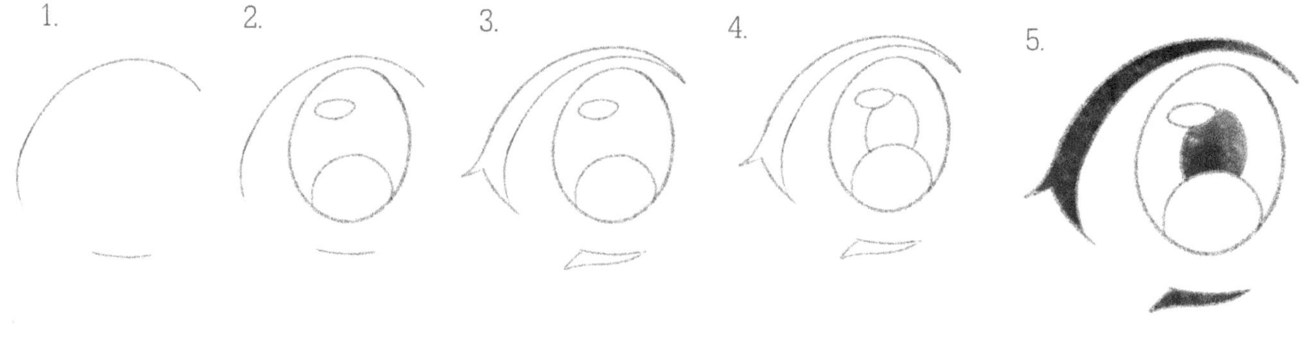

Mirrored version:

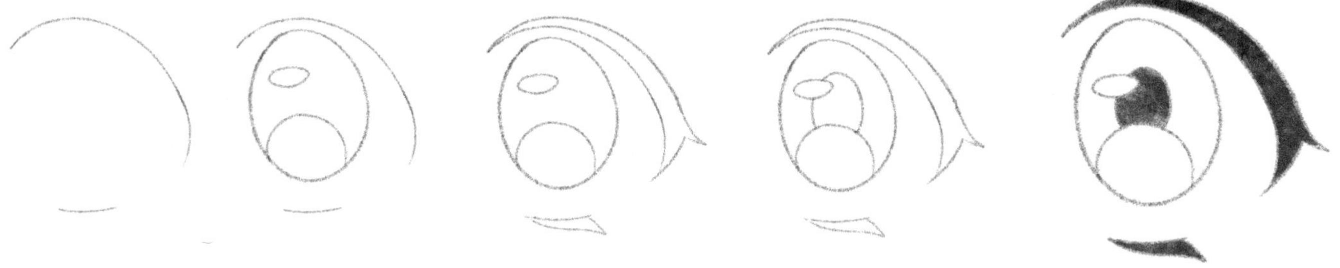

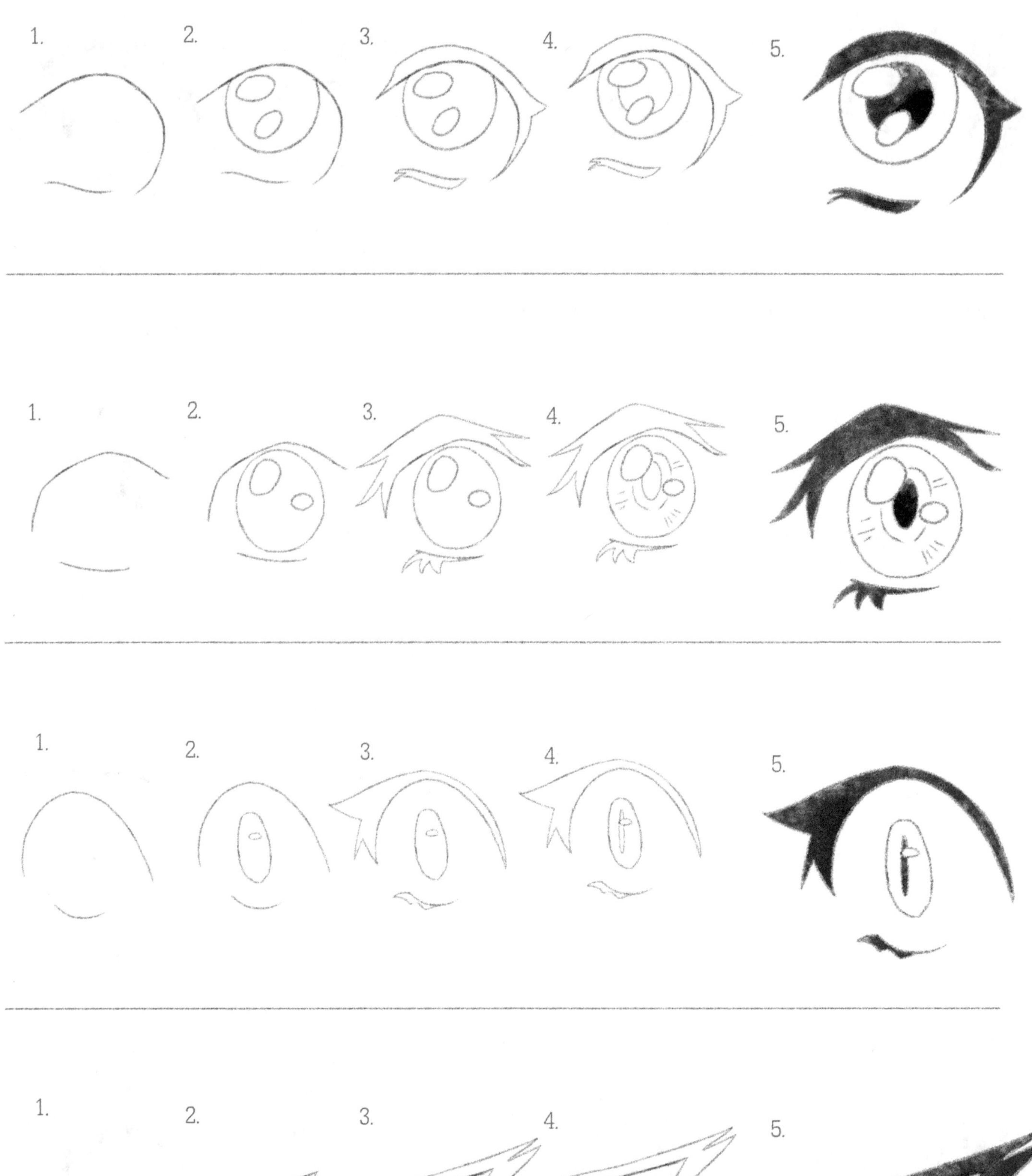

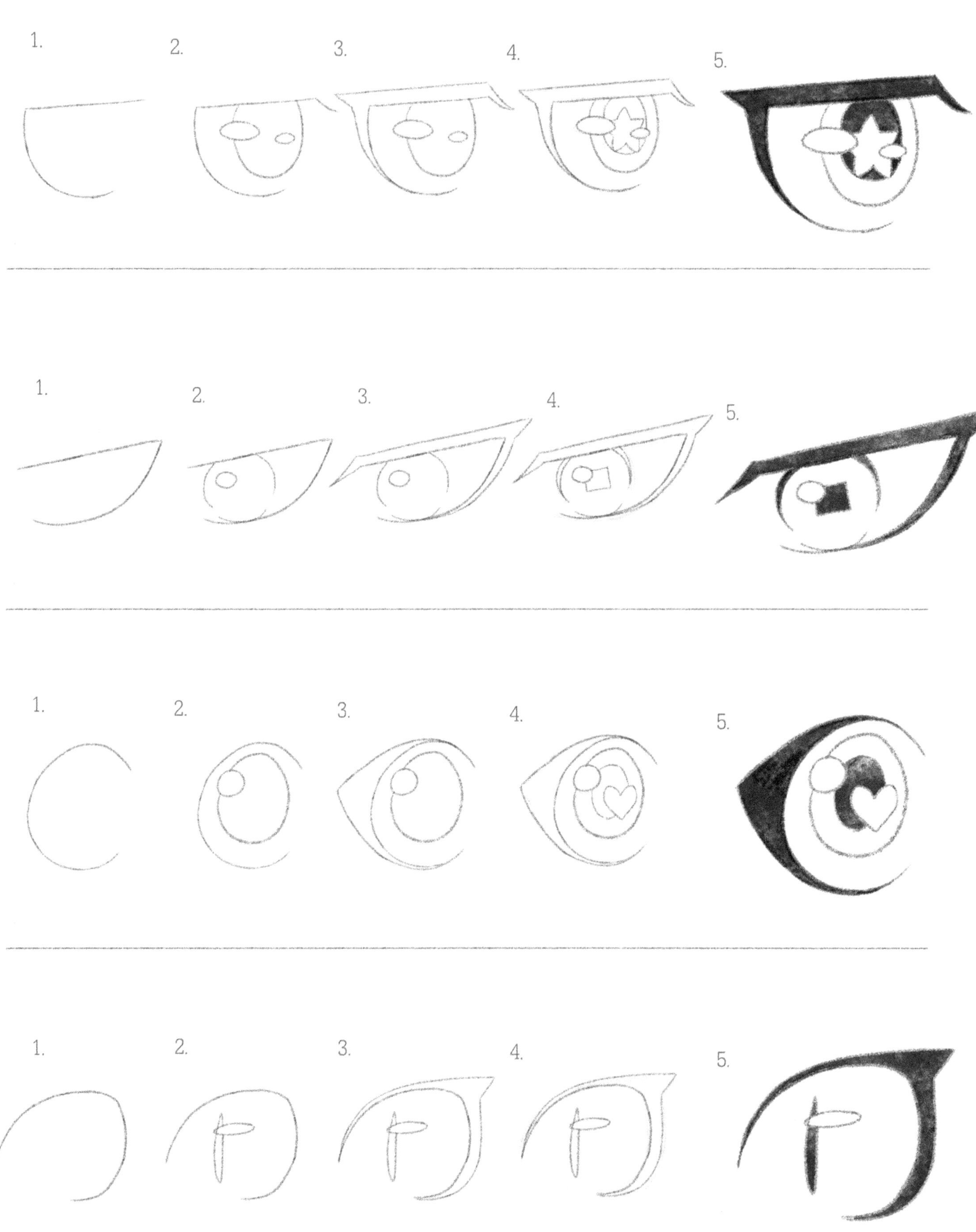

The eyes get squished into long ovals and the eyelashes begin
on one end and then are gone on the other side.

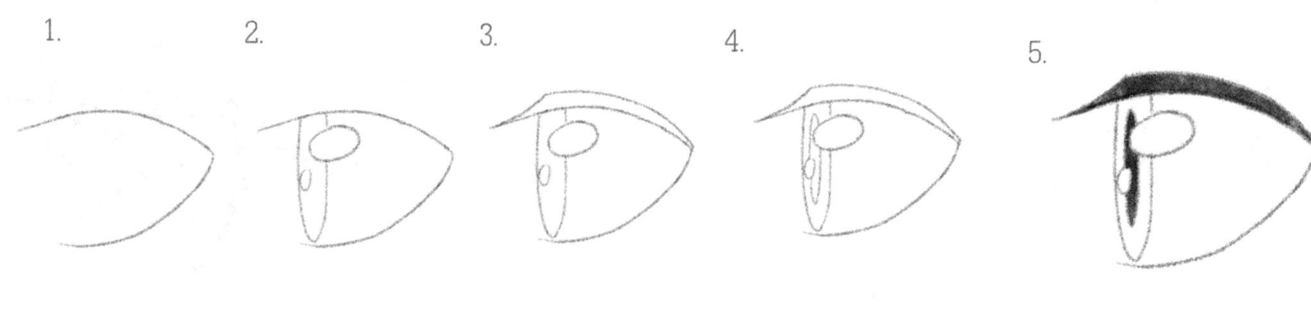

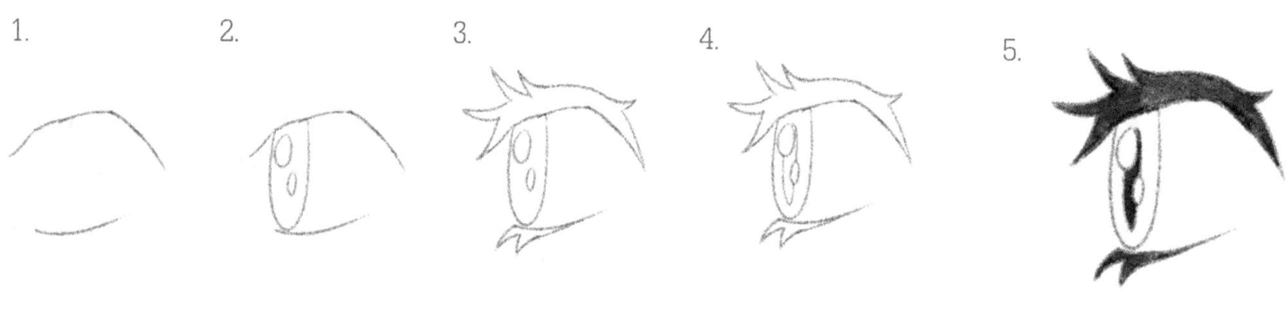

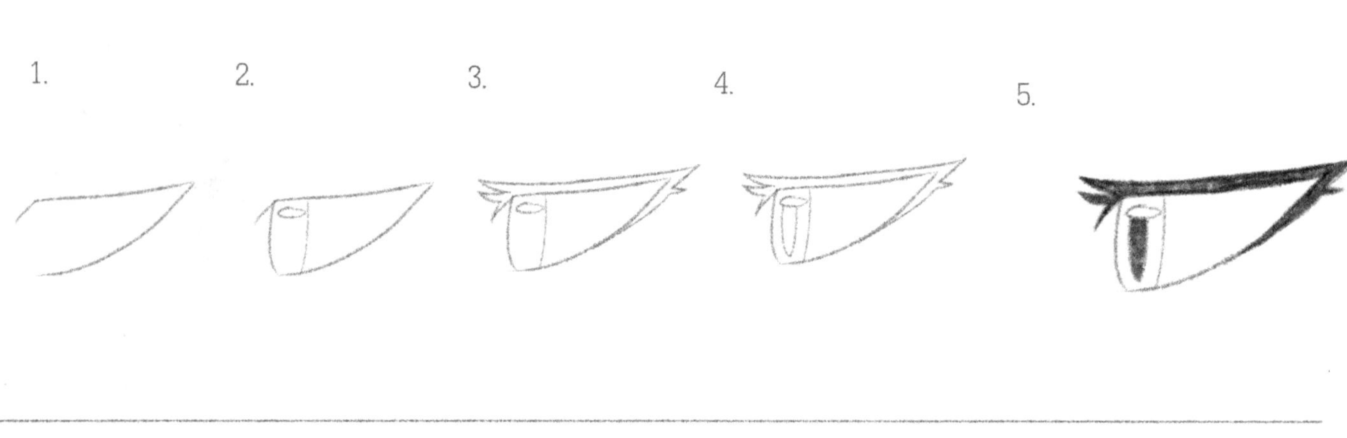

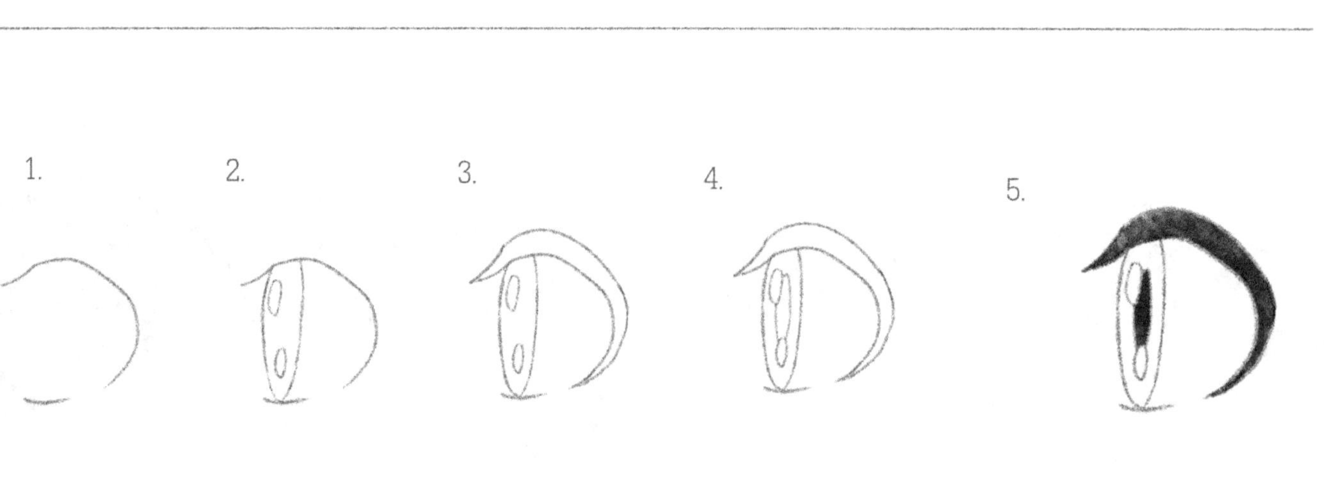

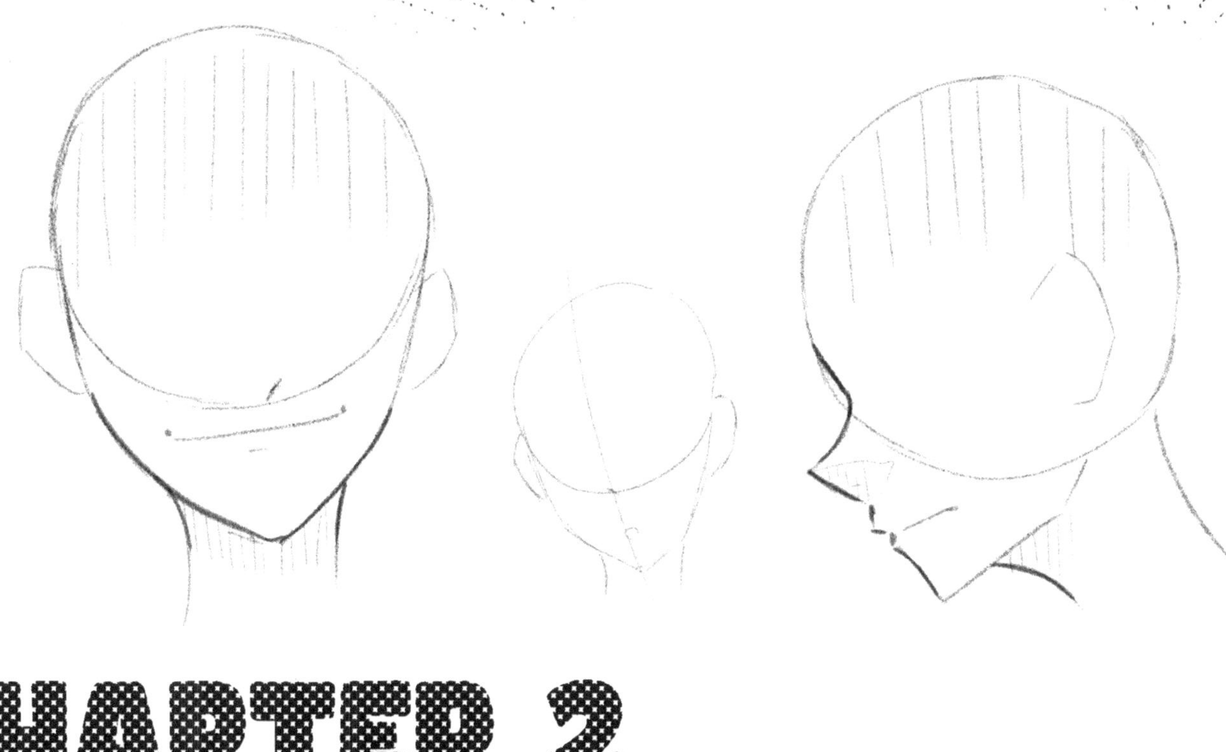

CHAPTER 2

Head, Noses, & Mouths

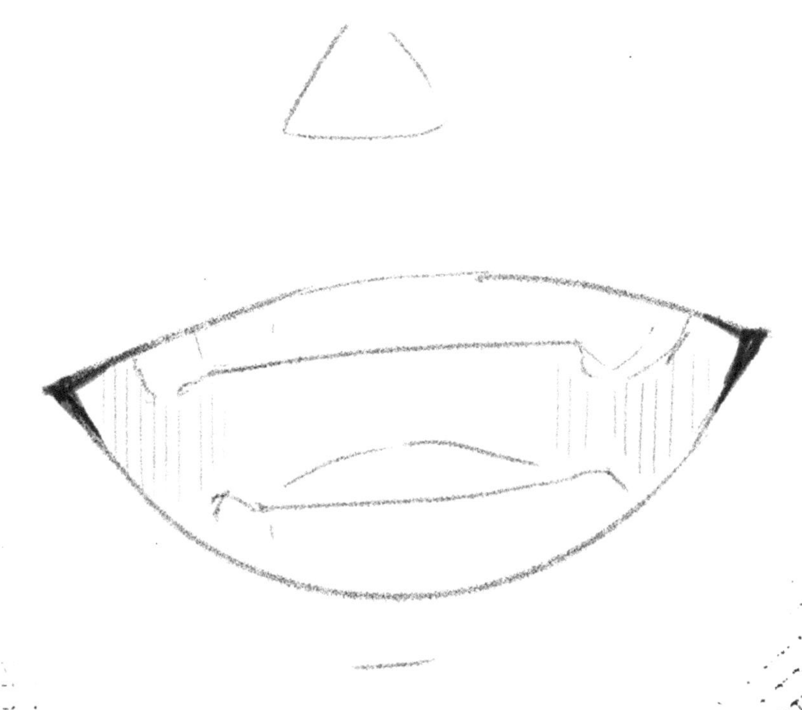

NOSES

Alright, there are a few noses that can be drawn for the anime genre, such as:

The dot

The comma

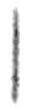

The line

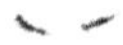

The two commas

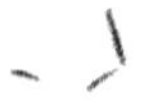

The more detailed nose

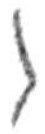

The flat arrow

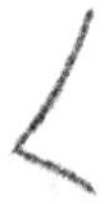

The side profile *

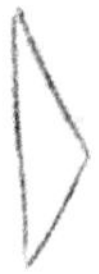

The nose shadow (side)

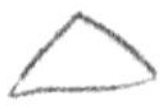

The nose shadow (down)

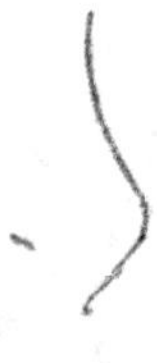

More detailed nose

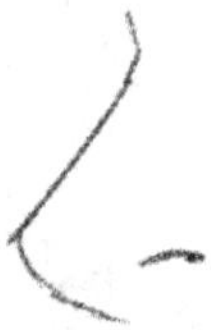

Side profile detailed nose *

* = The side profile noses

Any of these noses are fine to use. It all just depends on your preference!

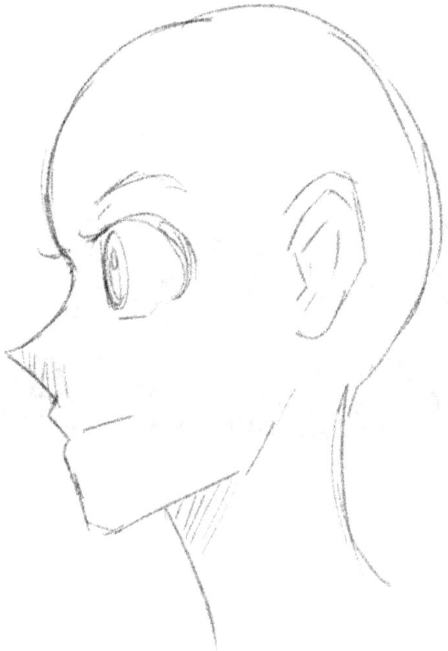

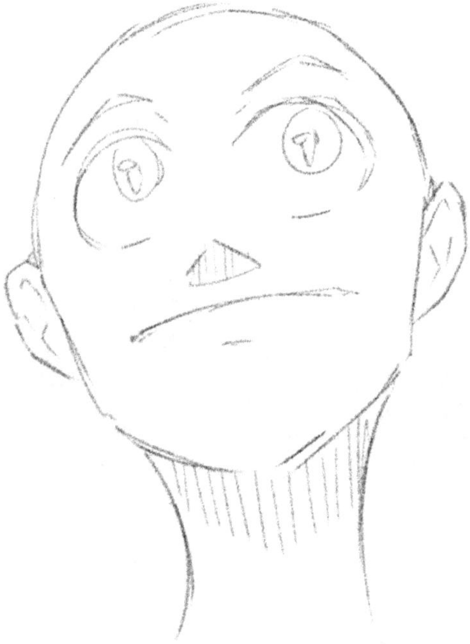

MOUTHS

Alright, now on to the mouth. I know it is scary, you have got teeth and a lot more in there to scare you, but no worries, I will help you draw it all.

Let's start easy and then up the level each time!

Level 1

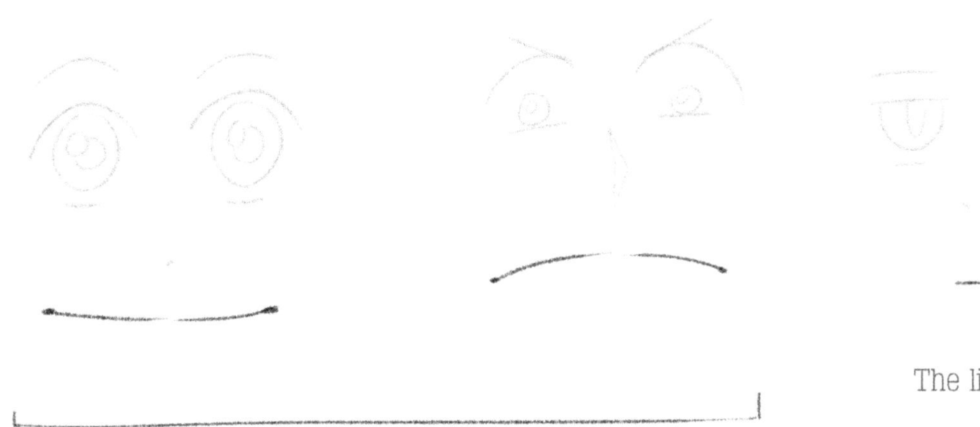

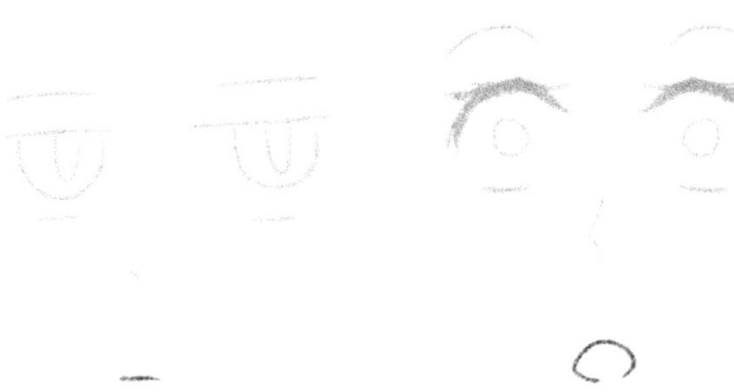

The line.

Circle with bottom missing.

STEP 1 : Draw two dots! It will help you map out the length of the mouth!

STEP 2 : Try to connect them but not all the way.

Level 2

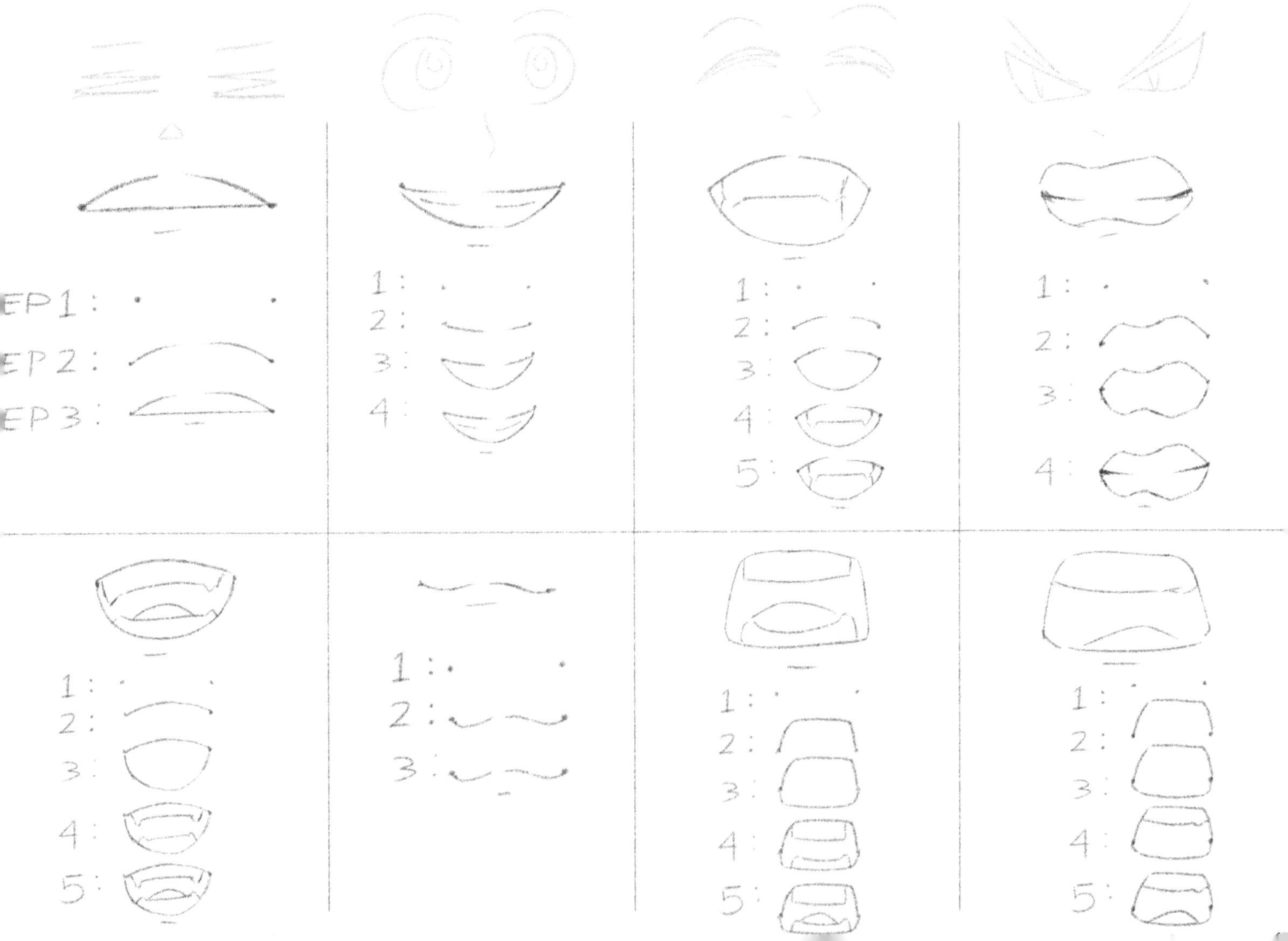

EP 1 :
EP 2 :
EP 3 :

1 :
2 :
3 :
4 :

1 :
2 :
3 :
4 :
5 :

1 :
2 :
3 :
4 :

1 :
2 :
3 :
4 :
5 :

1 :
2 :
3 :

1 :
2 :
3 :
4 :
5 :

1 :
2 :
3 :
4 :
5 :

HEADS   Now on to the head.

1. Draw your best circle.

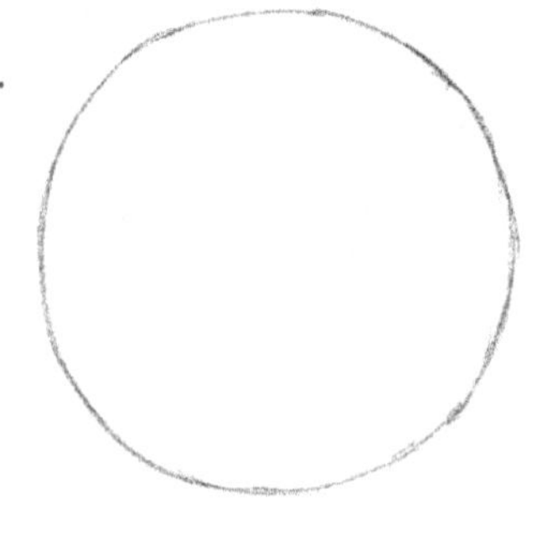

2. Now a line through the middle.

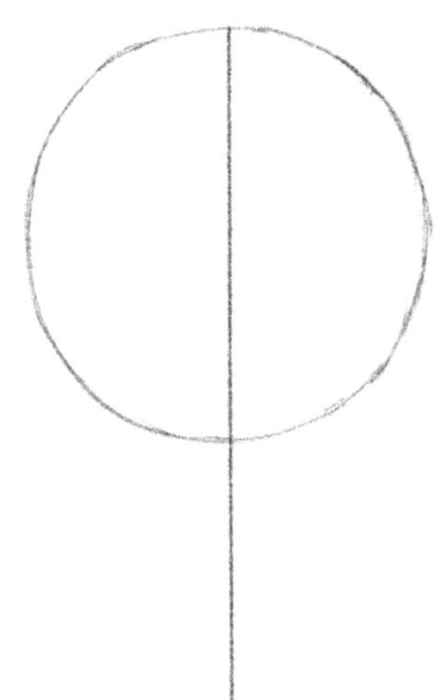

3. Again, through the middle.

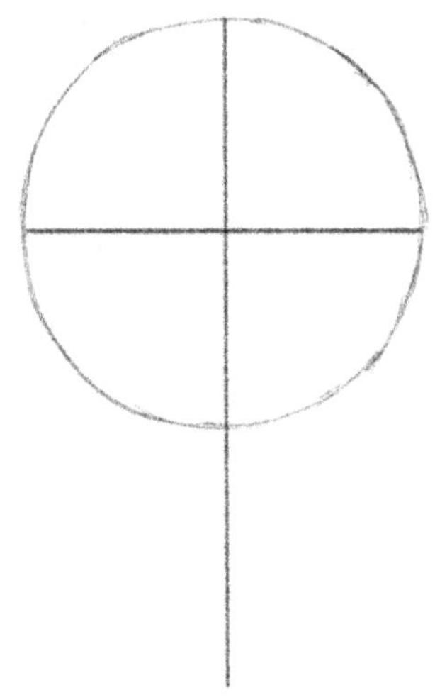

4. Now add these three little lines to help find the chin.

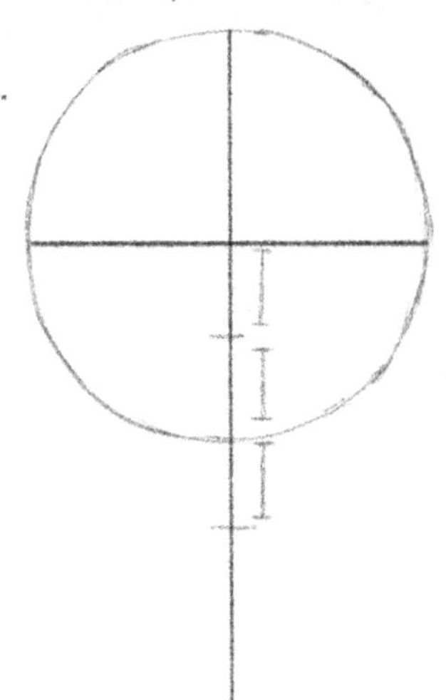

5. Draw the chin part of the face. The side bits end where the second line of the face is.

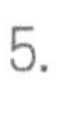
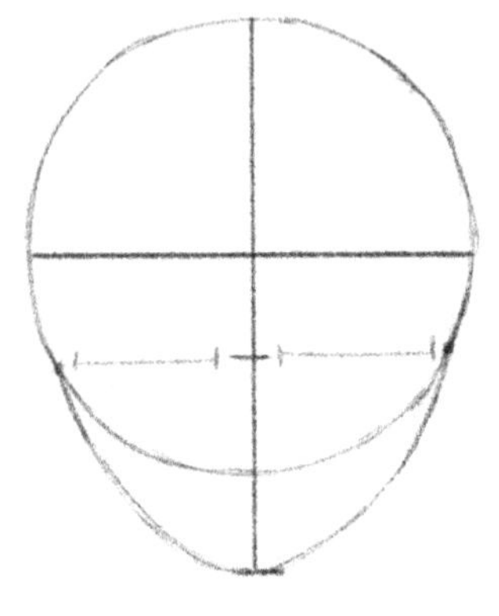

6. Draw the eyes below the line.

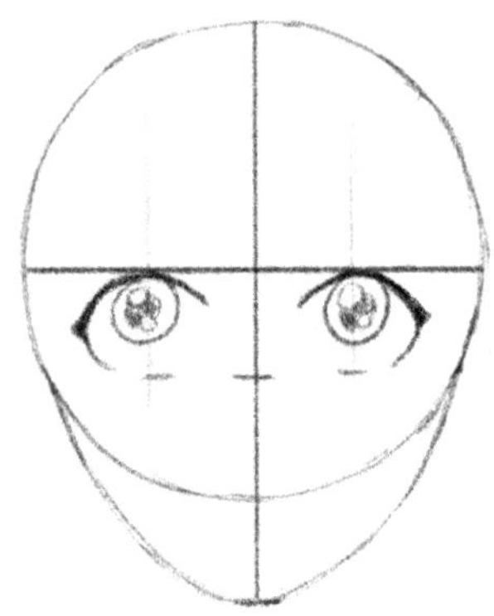

7. Now the mouth, eyebrows, and nose.

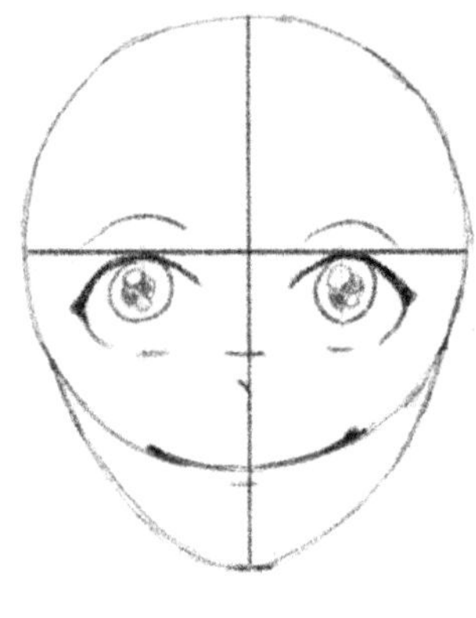

8. Neck and ears go in these areas.

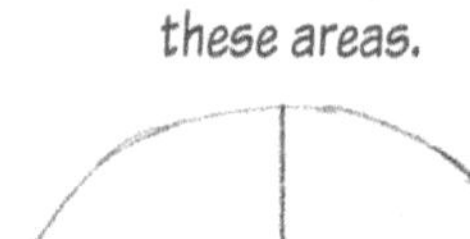
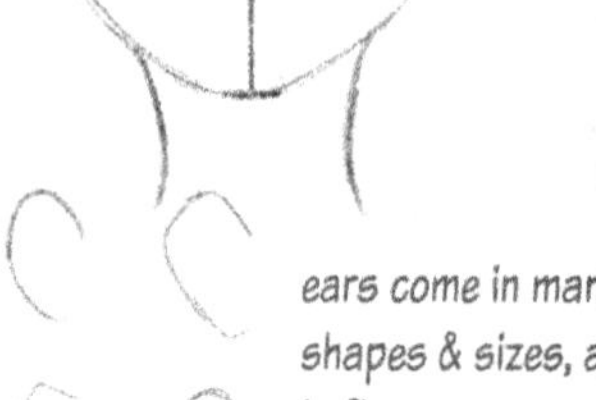

ears come in man[y] shapes & sizes, a[nd] is fine.

9. Erase all the lines.

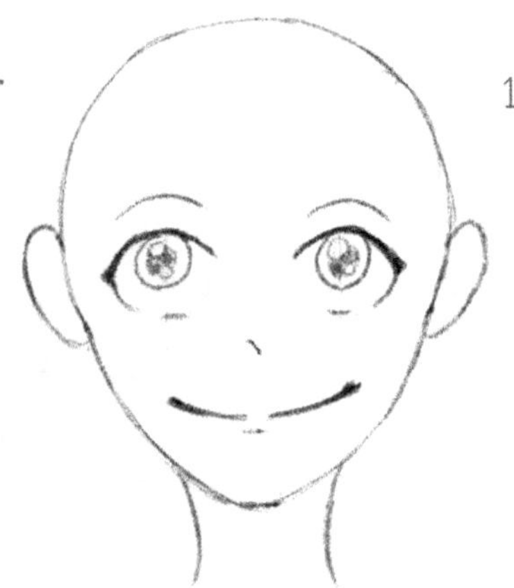

10. The inside of the ear isn't that complex. Just draw simple curves inside.

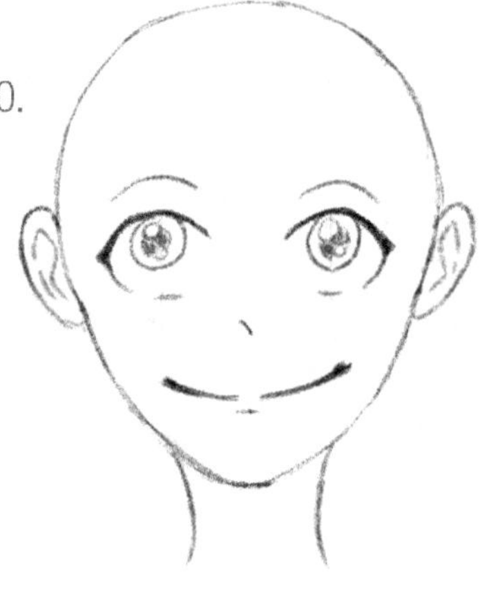

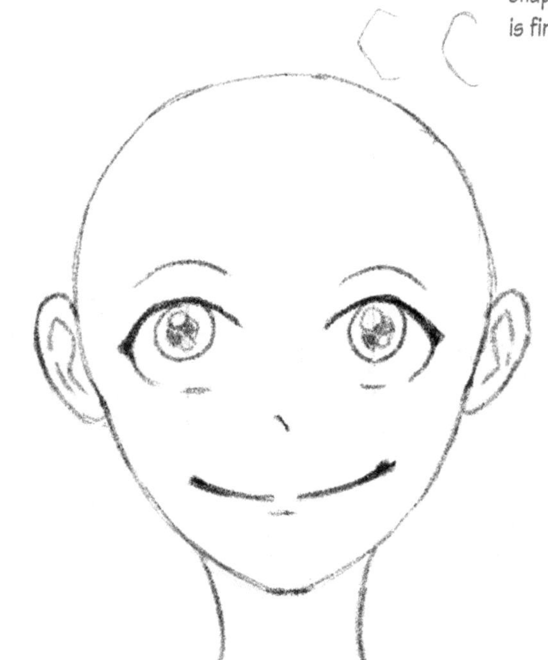

DONE!! You've done it!

ON TO THE SIDE PROFILE!

Draw your best circle.

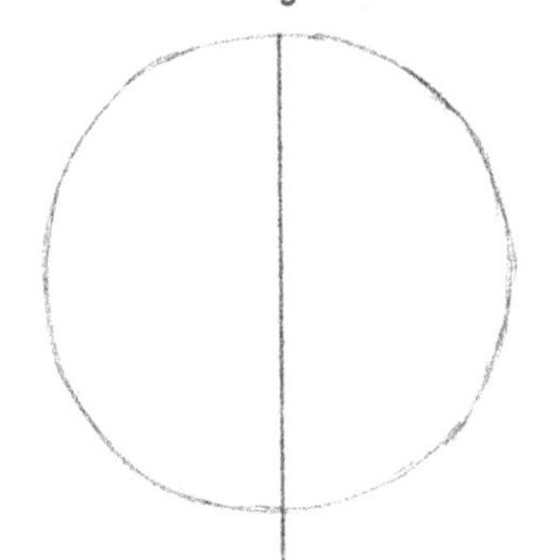

1.

Now a line through the middle.

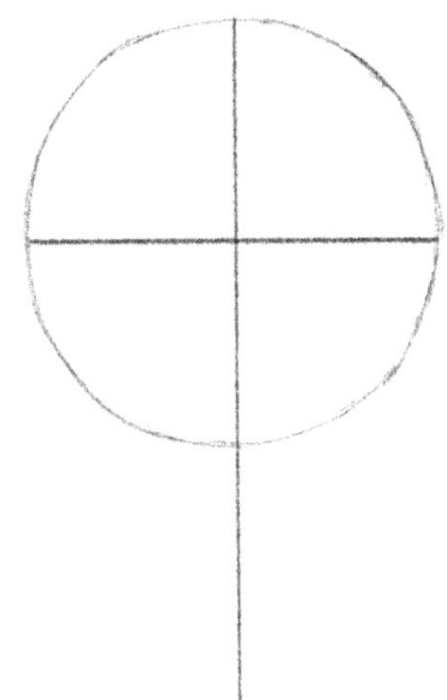

2.

Again, through the middle.

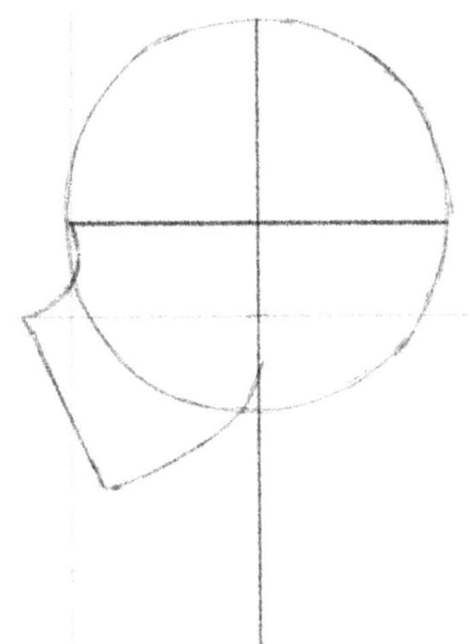

3.

Try your best to get this shape, and pay attention to the placement. You can add these lines to help you.

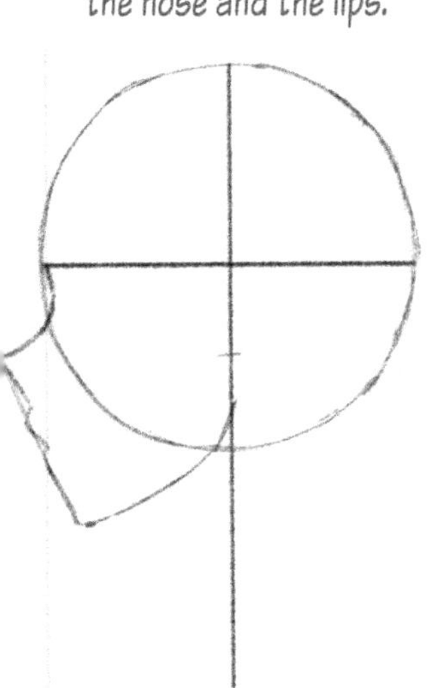

4.

Now let's mold the face, the nose and the lips.

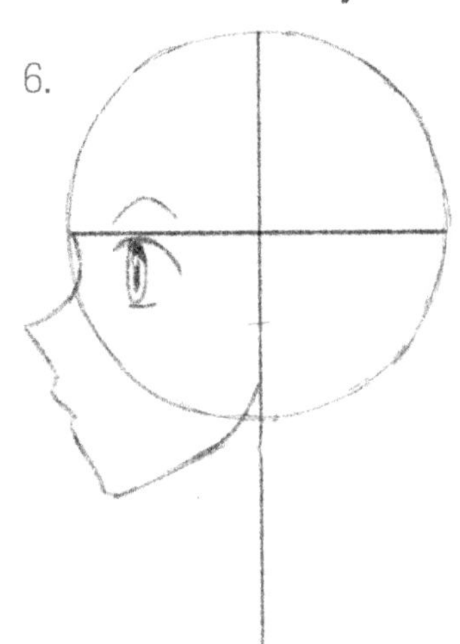

Add the side eye.

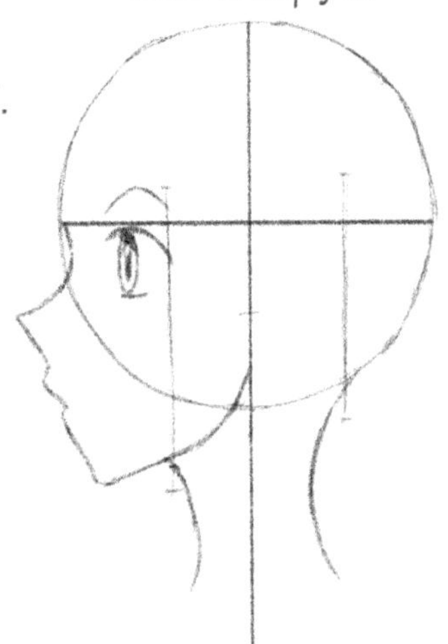

6.

Now the neck. Lines are there to help you.

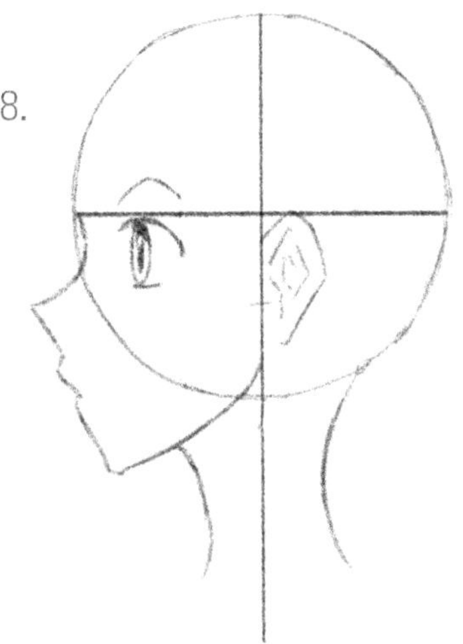

7.

Now the ear; any ear shape or type is fine.

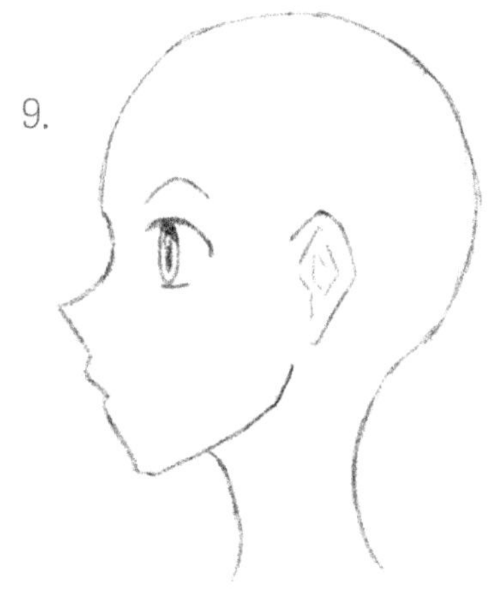

8.

Erase the lines.

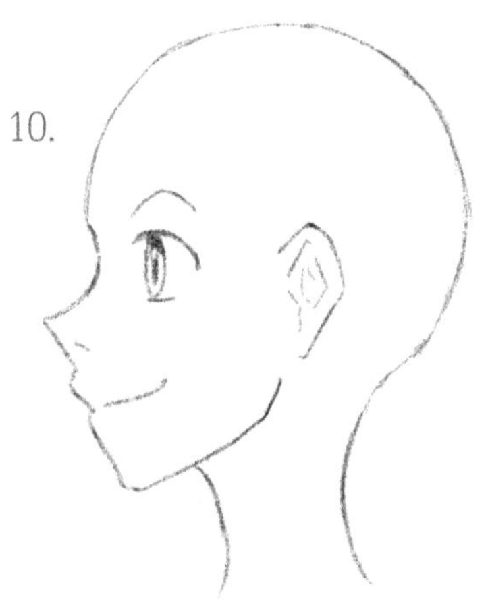

9.

Add the lip and nose detail.

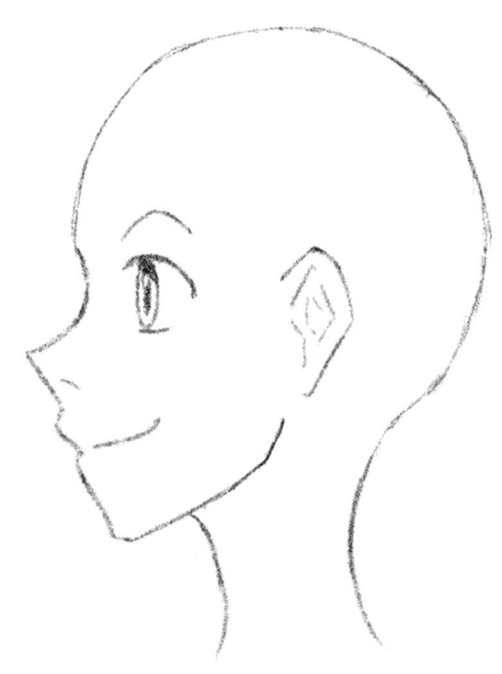

10.

You're done! So proud of you.

THEN THE THREE-QUARTER VIEW!

Reminder: The more to the side
you are. the more the eyes get squished.

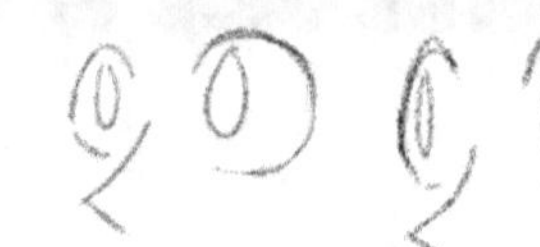

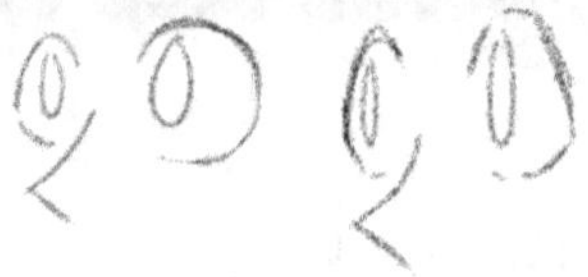

Draw your best circle.

1.

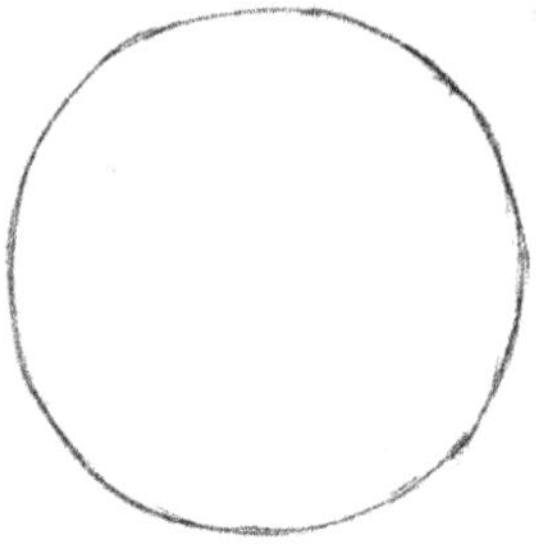

Then a curved line through
the middle.

2.

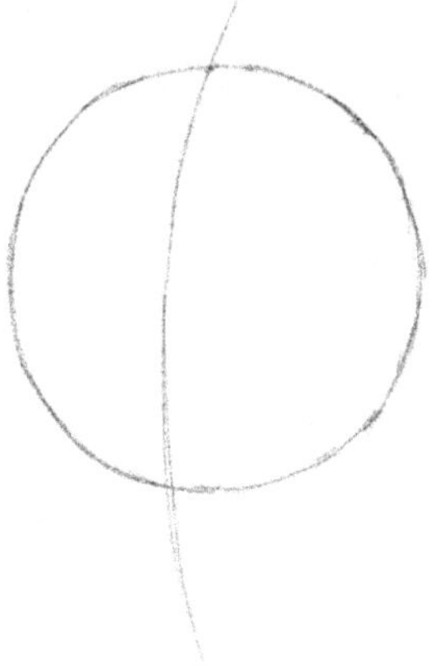

Again, a line through the middle.

3.

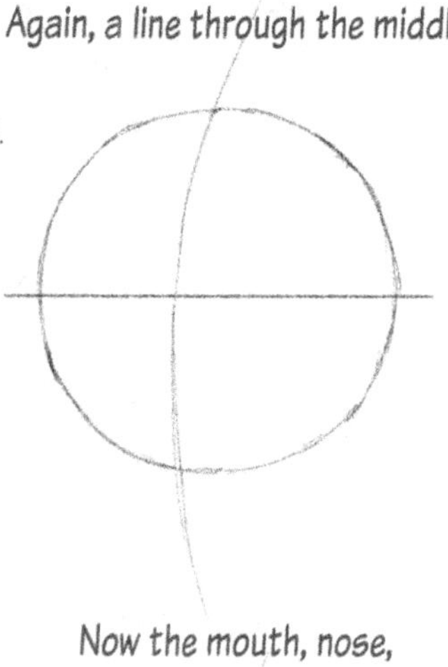

Draw your chin area and
look how this part goes in and
the cheek comes out.

4.

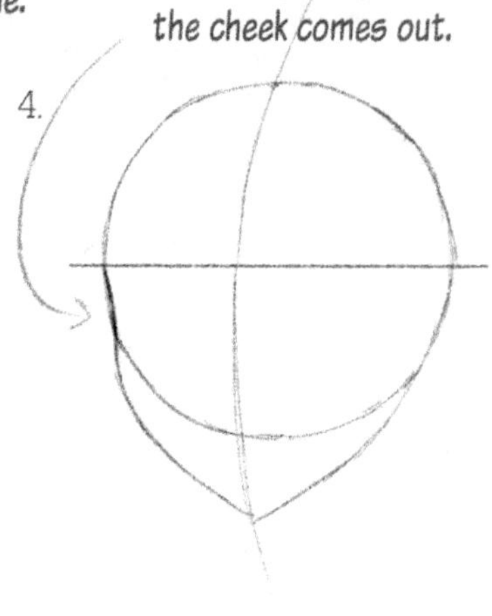

Now the eyes.

5.

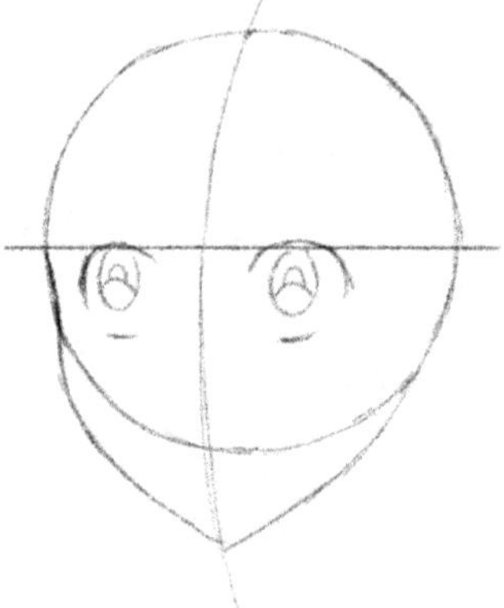

Add the side ear, it's
overlapping the head this time.

6.

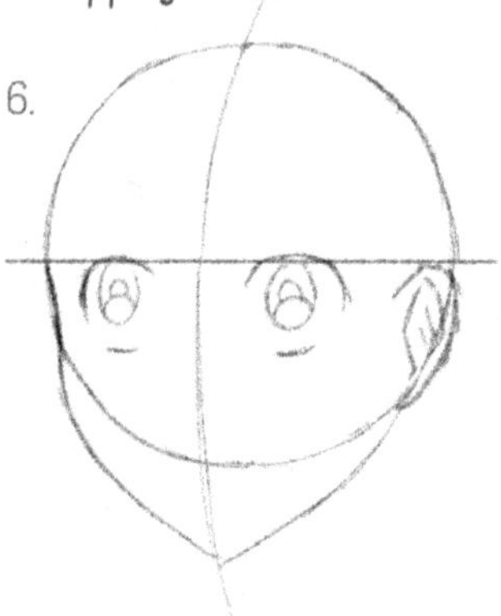

Now the mouth, nose,
and a neck.

7.

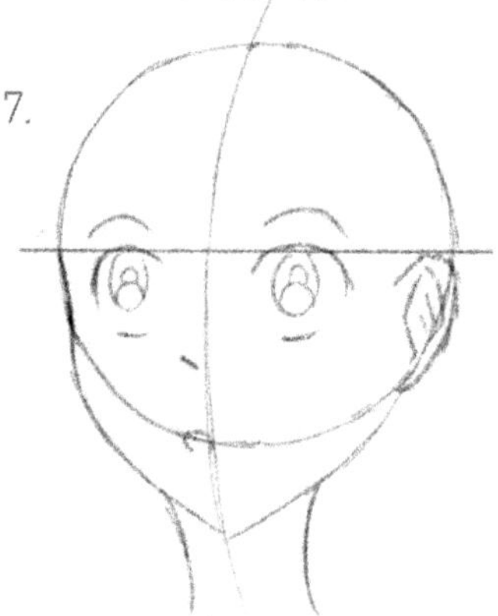

Erase and you're done.

8.

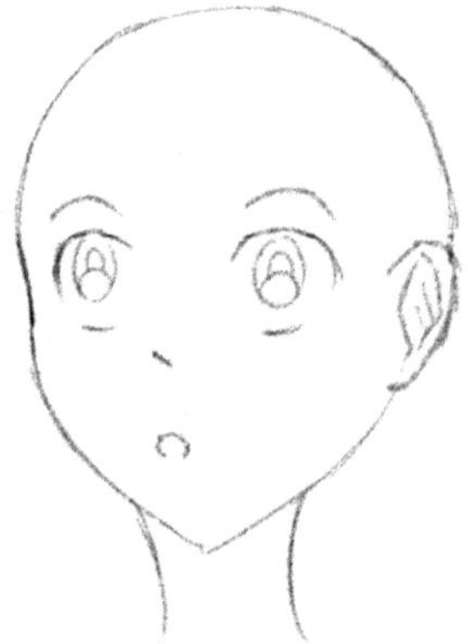

Mirrored version:

1.

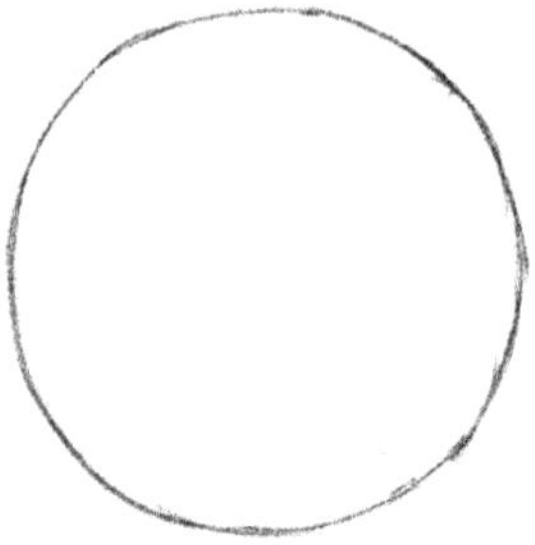

2.

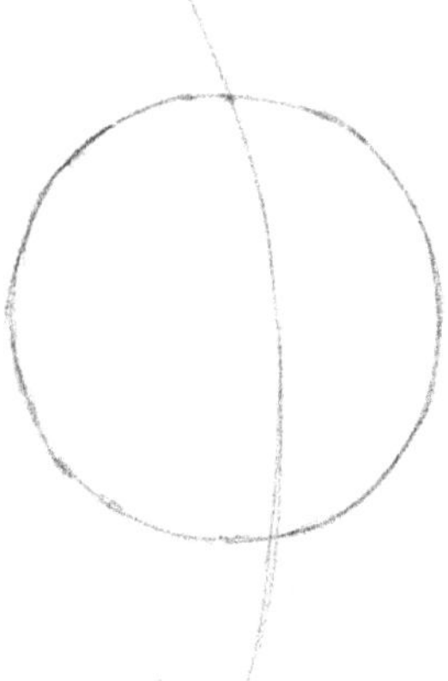

3.

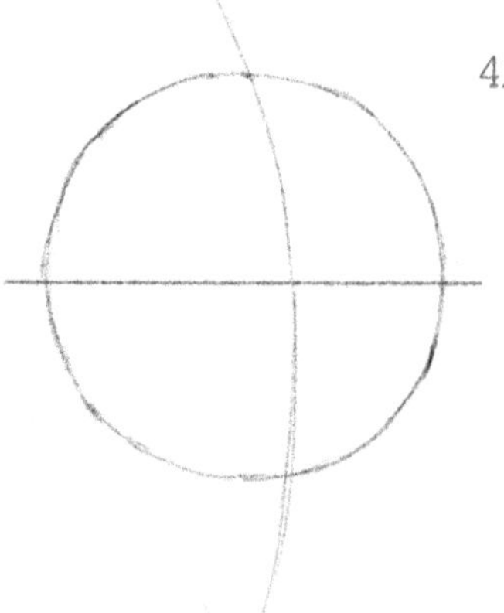

4.

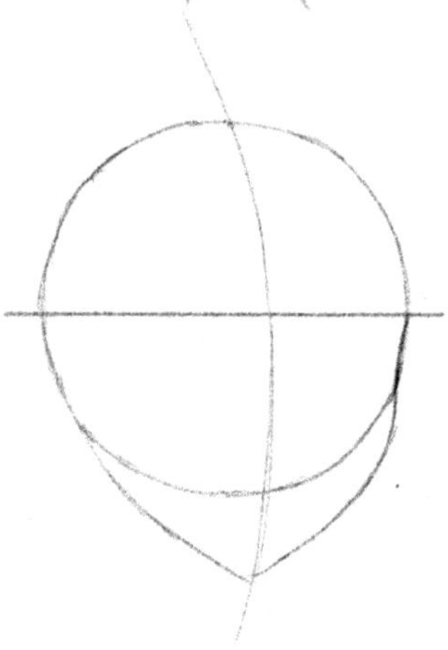

5.

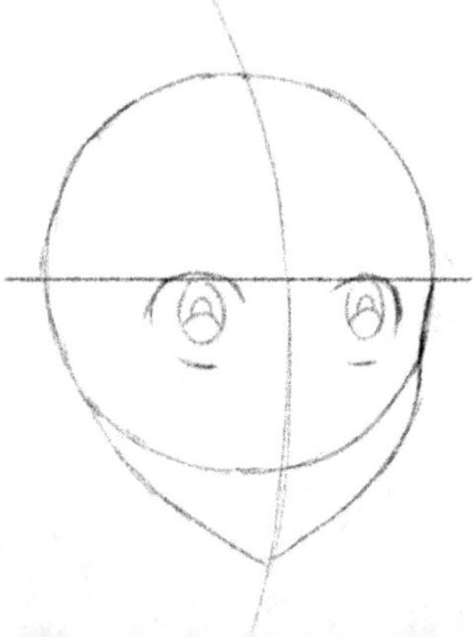

6.

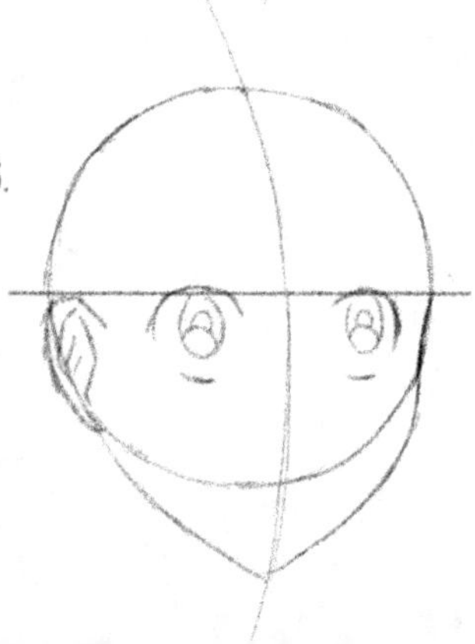

7.

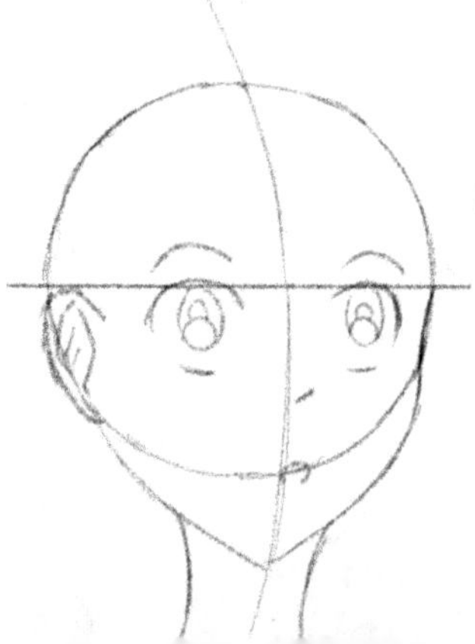

8.

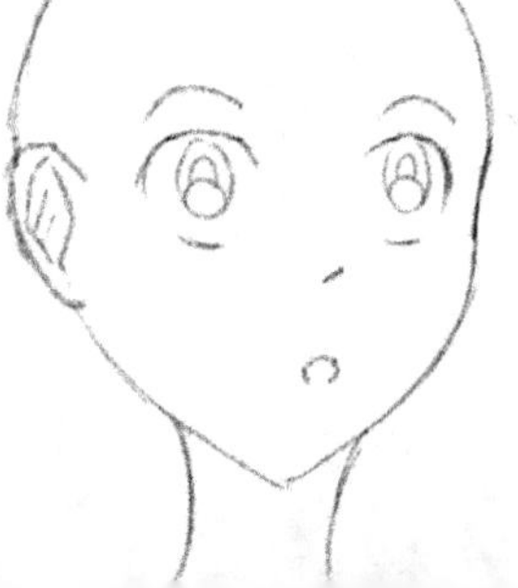

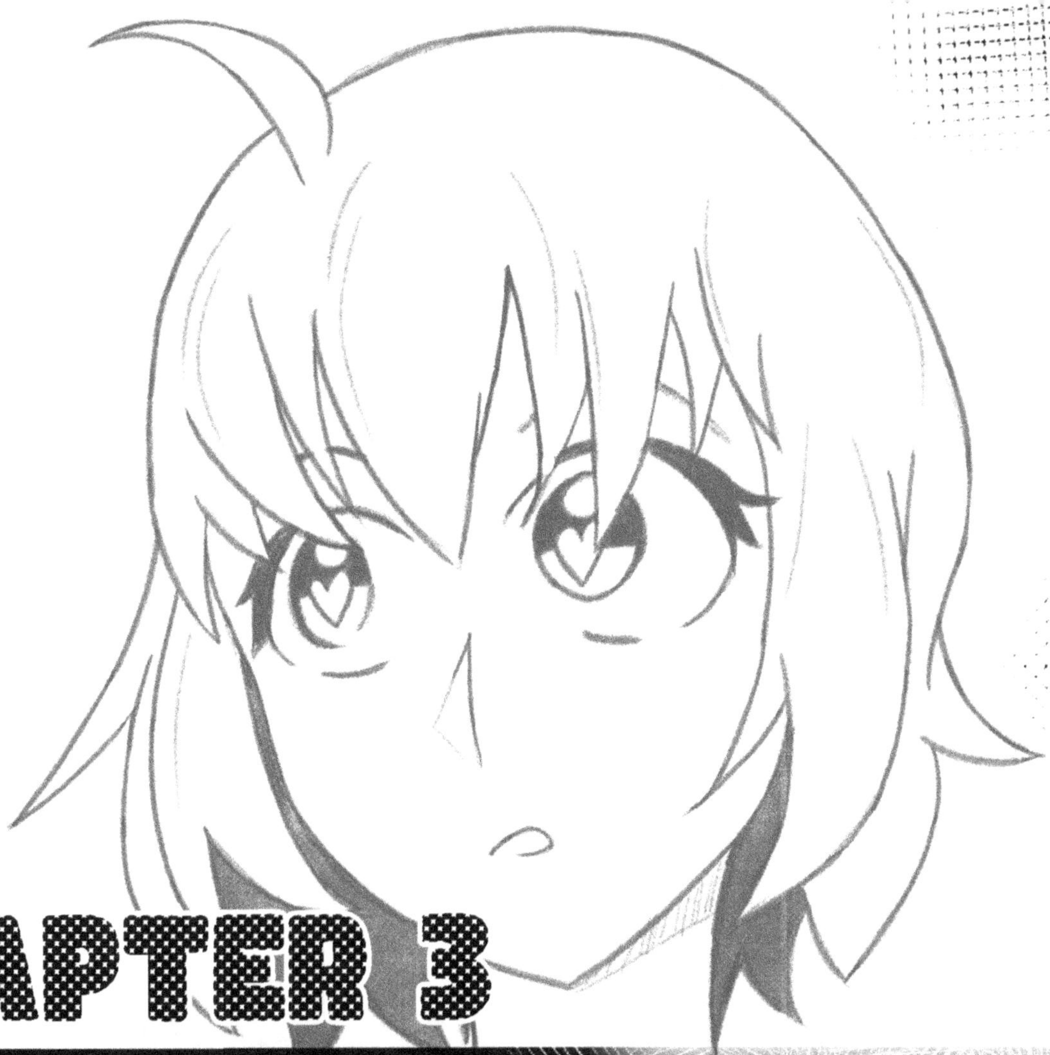

CHAPTER 3
Drawing Hair

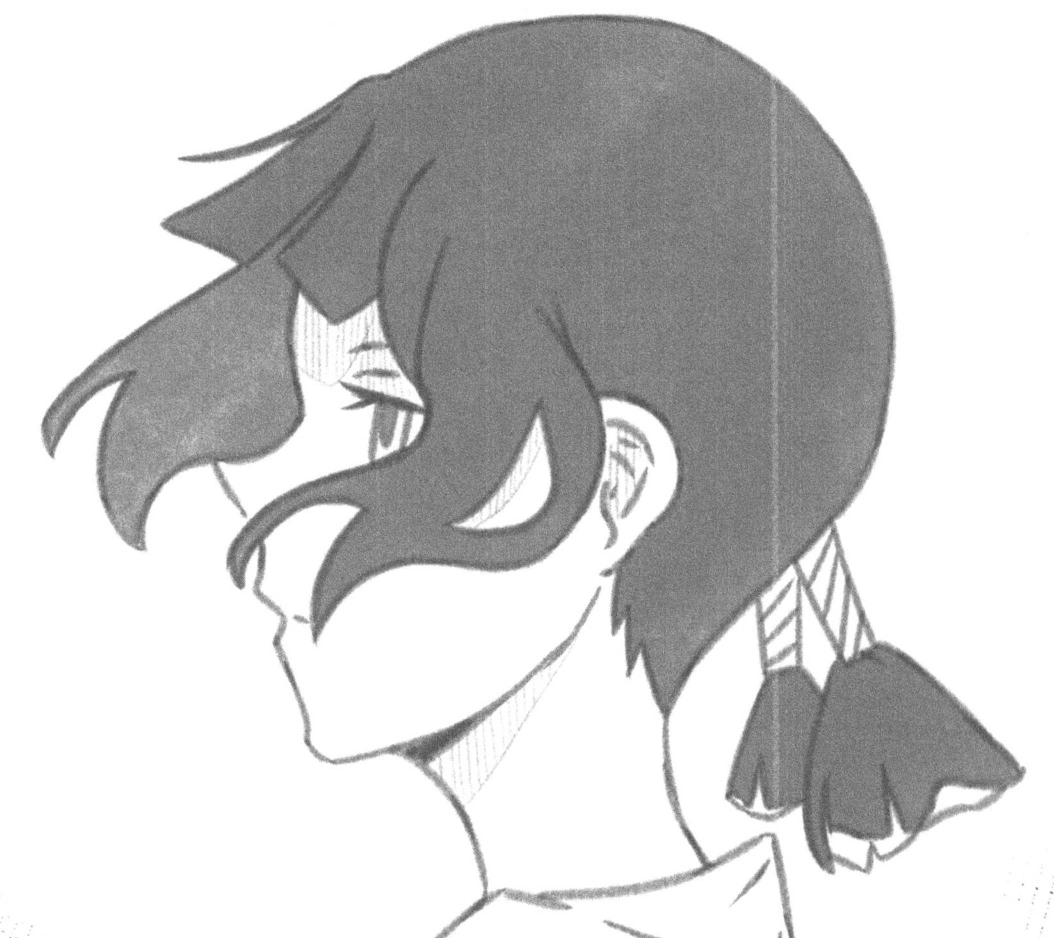

HAIR

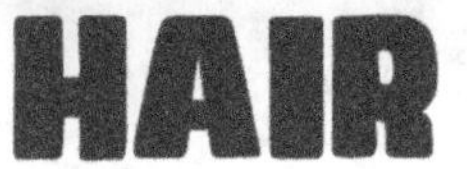

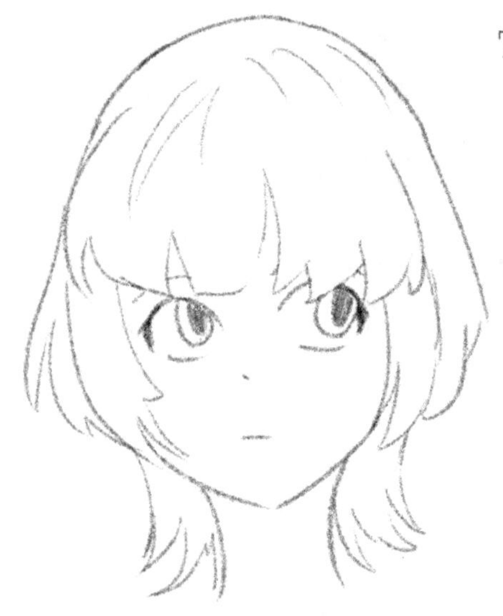

The hair might seem challenging, and it is at first, but you have got to look at the overall shape.

And remember the head is in there, just not as big. The hair is much higher than the head.

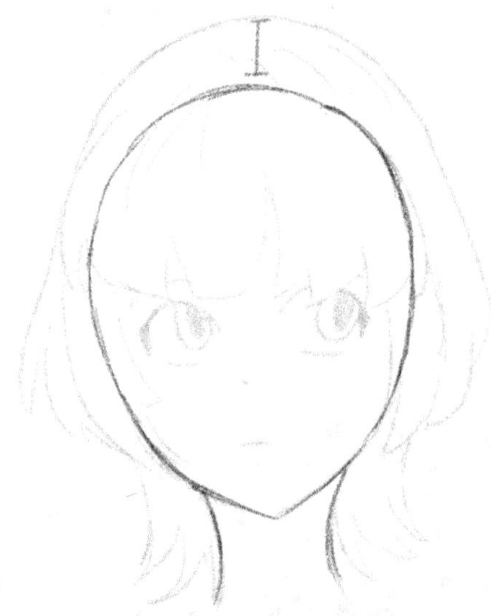

Just think of the hair as shapes first, then go ahead and do details later, after you are happy with the shape.

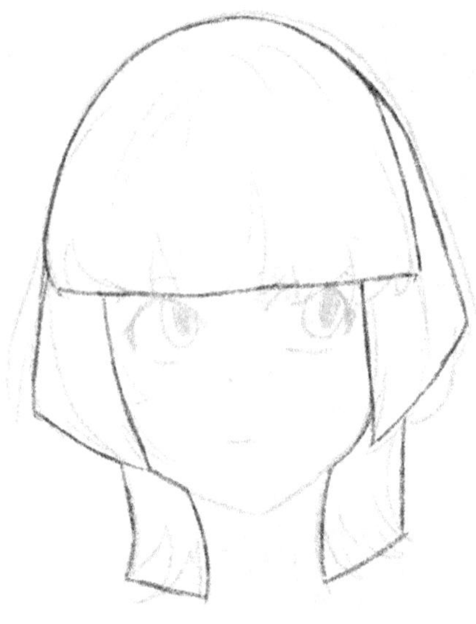

Remember, hair is thick! It has shape! Anime isn't advanced enough to animate all the strands of the hair and still look good.

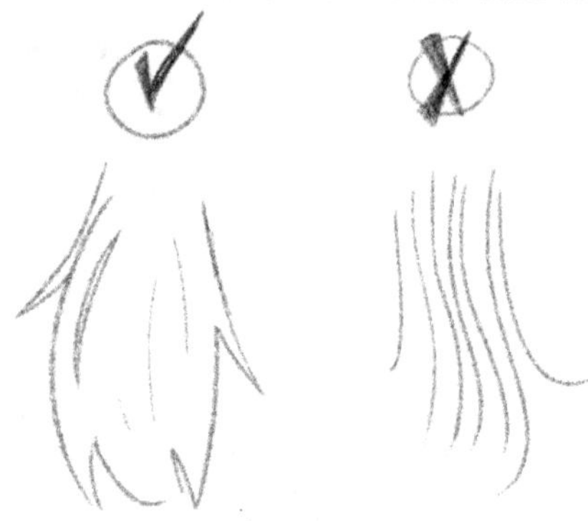

All we're doing is adding details to shapes.

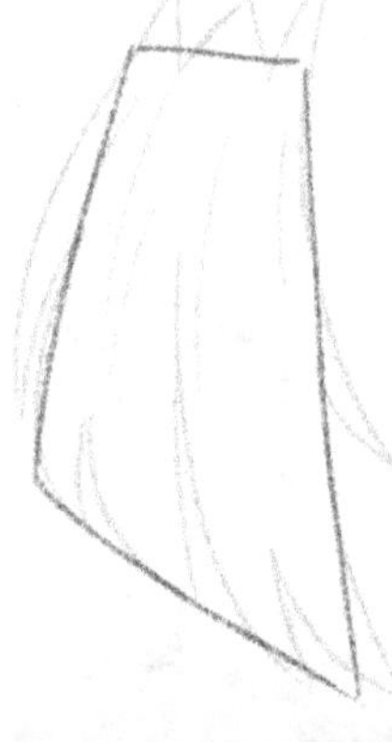

Hair is free flowing, it doesn't have to be exactly like the shape.

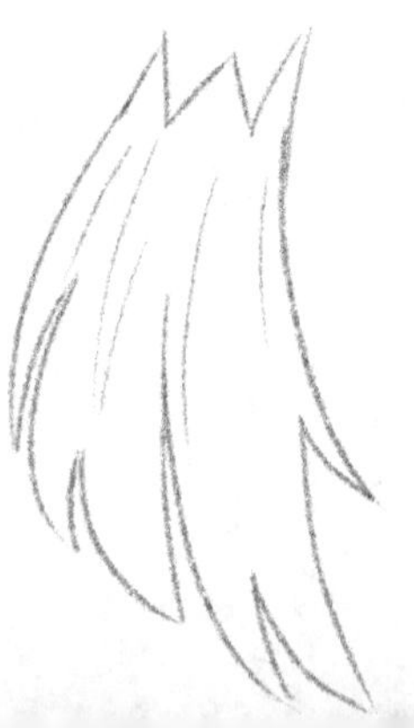

HAIR (PRACTICE)

Let's practice a bit before we dive into drawing the whole head.

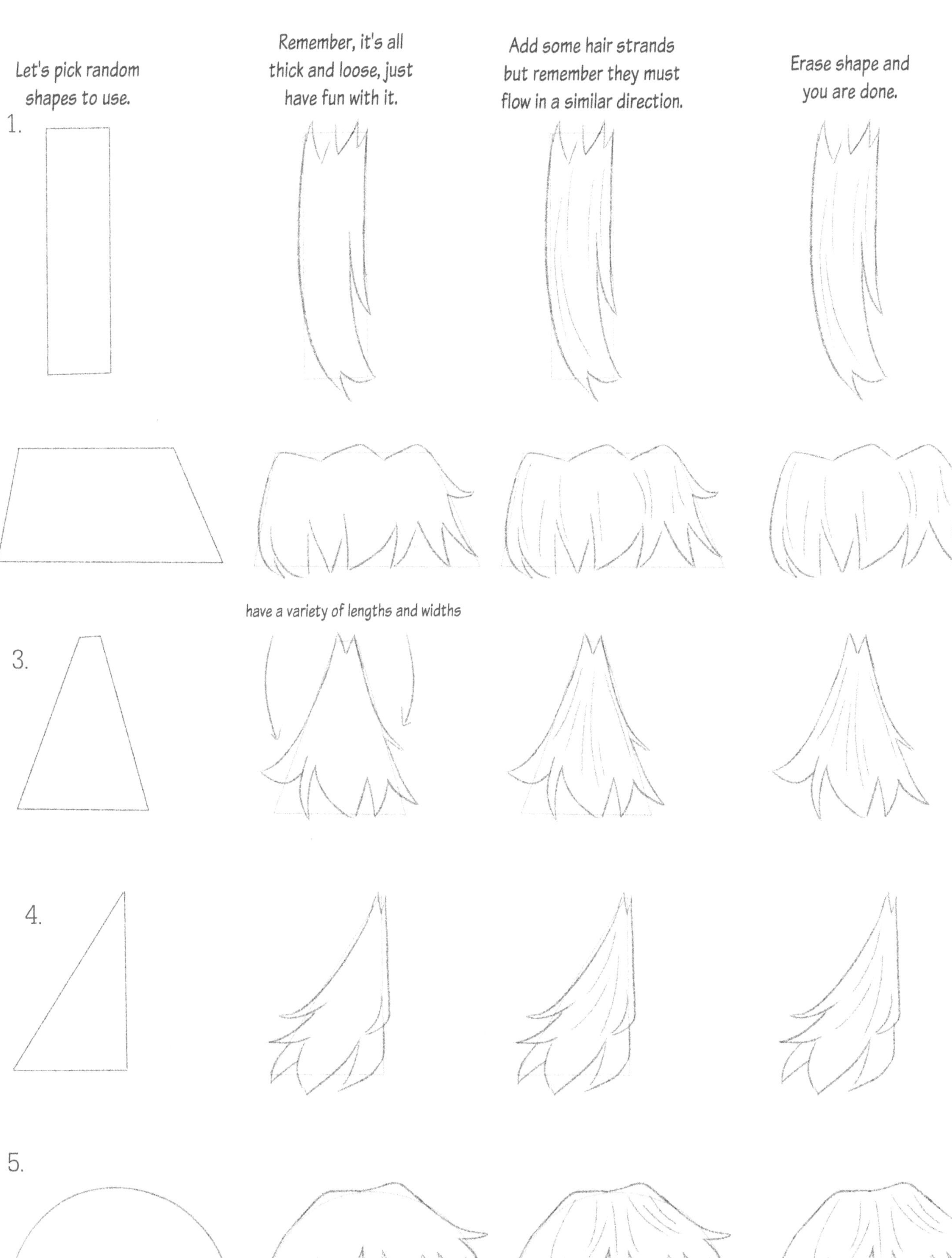

Let's take this completed head
from a few pages back
that you have done.
Let's add the shape.

1.

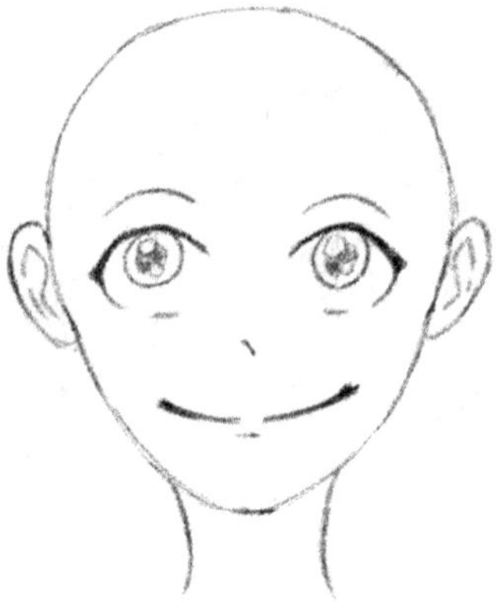

Let's add the planned shape.

2.

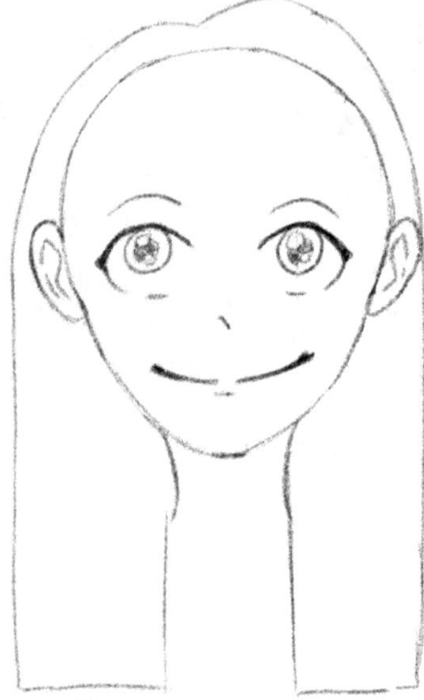

Now the bangs and extra shapes.

3.

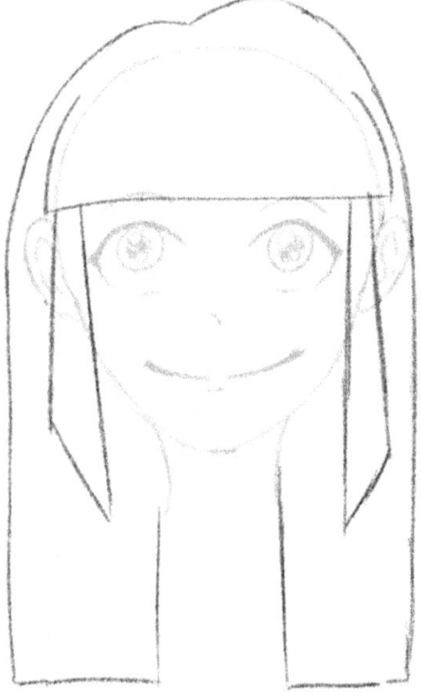

Erase any part that's
under the lines.

4.

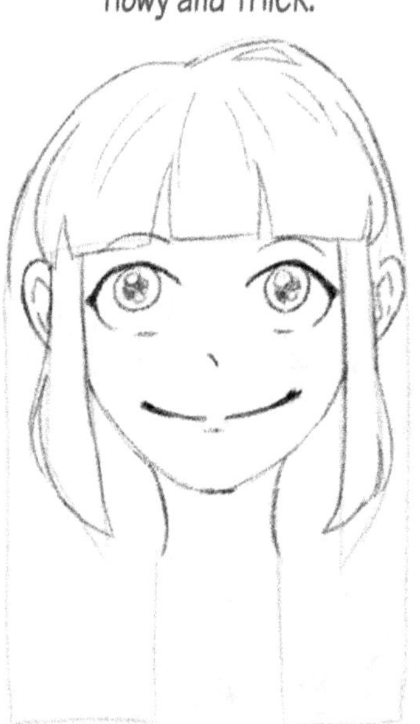

Now the details. Keep them loose,
flowy and THICK.

5.

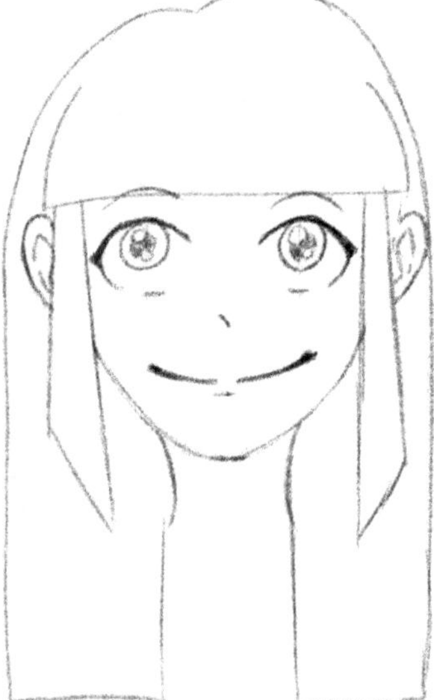

I WENT OUTSIDE THE LINE!
Oh no! Why did I? Because this
piece looks like it's a long
strand that sticks out with the top part.

6.

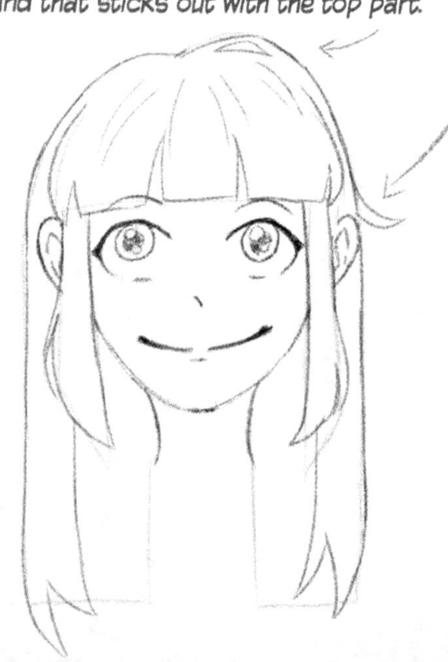

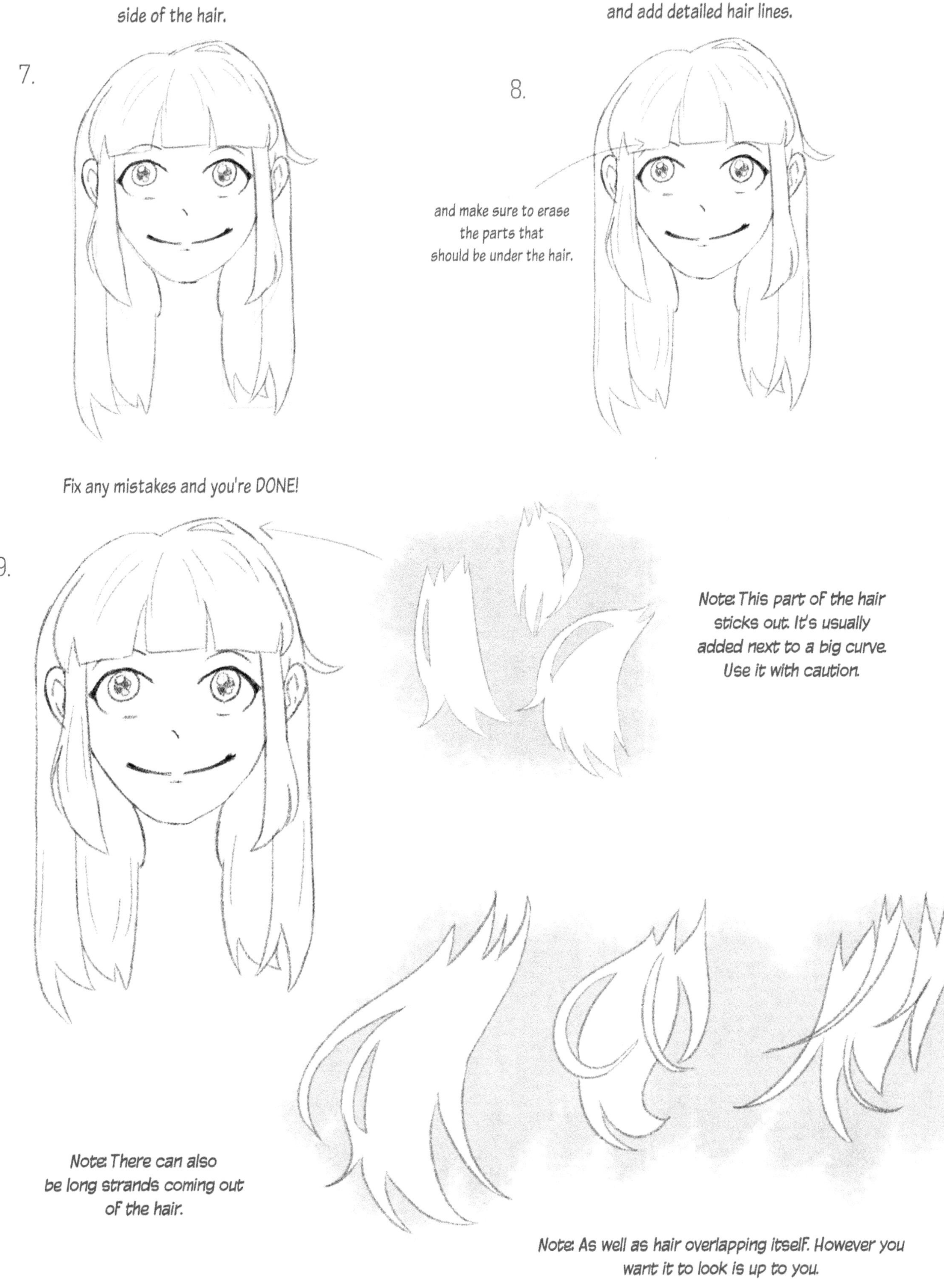

Now finish the back
side of the hair.

7.

Now lastly, erase the shape in the back
and add detailed hair lines.

8.

and make sure to erase
the parts that
should be under the hair.

Fix any mistakes and you're DONE!

9.

Note: This part of the hair
sticks out. It's usually
added next to a big curve.
Use it with caution.

Note: There can also
be long strands coming out
of the hair.

Note: As well as hair overlapping itself. However you
want it to look is up to you.

Let's take this completed head
from a few pages back
that you have done.
Let's add the shape.

1.

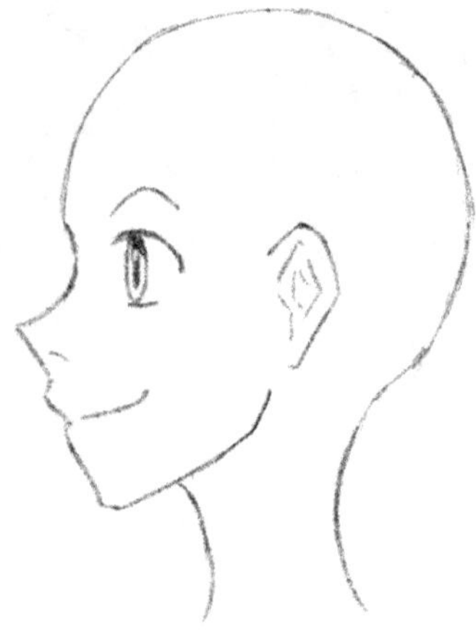

Let's add the planned shape.

2.

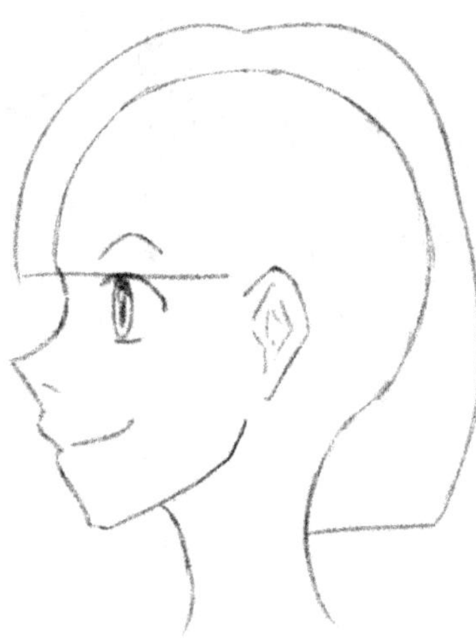

Now the extra shapes
to finish the style.

3.

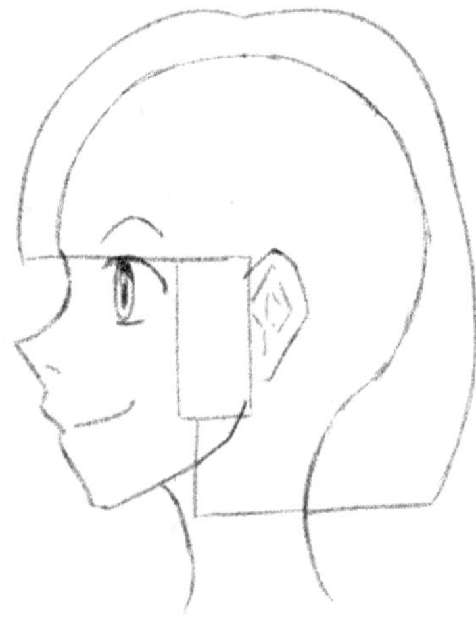

Erase any part that's
under the lines.

4.

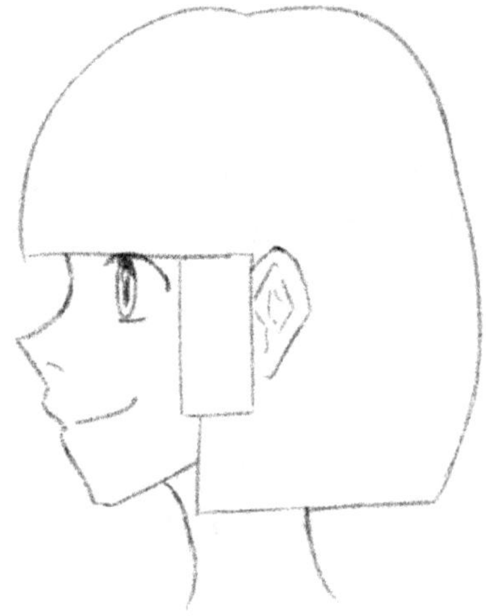

Now the details. Keep them loose,
flowy and THICK.

5.

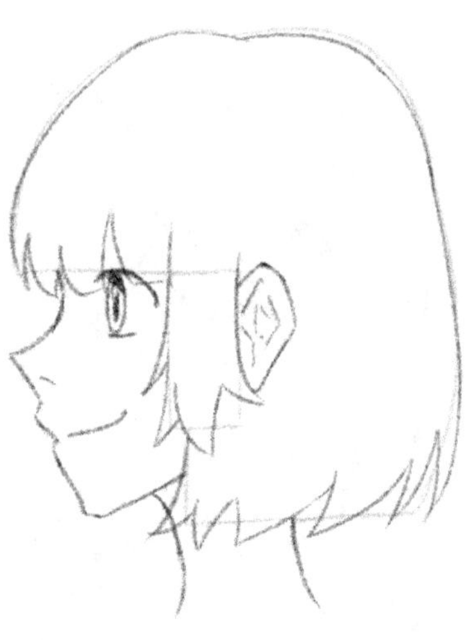

Now erase the shape in the back
and erase anything that might be
above the hair.

6.

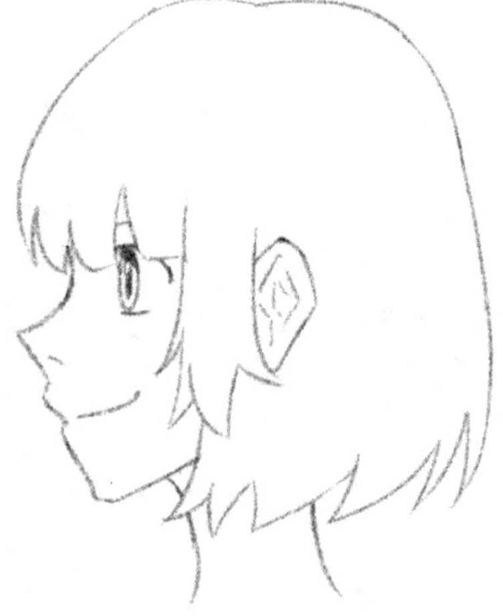

Now add a bit of the back
side of the hair poking out.

7.

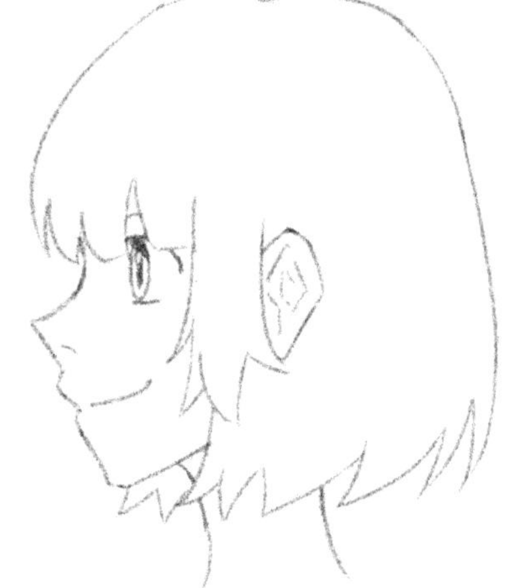

Let's add in the hair detail lines.

8.

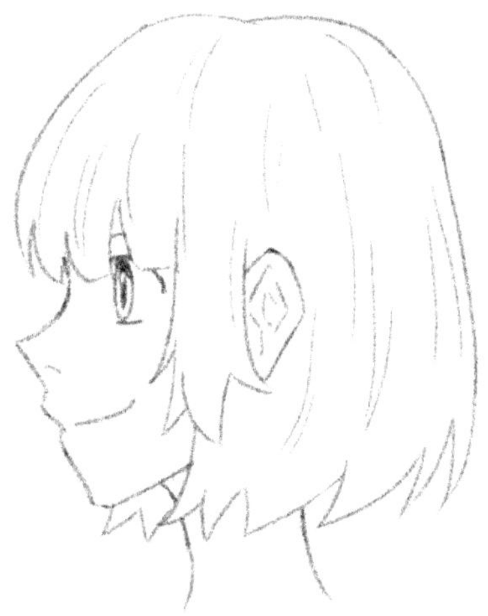

Done! Great work!

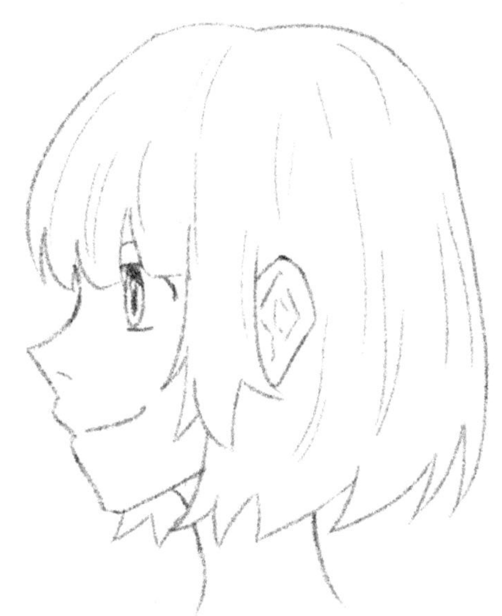

*ADVANCED TIP: IF you want to add more detail to your hair,
you can add a slight shadow to every hair part in the back!*

Like this:

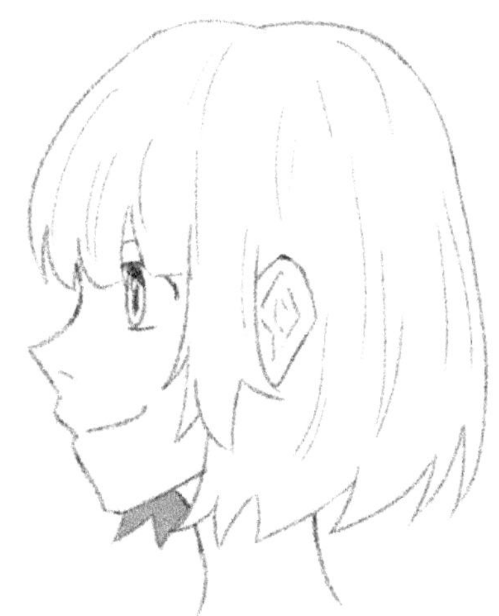

And this:

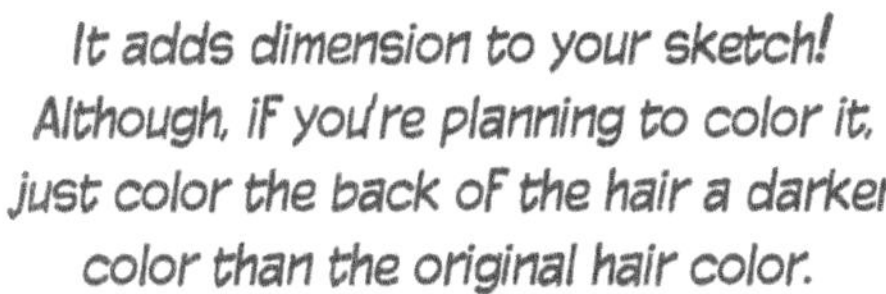

*It adds dimension to your sketch!
Although, if you're planning to color it,
just color the back of the hair a darker
color than the original hair color.*

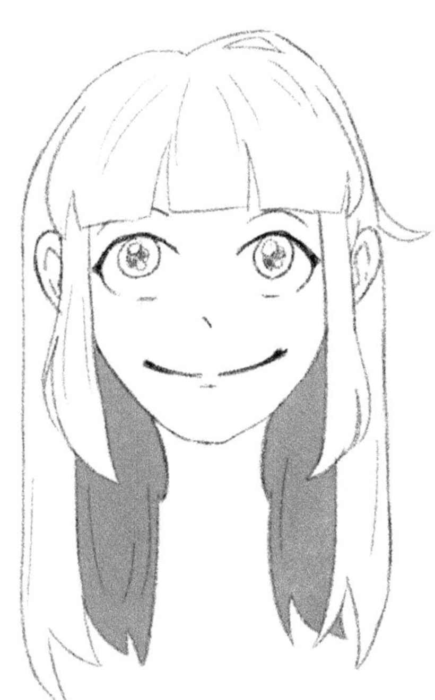

TYPES OF HAIR...

"Straight"

Straight hair is the easiest. The weight is heavy so it all just slumps down and doesn't stick out.
It's the type that follows the boxy shapes the best.

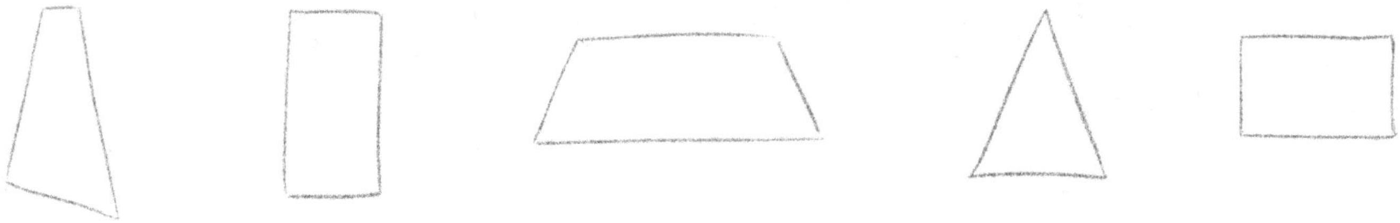

They can have curves but very MINIMAL ones.

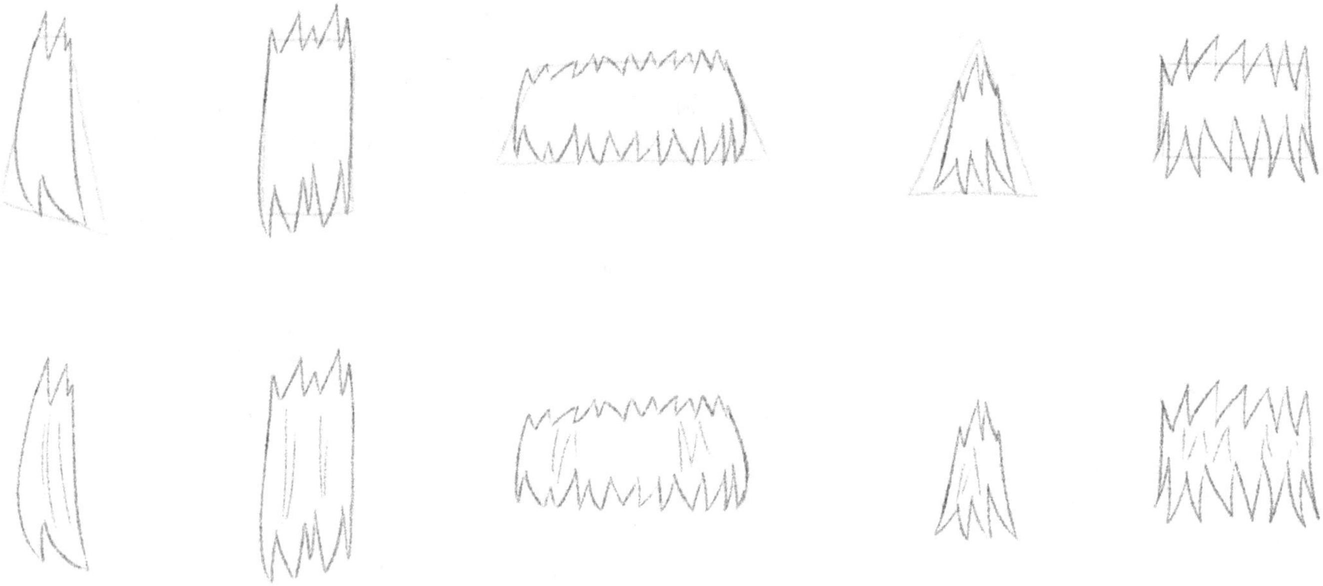

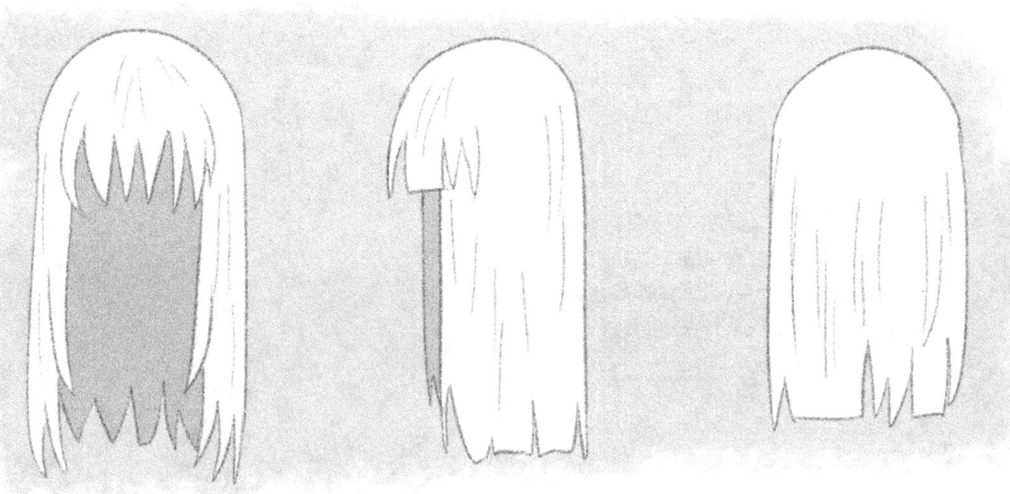

"Wavy"

Wavy hair is a bit more challenging. The physical idea is that it's slightly bouncy.
It's a mix of straight and curly.
It doesn't fully slump down and does have some parts sticking out.
It's the type that follows the triangular shapes best.

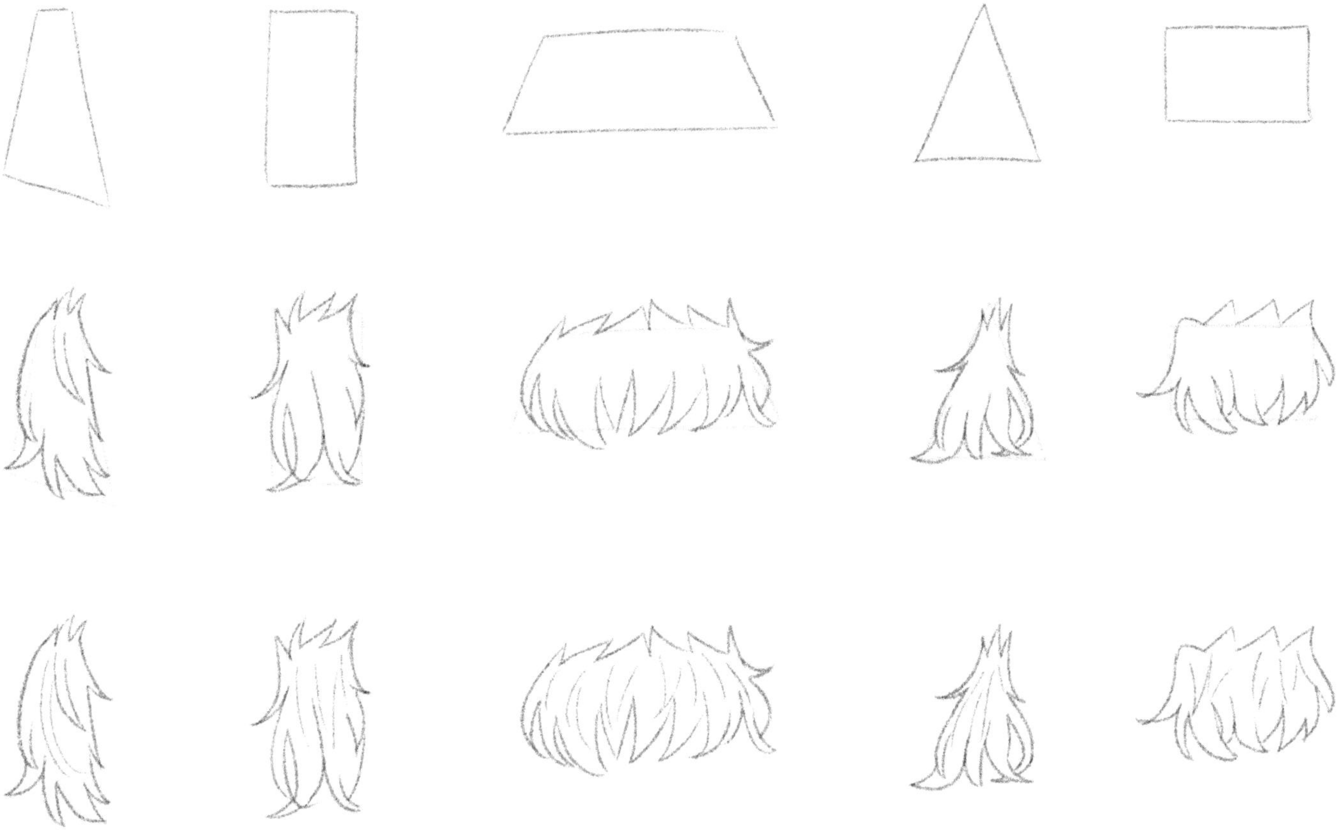

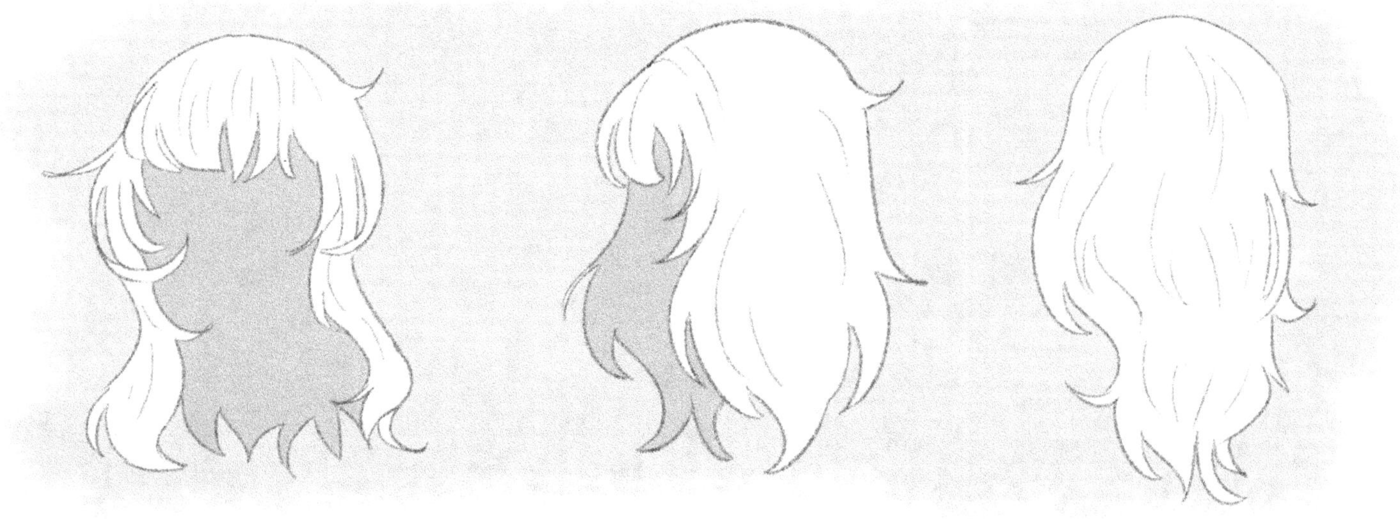

"Wavy"

"Curly"

Curly hair is challenging. The physical idea is that it's very light & bouncy.
It doesn't slump down and doesn't follow the shapes too well.
This one requires more thinking in the shapes.
I believe in you. Let's go!

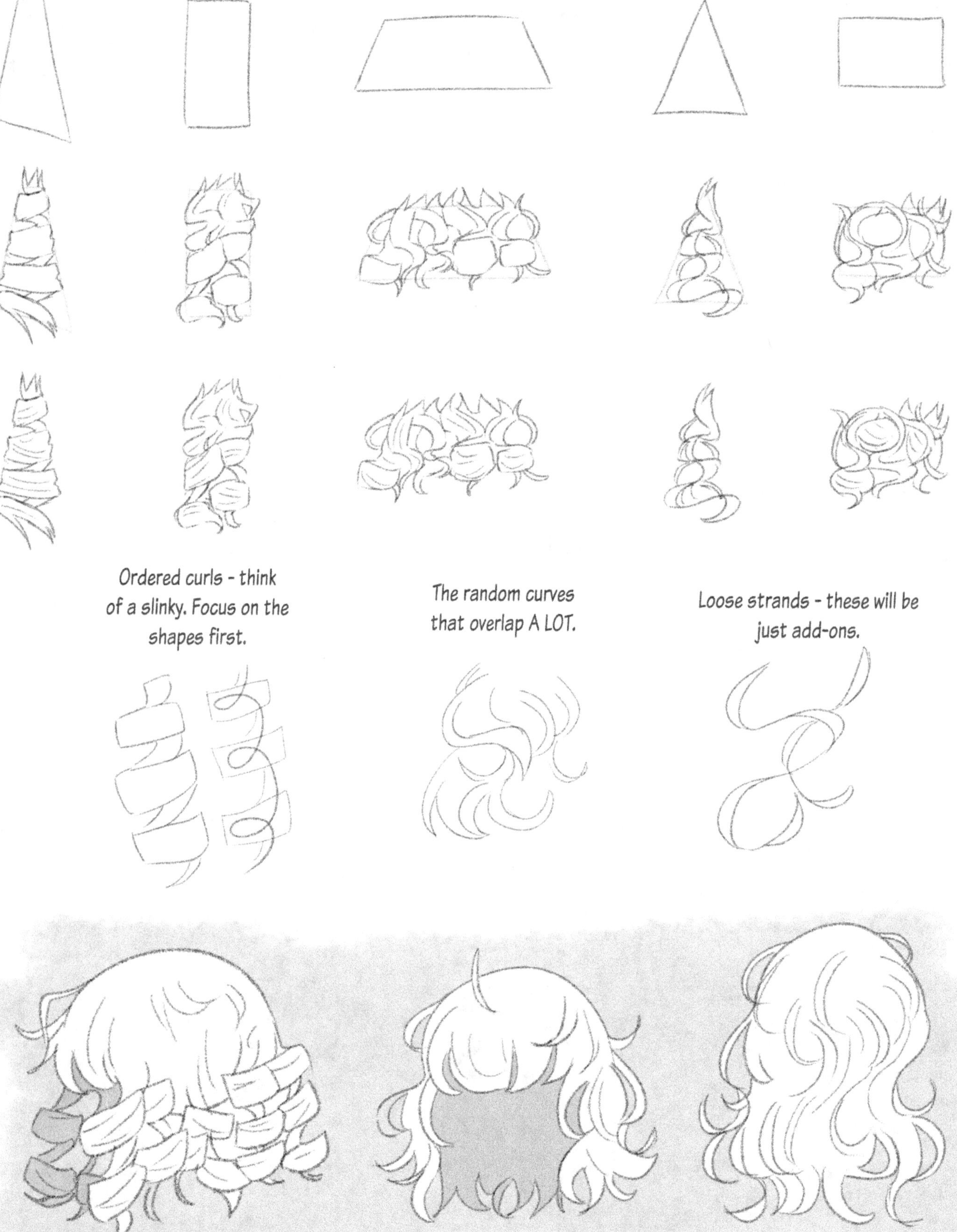

DIFFERENT HAIR STYLES:

Our model for this exercise is:

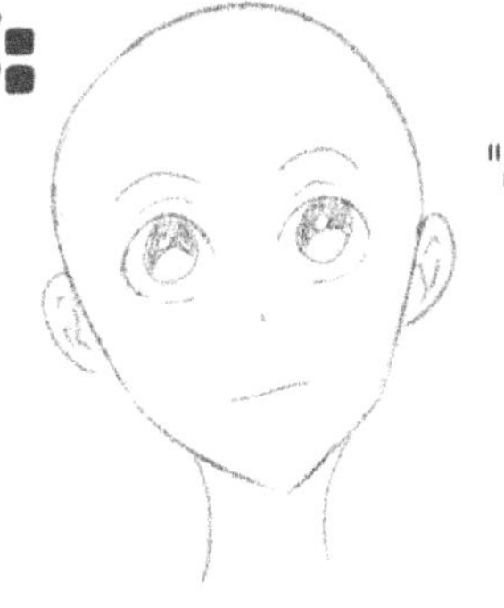

Let's call her
"Futaba-yochino-san"

...

Fine.

Stacy.

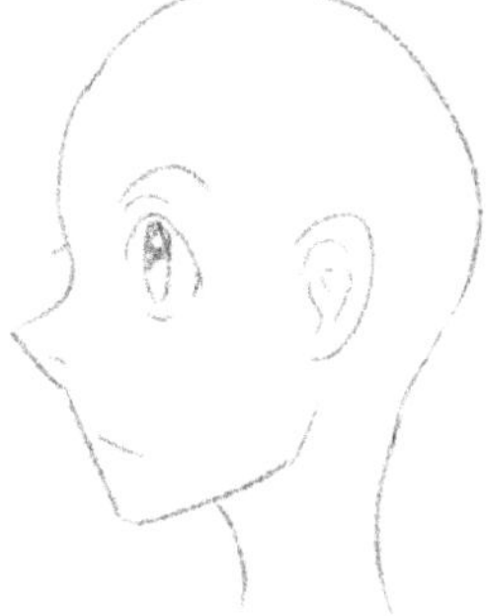

Side profile:

Front profile:

Ponytail

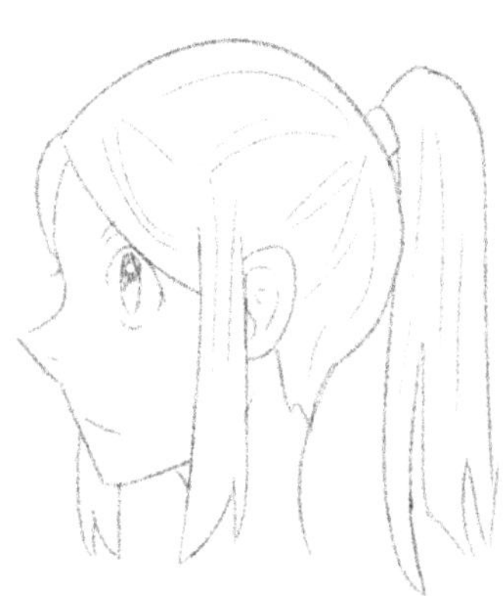
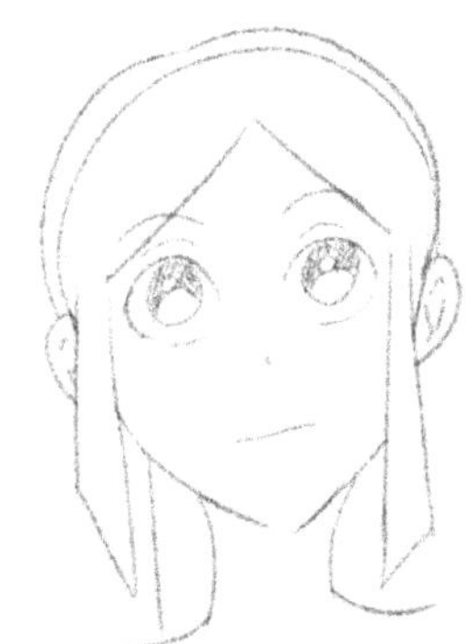
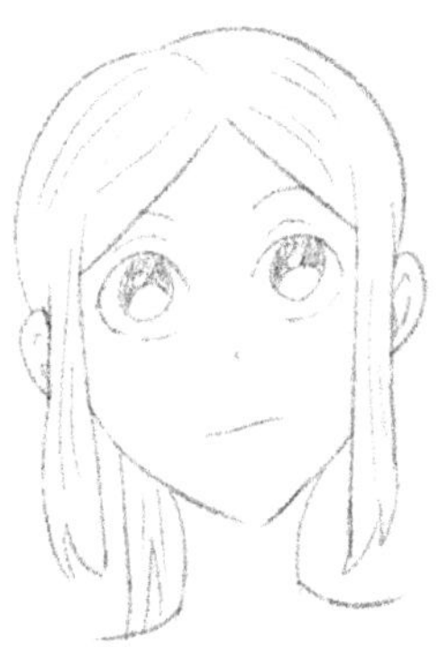

Bun

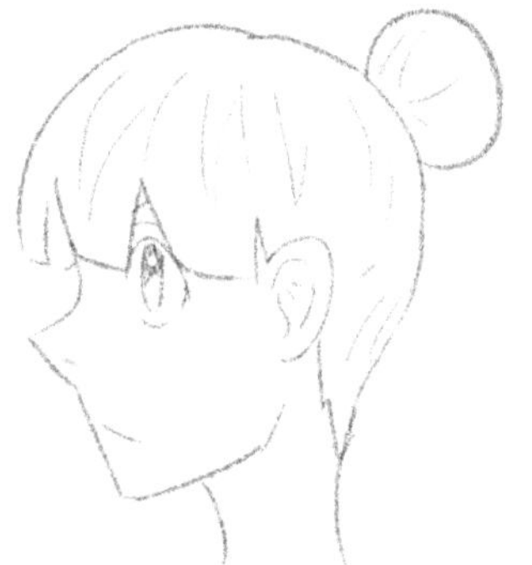
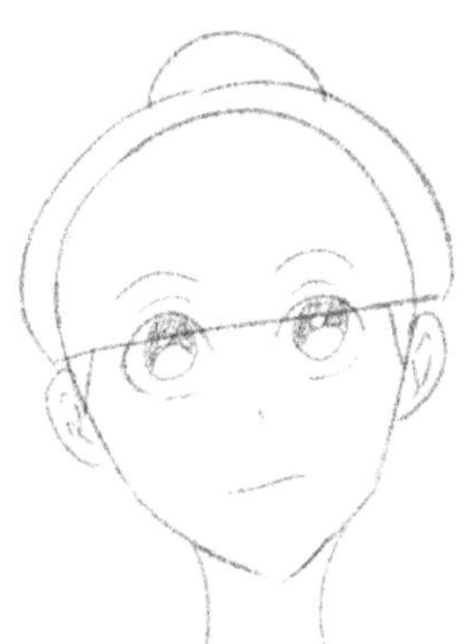
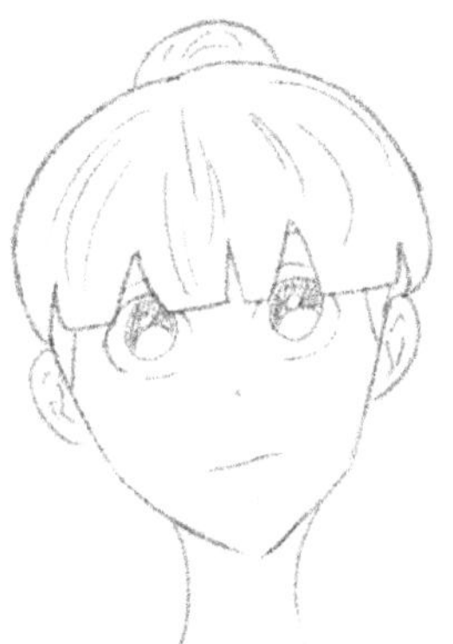

Braids

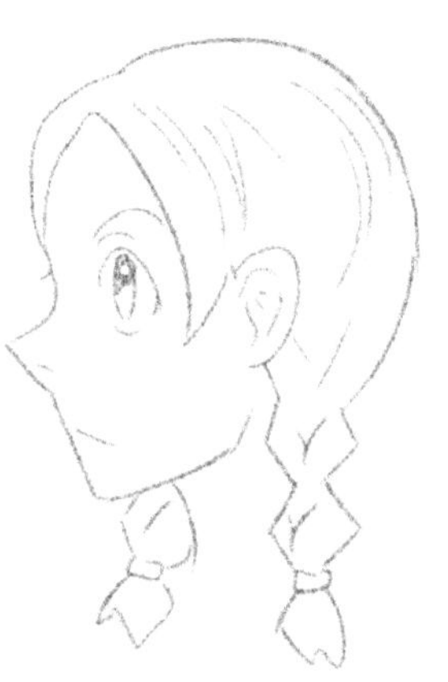
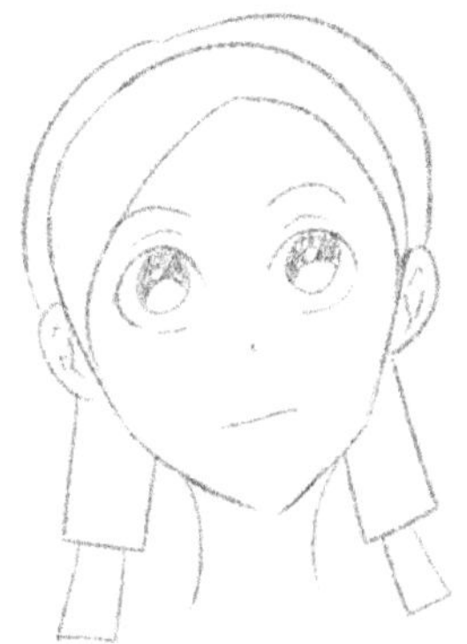
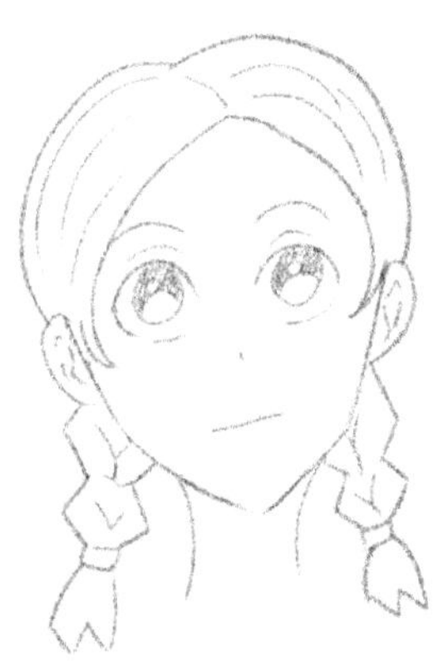

Twin ponytail (short hair)

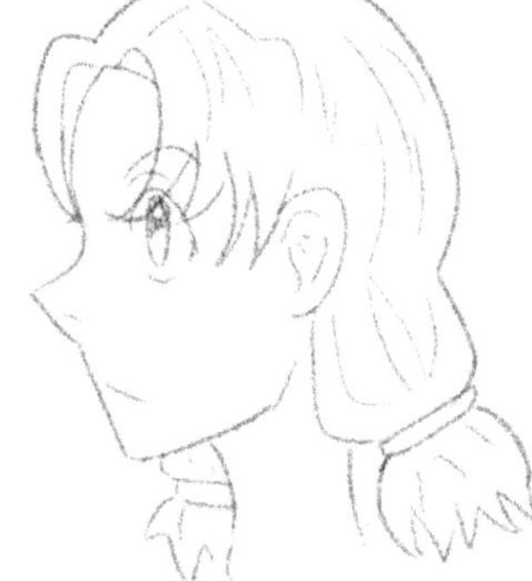
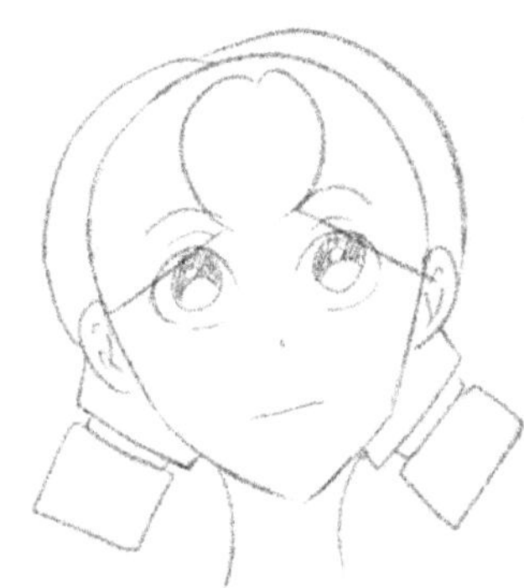
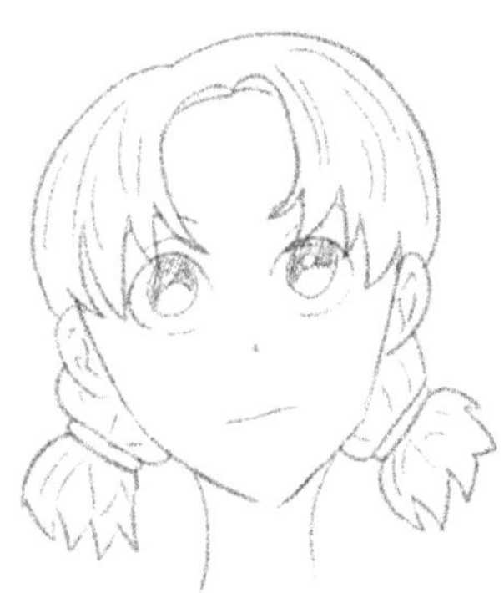

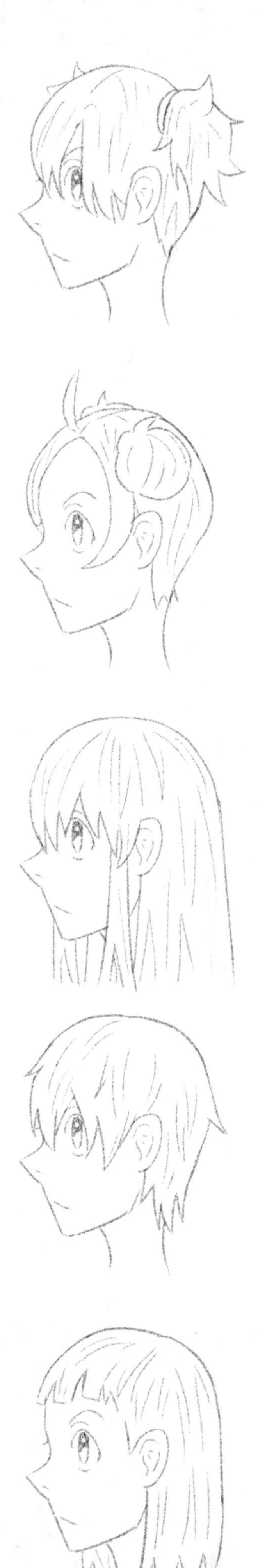

Twin ponytail

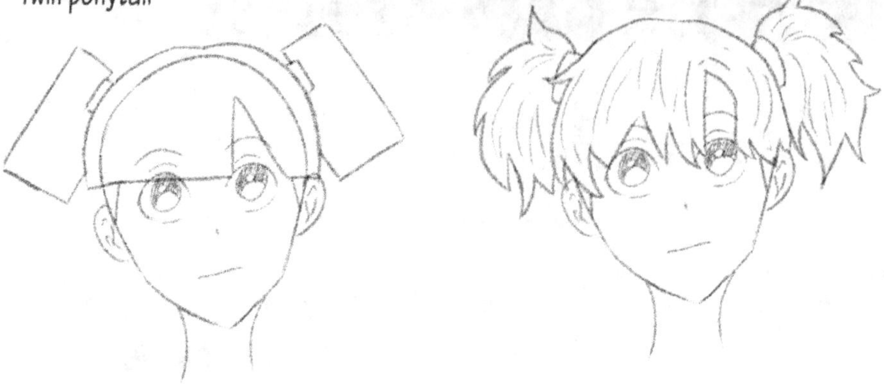

Twin buns

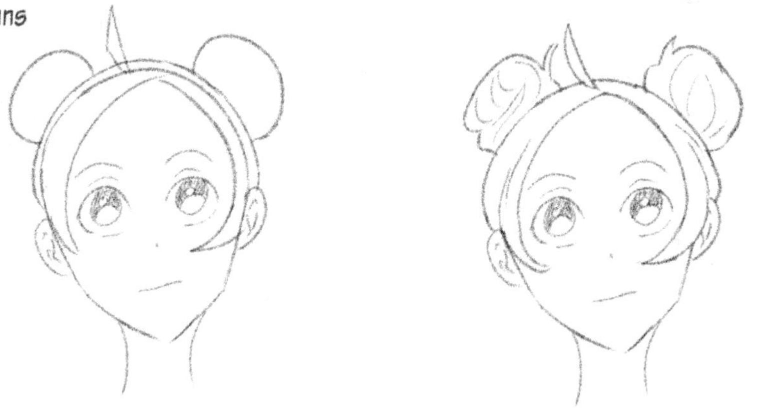

Long

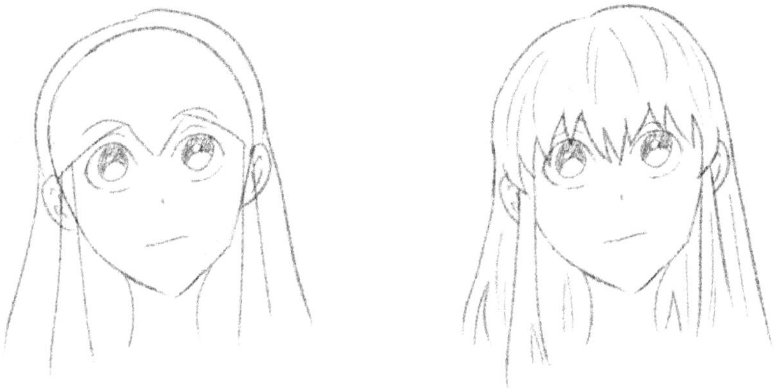

Short

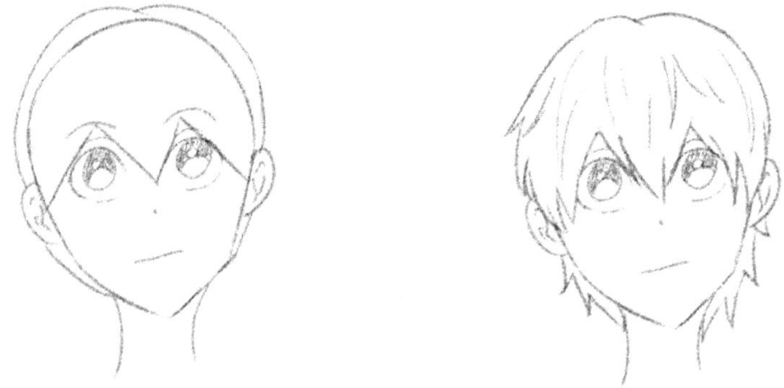

Medium length

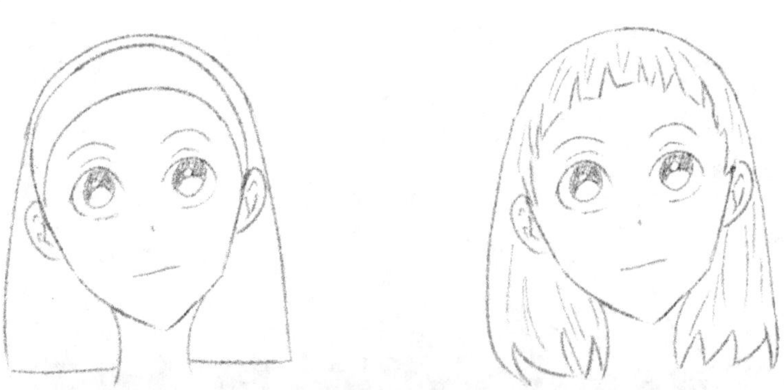

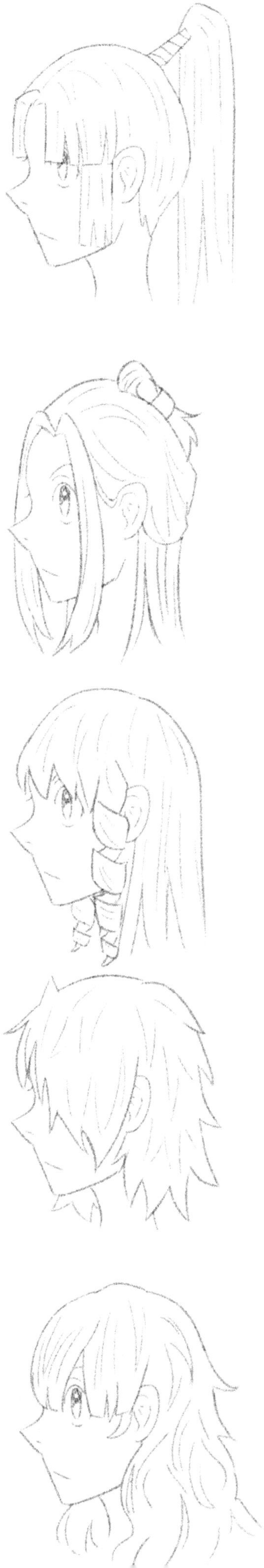

Shrine-inspired

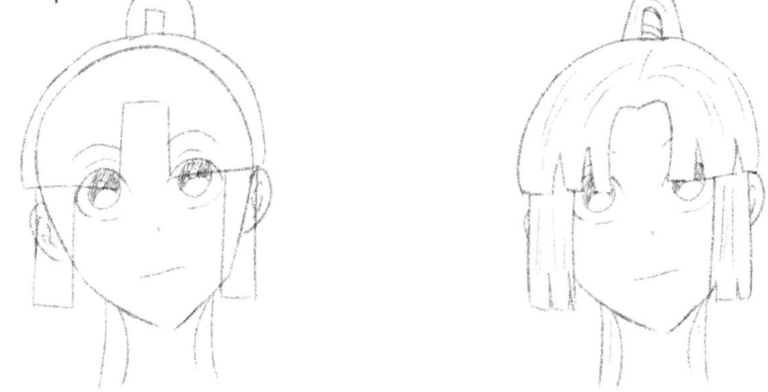

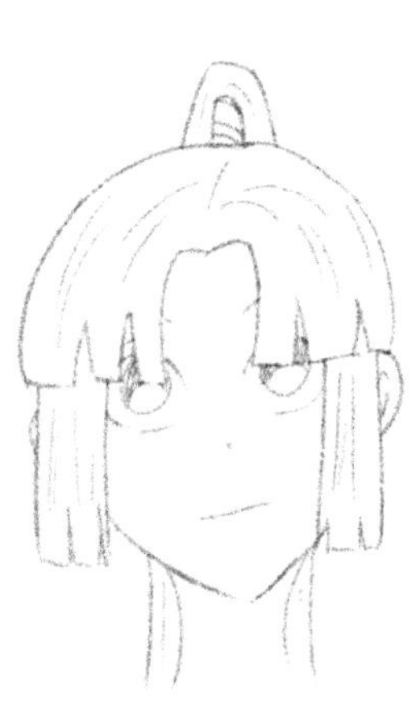

Elegant style

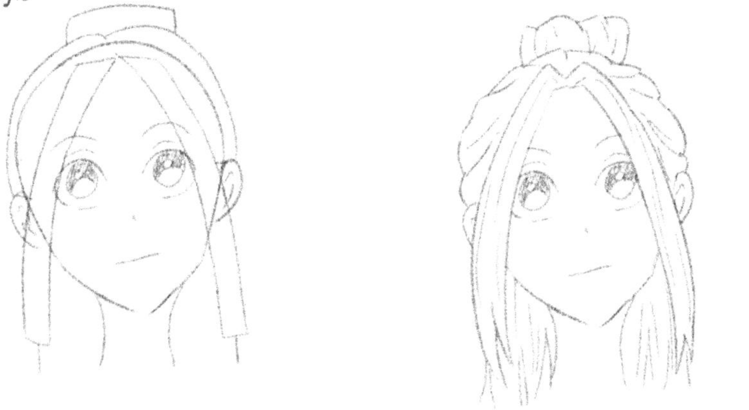

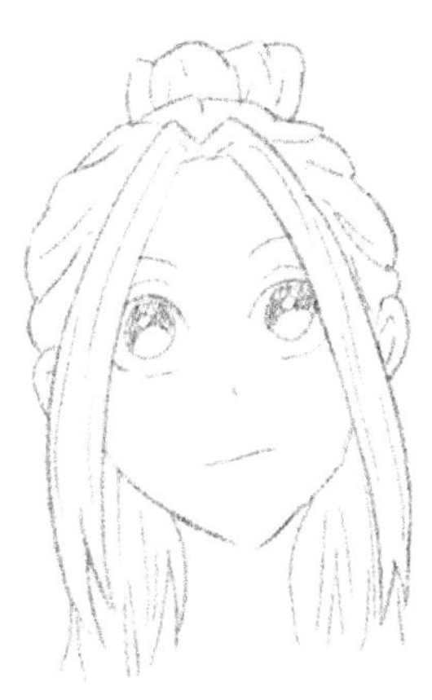

Front curl

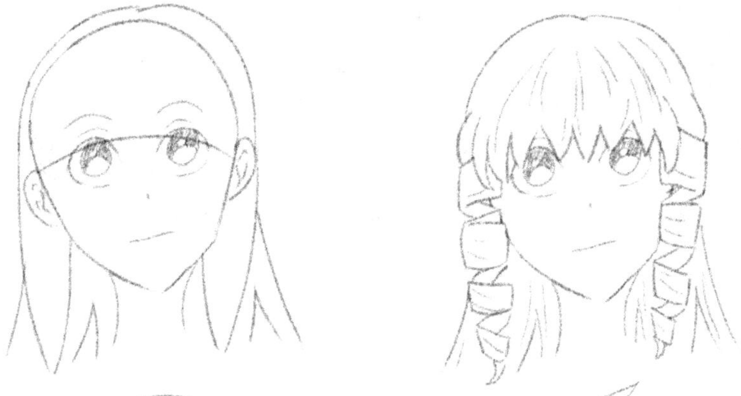

Covered eye

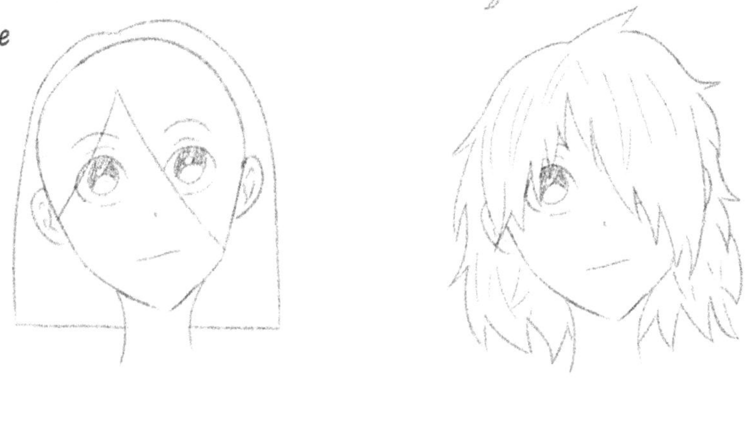

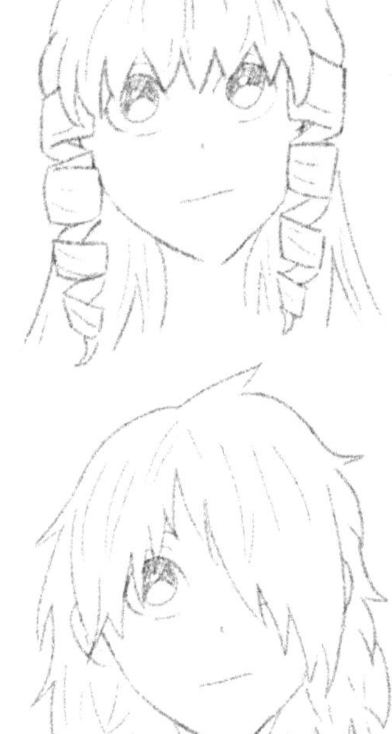

Curly

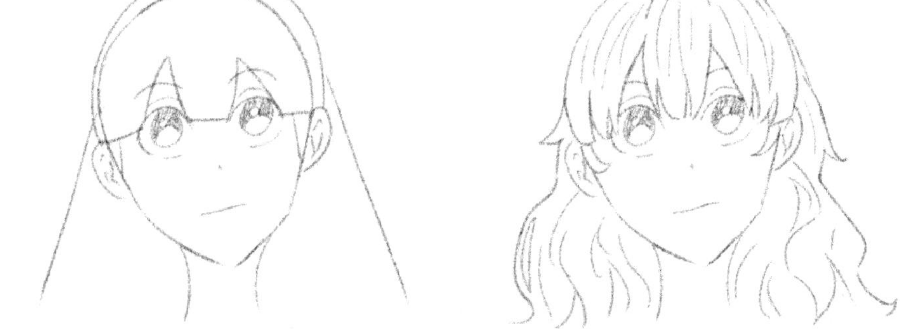

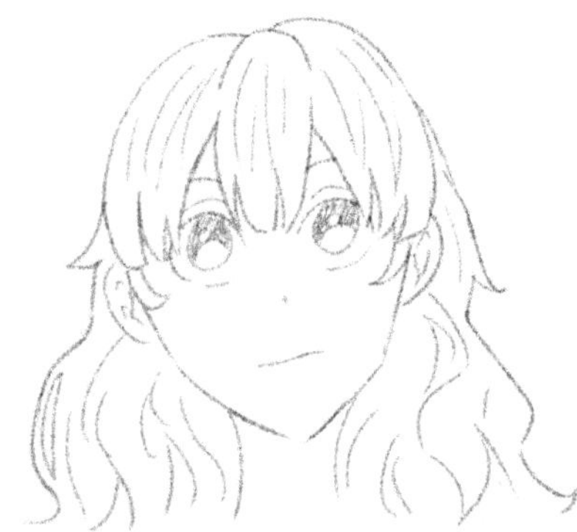

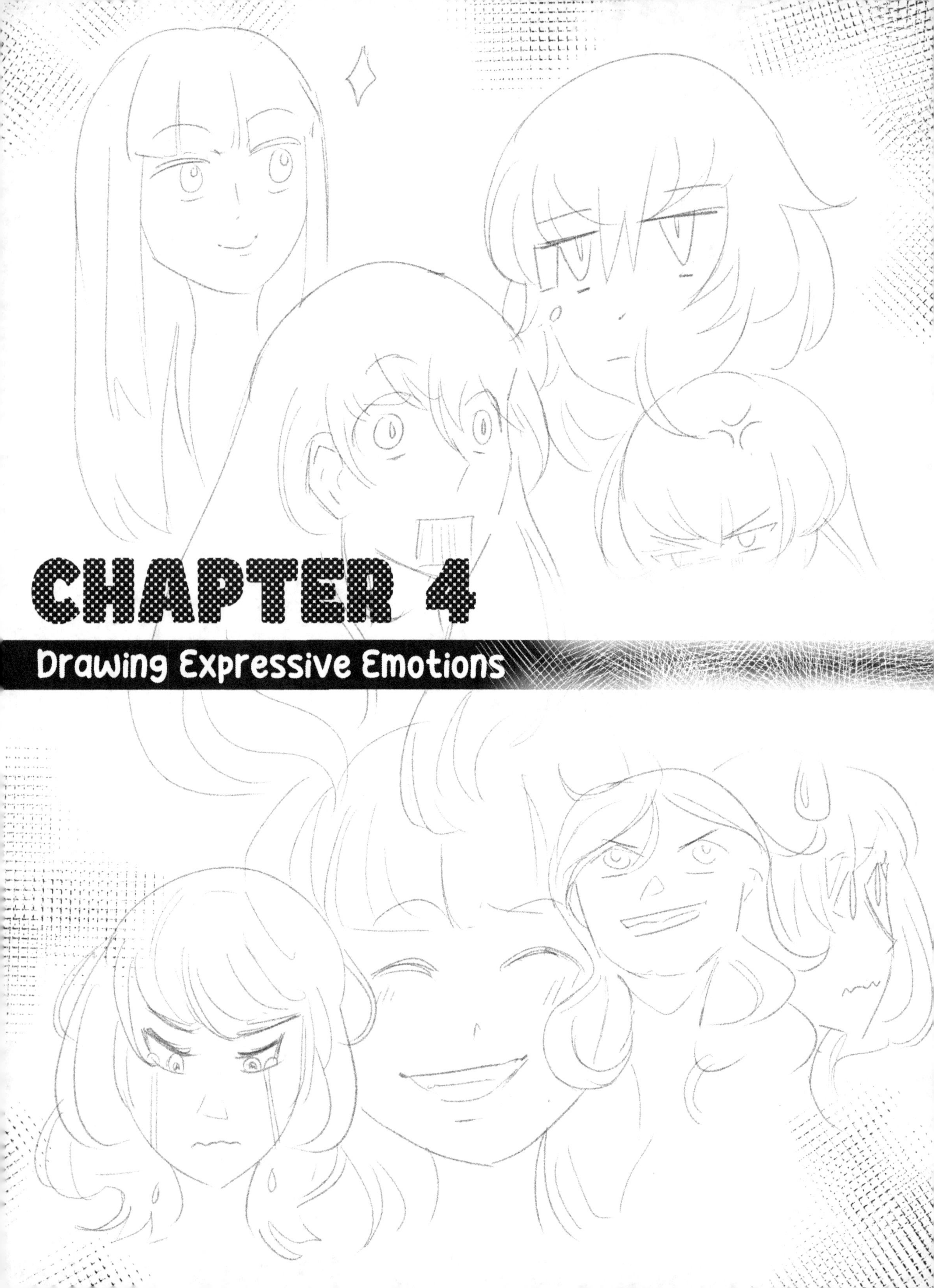

CHAPTER 4
Drawing Expressive Emotions

EXPRESSIONS

You want your character to show different emotions, and to do that you need to imagine what these emotions would look like.

Make the expression you want to draw as you're drawing it, and don't worry too much about it not working. Only with risks will you learn to grow!

Let's get started:

Happy: There are a few ways to show happiness, but the main characteristic is the big smile.

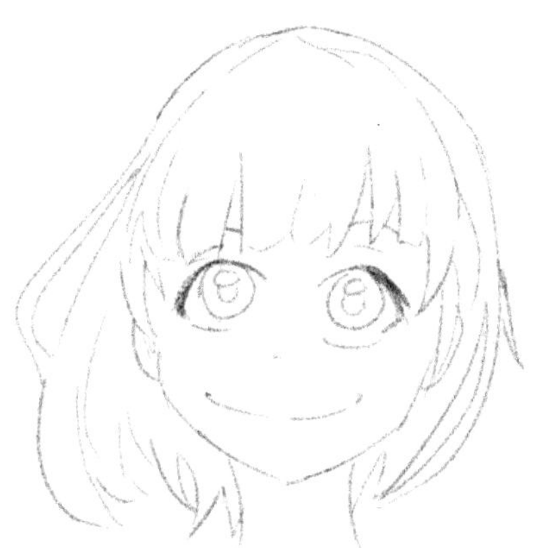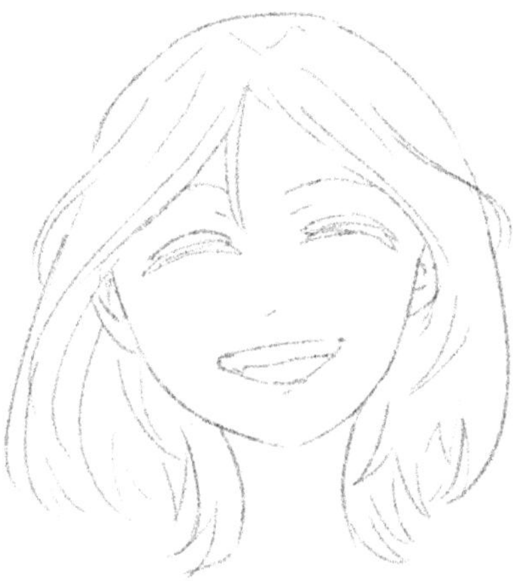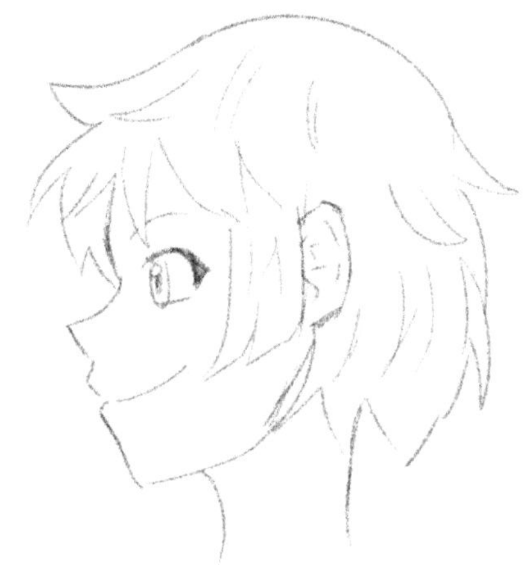

Angry: The main characteristics are angled eyebrows and eyes.

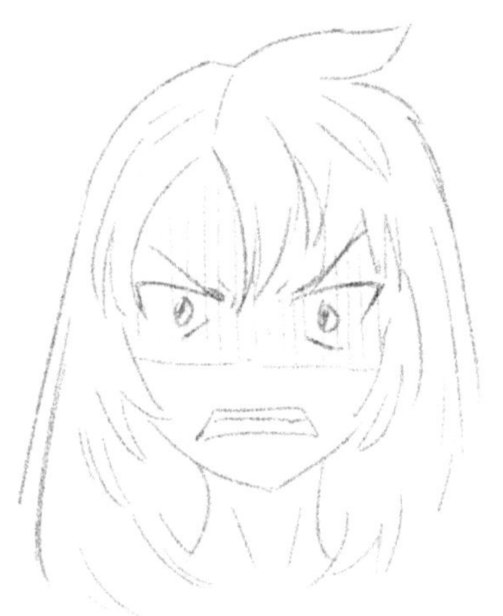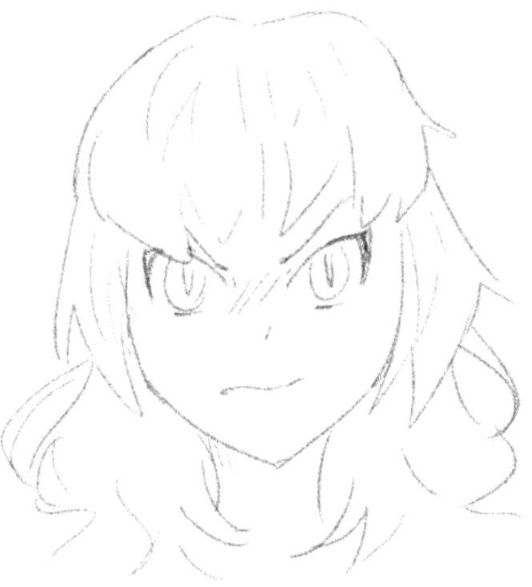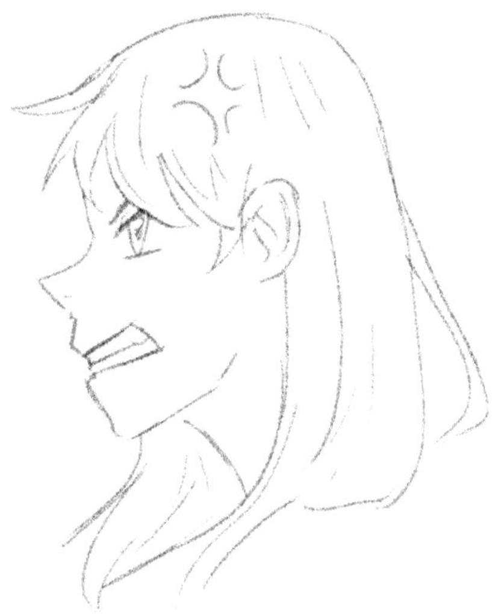

Sad: There are many sad faces. Here are some main characteristics; tears and squinted/closed eyes.

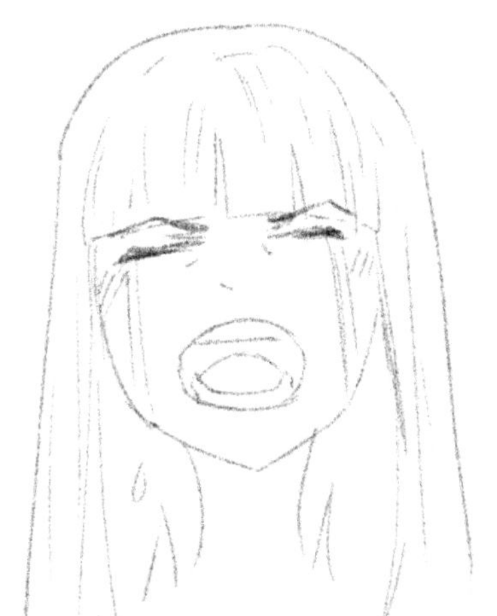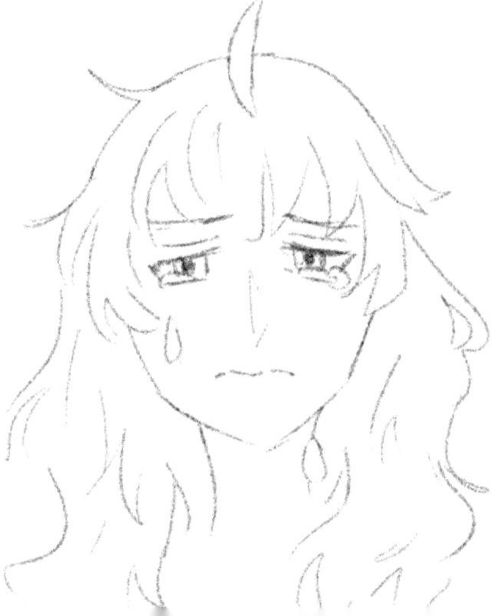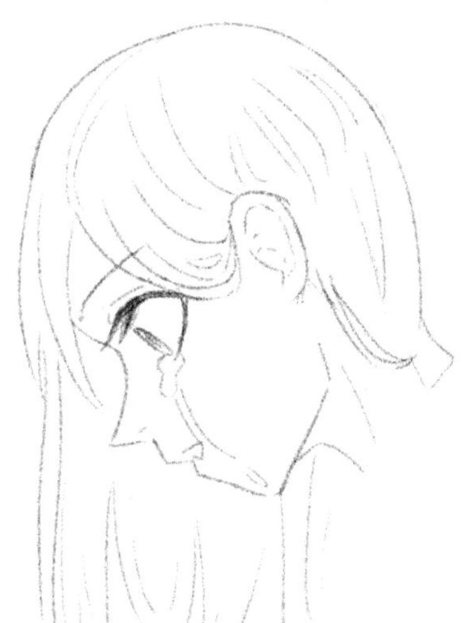

[...]: This expression usually has dilated eyes and a bit of sweat drops on the face.

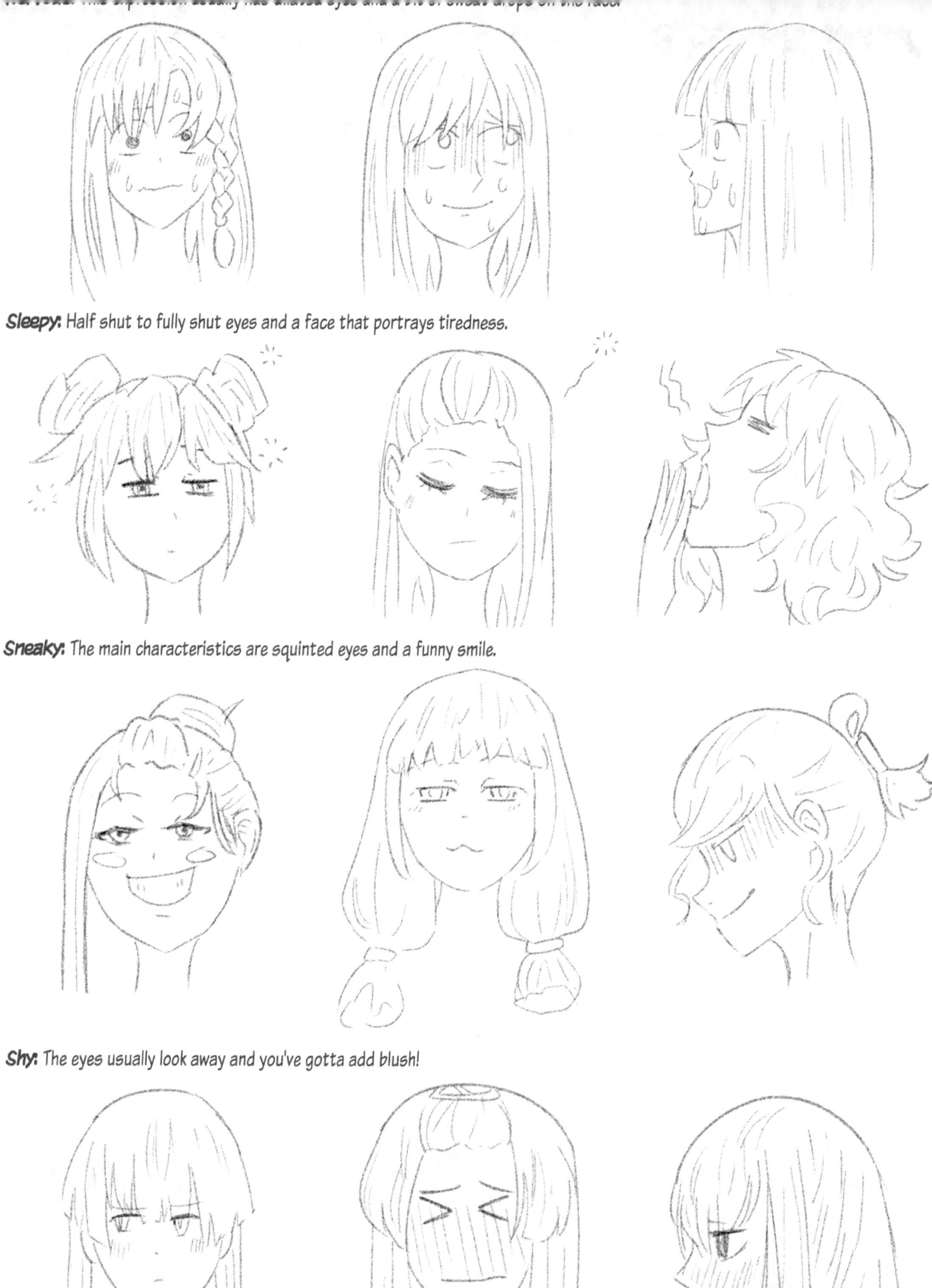

Sleepy: Half shut to fully shut eyes and a face that portrays tiredness.

Sneaky: The main characteristics are squinted eyes and a funny smile.

Shy: The eyes usually look away and you've gotta add blush!

Excited: This expression usually has big sparkly eyes and a big smile.

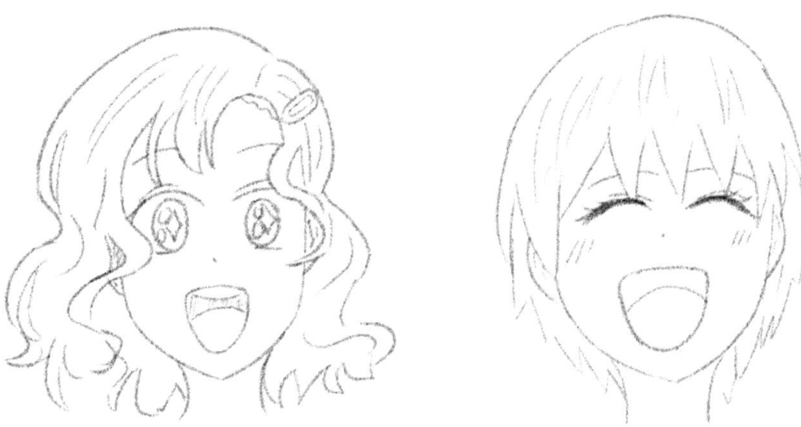

Eating: A full mouth, often with rice on the cheek.

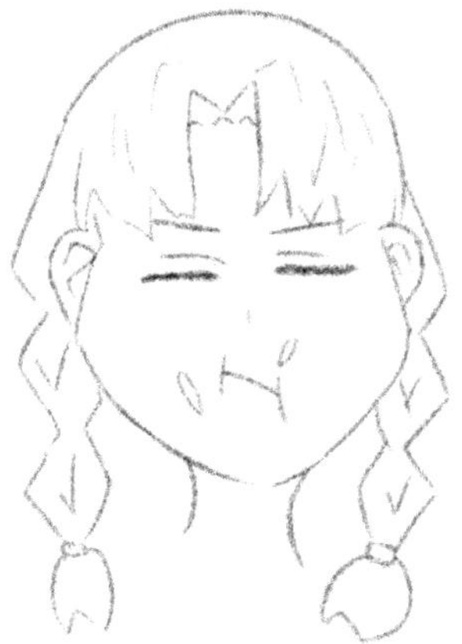 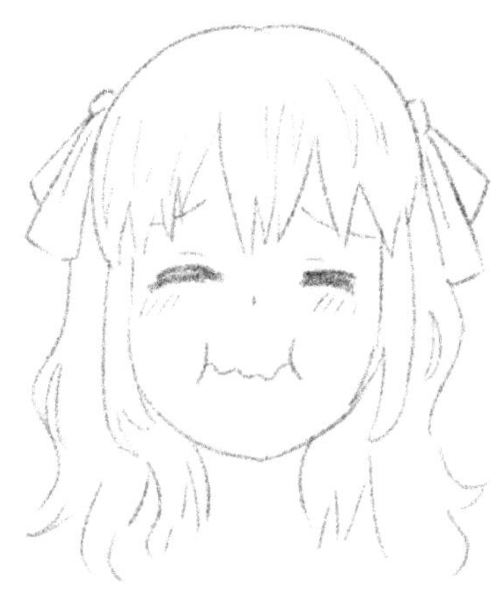 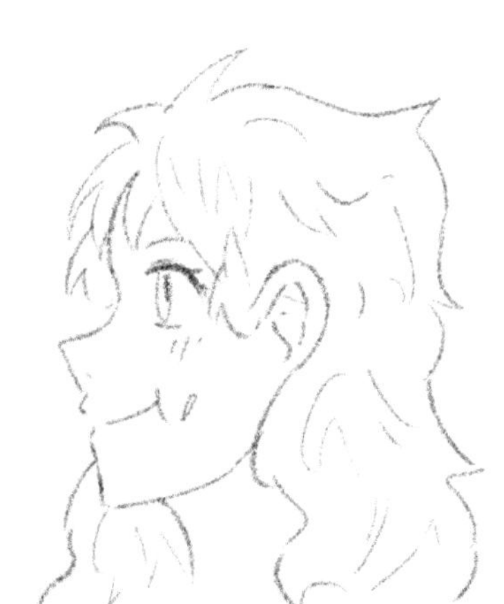

Surprised: Wide eyes and wide mouth with lines across the face to add effect.

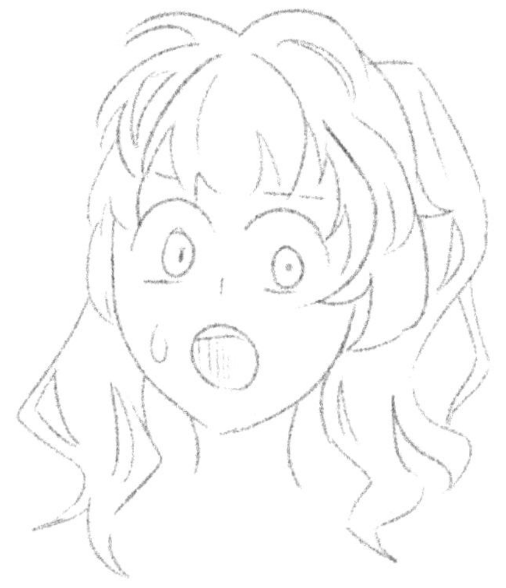 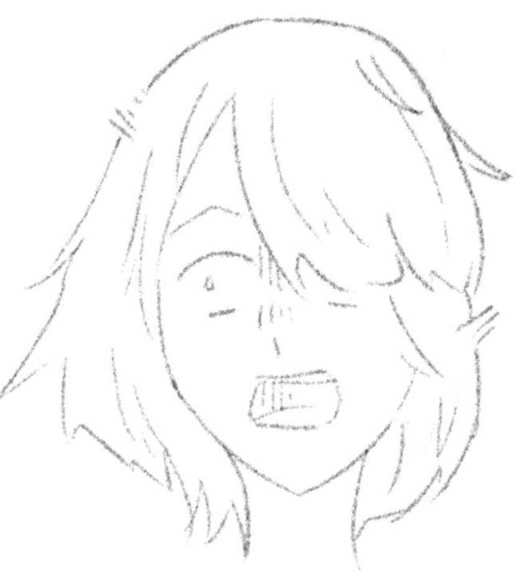 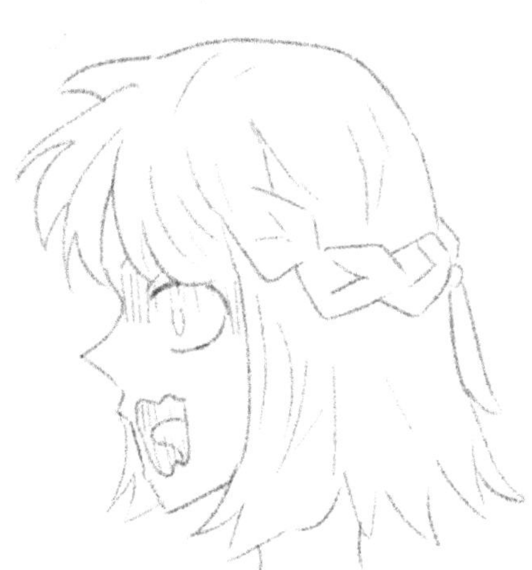

Fear: This one is similar to surprise but with less wide eyes and with different mouth variations.

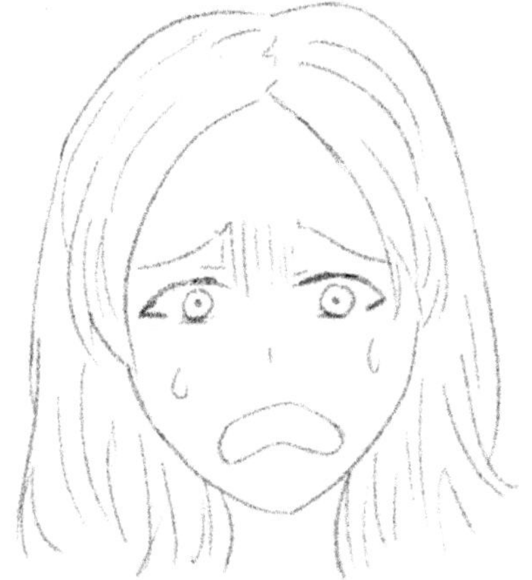 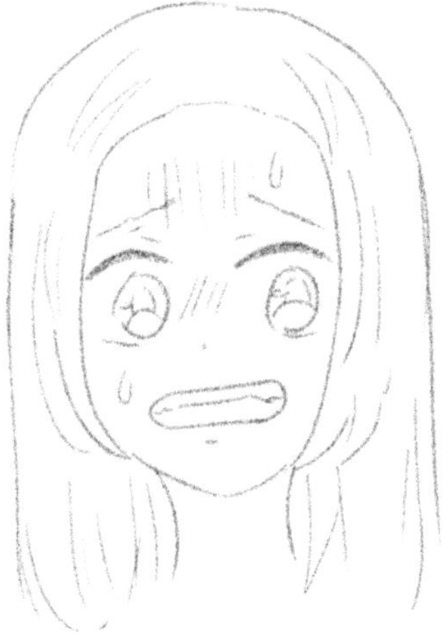 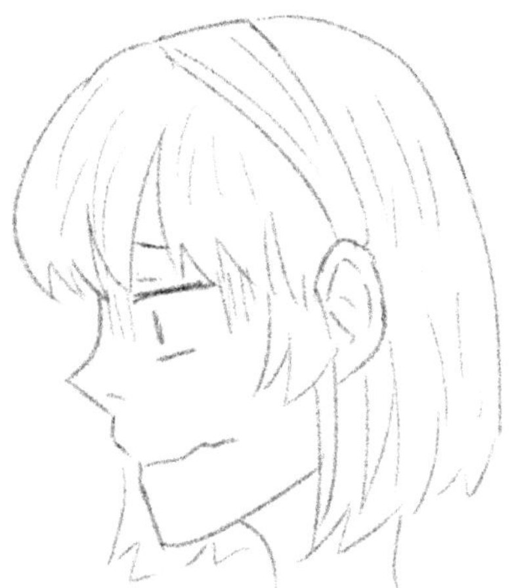

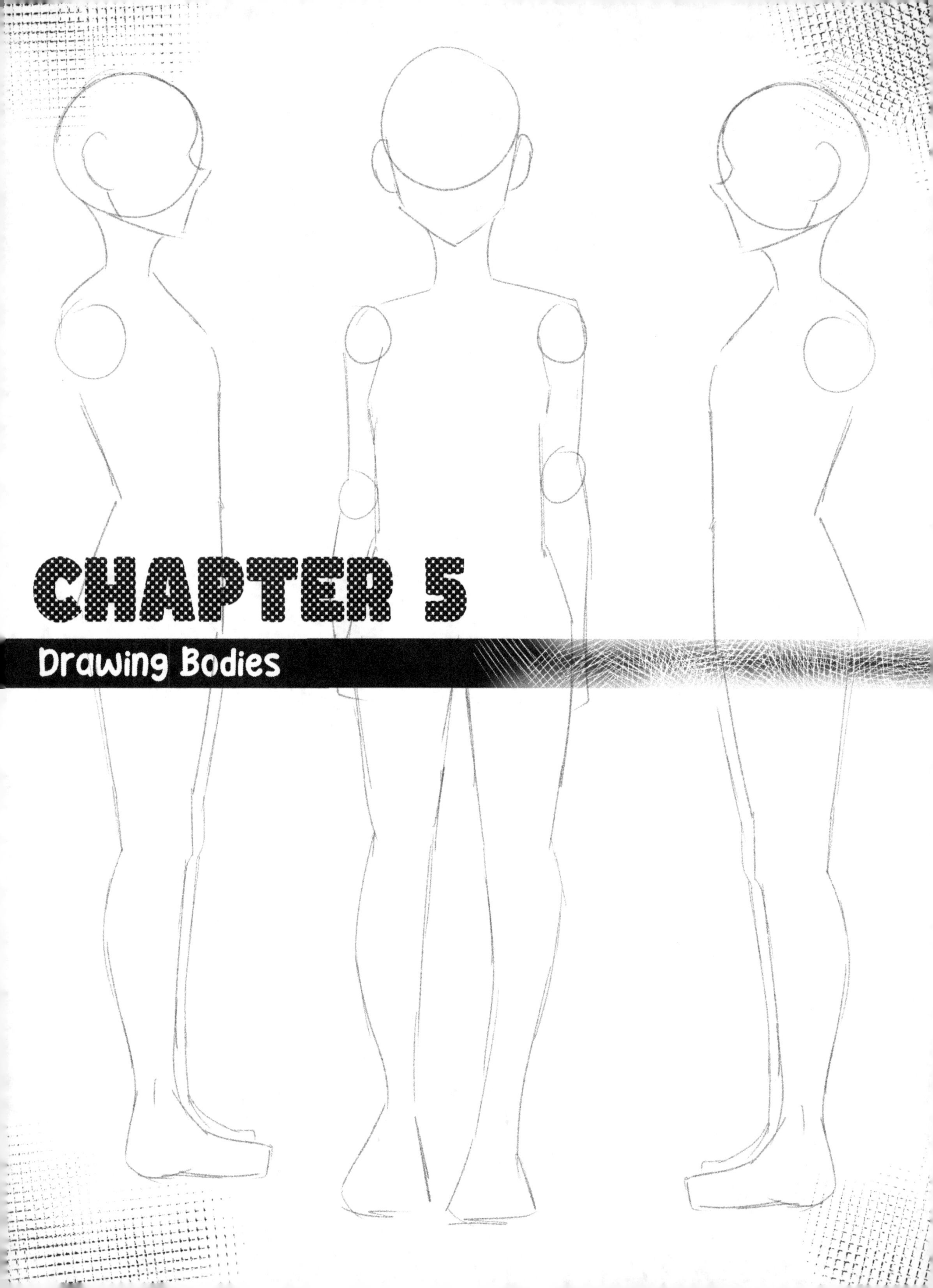

CHAPTER 5
Drawing Bodies

BODIES

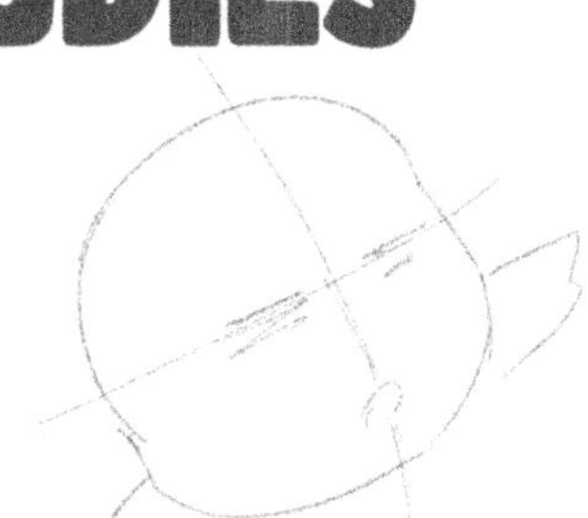

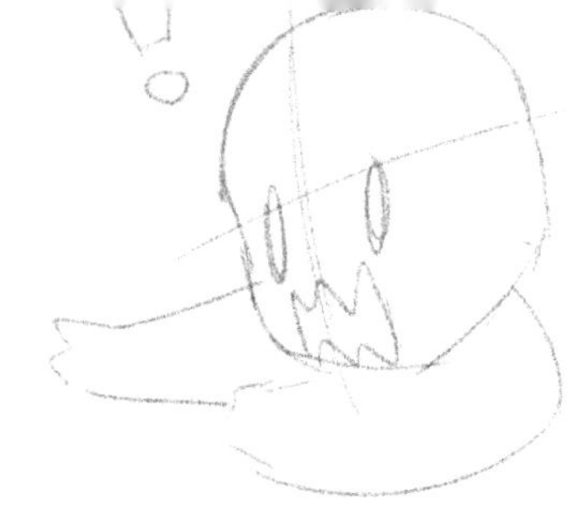

Important tip: Please sketch lightly!!!
You will erase parts of this later.
so trust me when I say, LIGHTLY!

Alright, body time. You have mastered the head and now wish to draw the body.
Well, it's not going to be a walk in the park, but let's give it our all.

Things to keep in mind!

1. The legs are a bit longer than the top half.
2. The arms stop around the hip/thigh area.
3. The shoulders are about as wide as the hips.
4. Oh, and I would highly suggest using REFERENCES.
Look up pictures of people in the pose you like or use yourself
in the mirror as reference.

**Also, be careful not to make the head too big.
That was my problem for so long!**

Let's go step by step by using our favorite
method: Shapes!

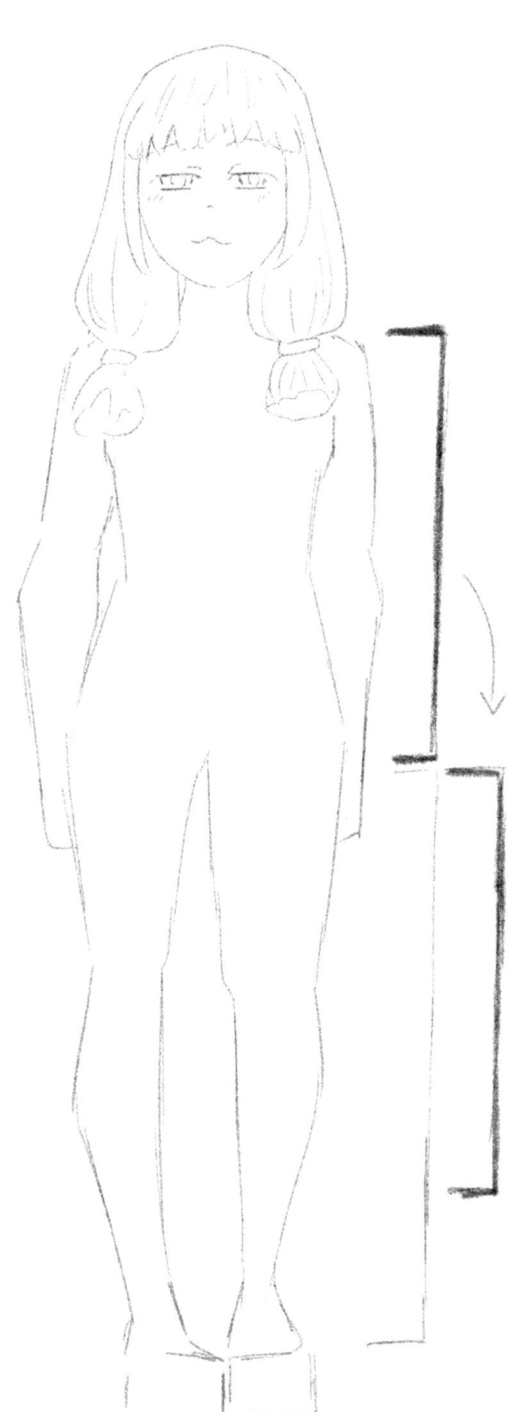

We'll use rectangles for the
body parts and circles where
the joints will be.

Now that's a bit easier to look at.
I'll describe
curves later, so her looking
boxy is not bad.

We just want the right
proportions.

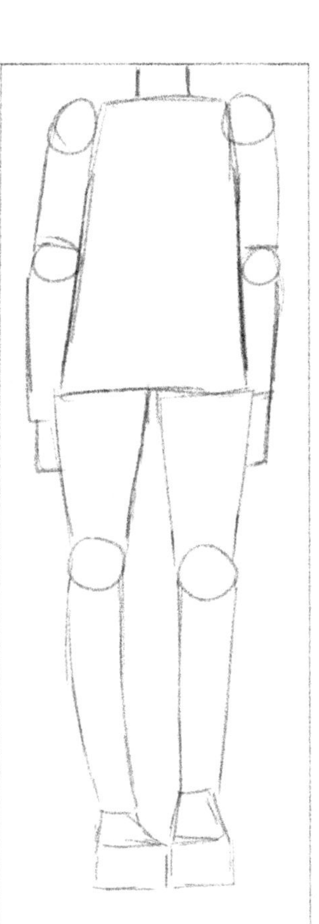

Alright, let's go!

Start by drawing a head.

1.

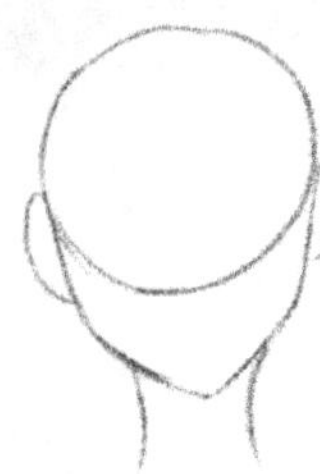

Plan your body where the hips
are and where legs end.

2.

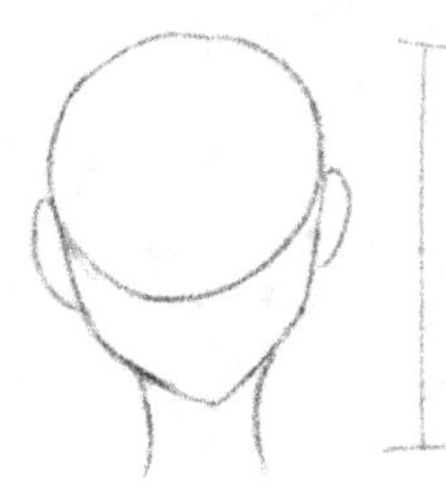

Draw a long trapezoid and stop
it where the hip line is.

3.

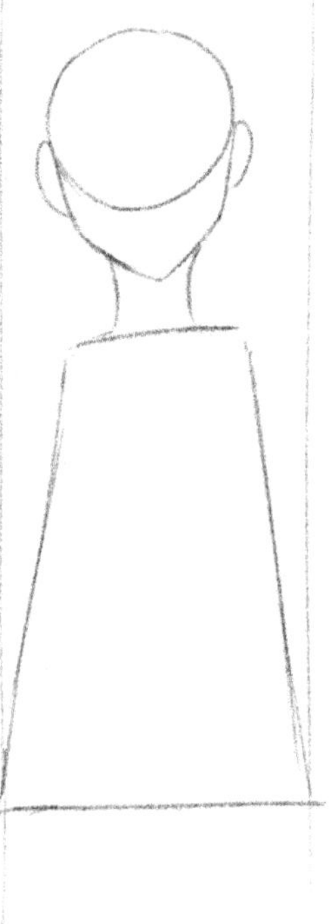

Now draw two rectangles about
halfway from the bottom line.

4.

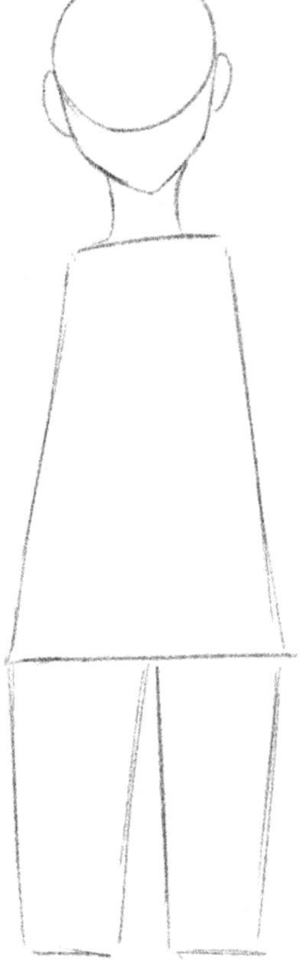

Now draw circles at the joints.

5.

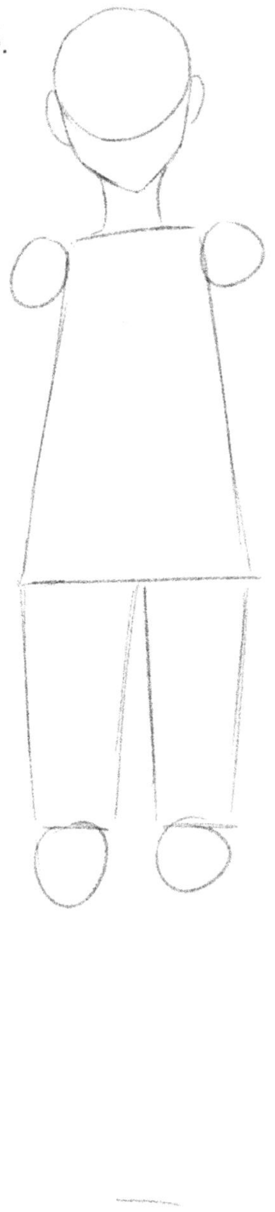

Another set of rectangles
right before the line.

6.

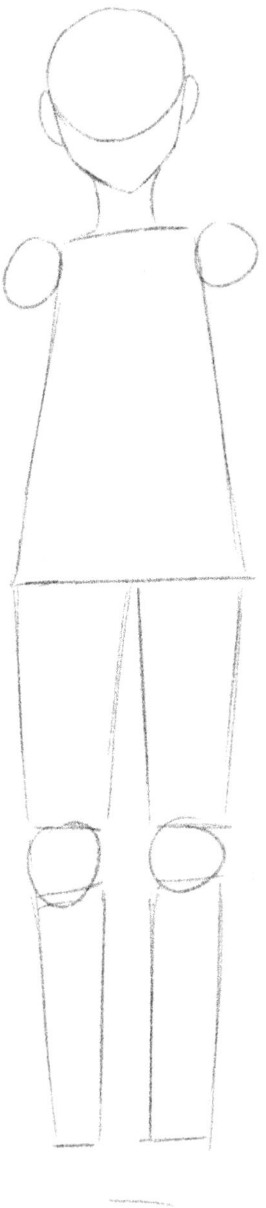

Draw two thin rectangles.
Those will be the toes.

7.

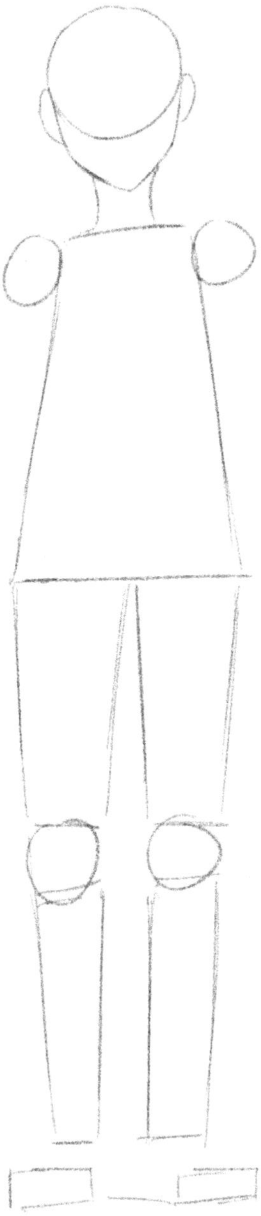

We will now finish the foot.
Remember that
naturally no one really
stands with their feet
perfectly straight,
so this pose looks
a lot more natural.

8.

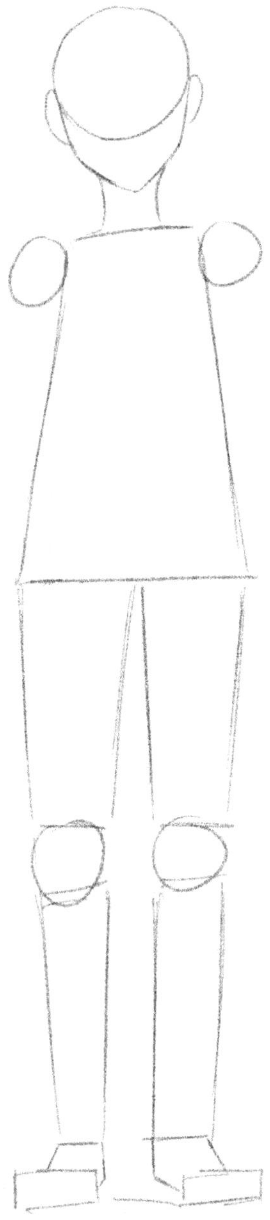

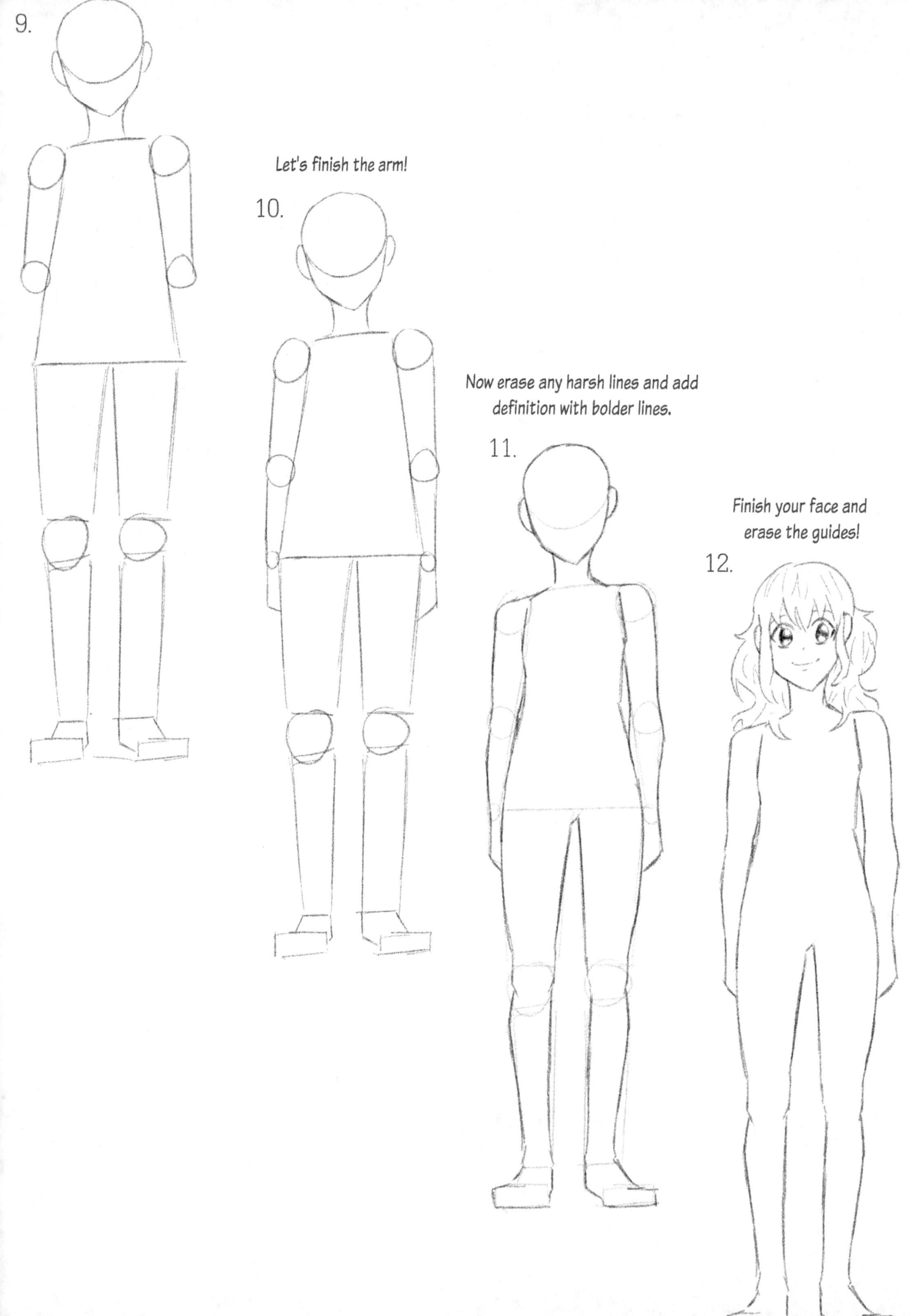

9.
Let's finish the arm!
10.
Now erase any harsh lines and add
definition with bolder lines.
11.
Finish your face and
erase the guides!
12.

Side View

Draw a head side profile.

1.

2. body ahead of time.

3. shape to the hip line.

4. then a trapezoid.

Mirror Version:

1.

2.

3.

4.

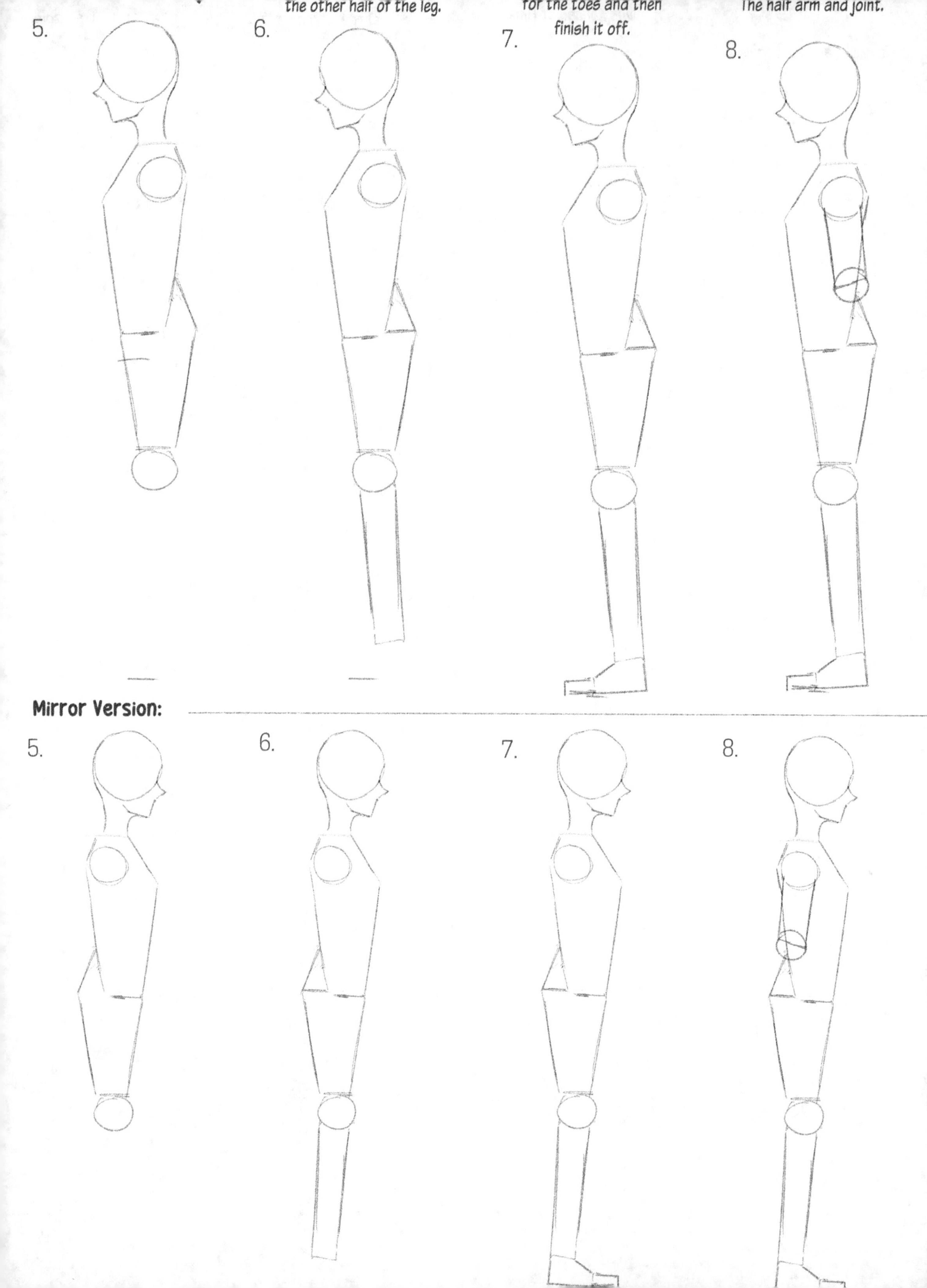

the other half of the leg.
for the toes and then
finish it off.
The half arm and joint.
5.
6.
7.
8.
Mirror Version:
5.
6.
7.
8.

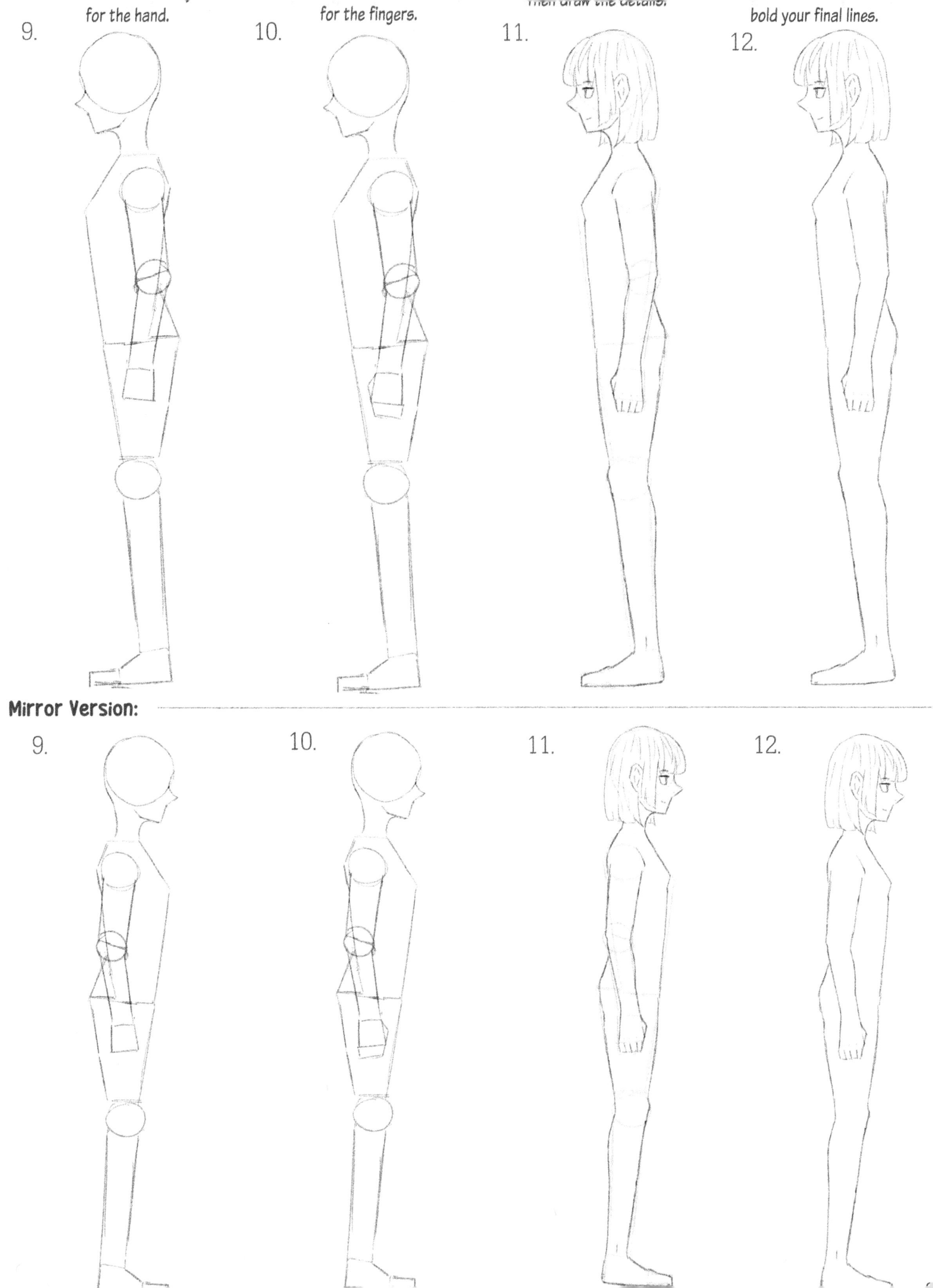
for the hand.
for the fingers.
bold your final lines.
9.
10.
11.
12.
Mirror Version:
9.
10.
11.
12.

HANDS

Start with parts of the hand, and I would HIGHLY SUGGEST that you use references. You can look up the pose you want or even use your own hand.

Remember the pinky is short and your middle finger is the longest. We need to get the proportions right. Don't worry and just have fun with it!

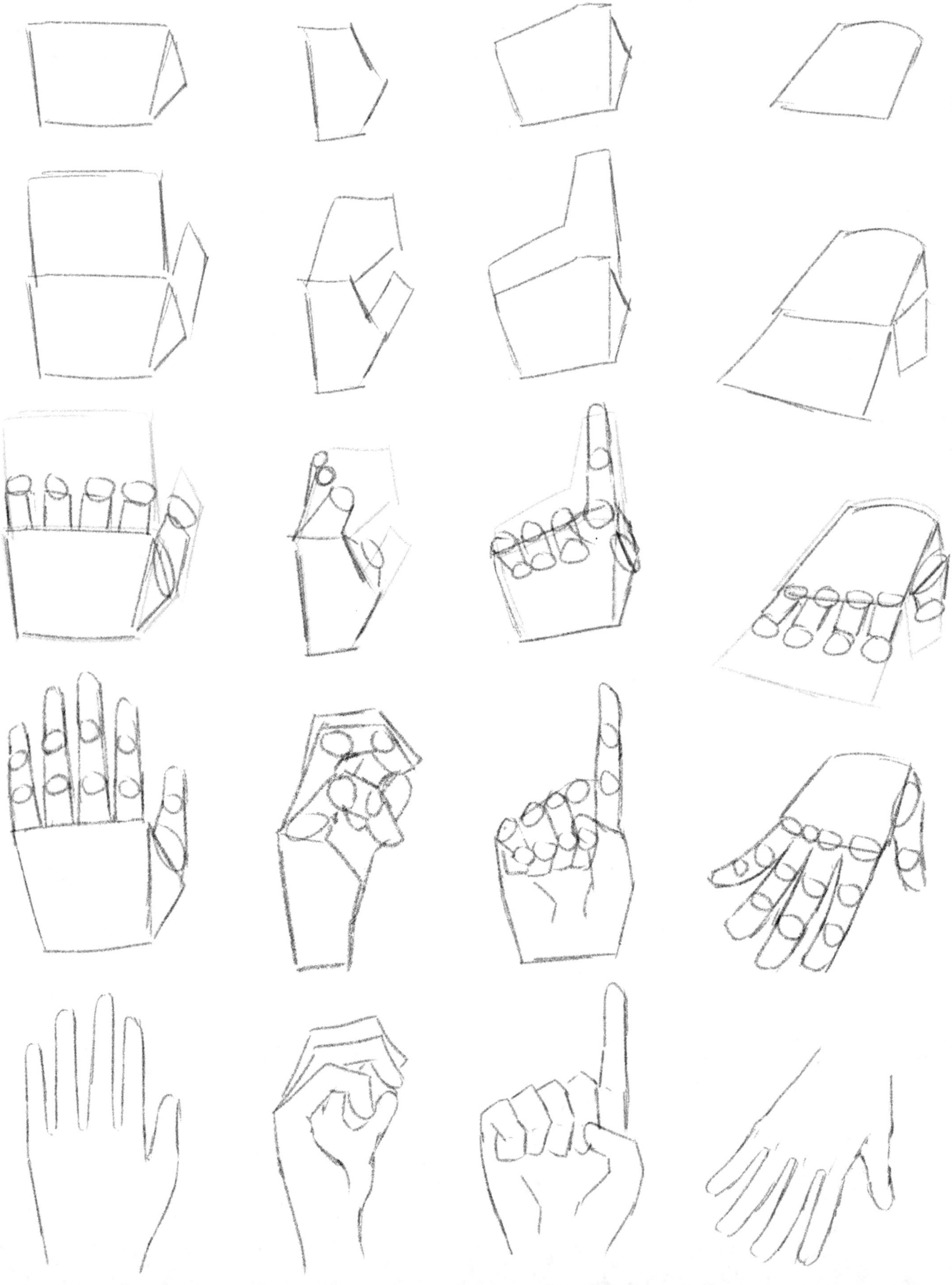

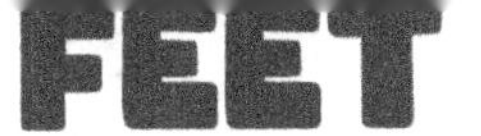

FEET

They aren't too bad as hands. Make a rectangle For the toes, then Finish the shape to get the right angle.

Good luck!

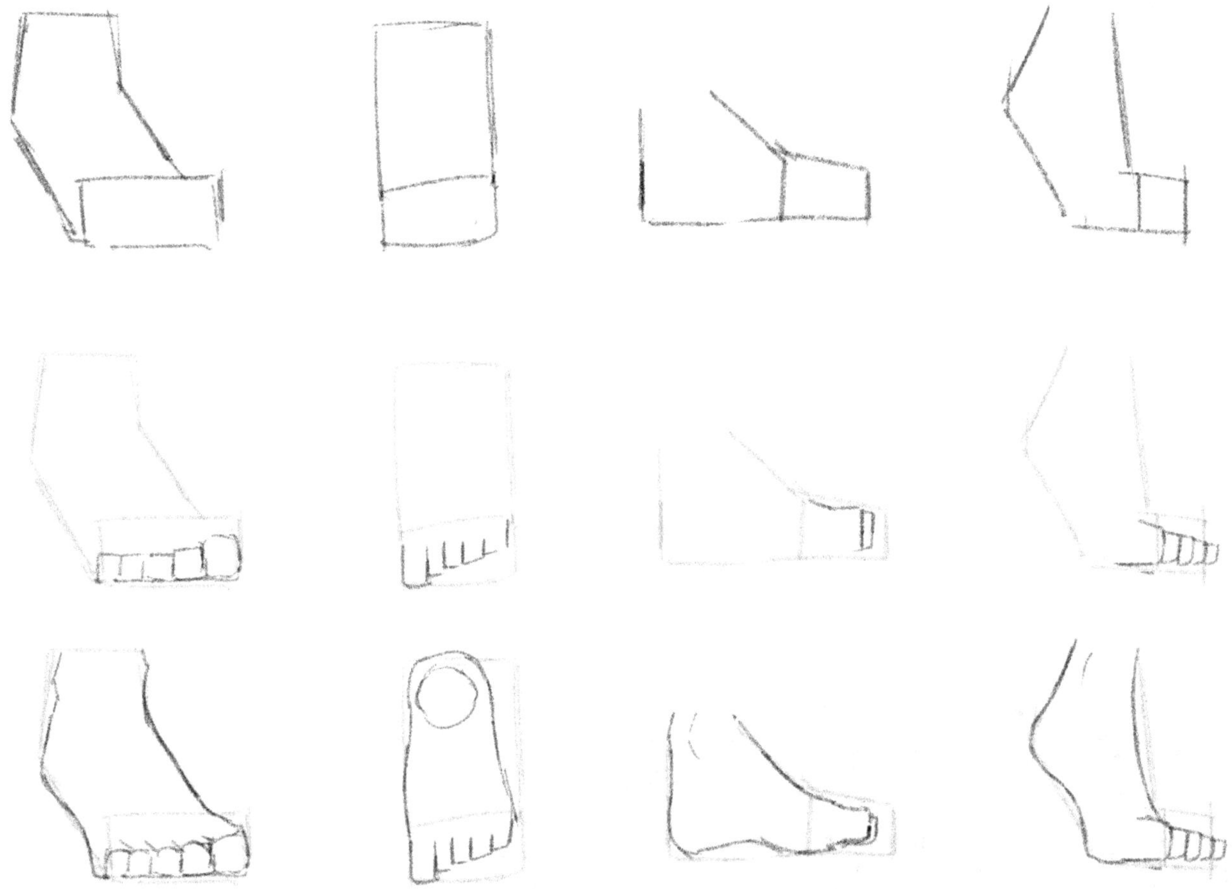

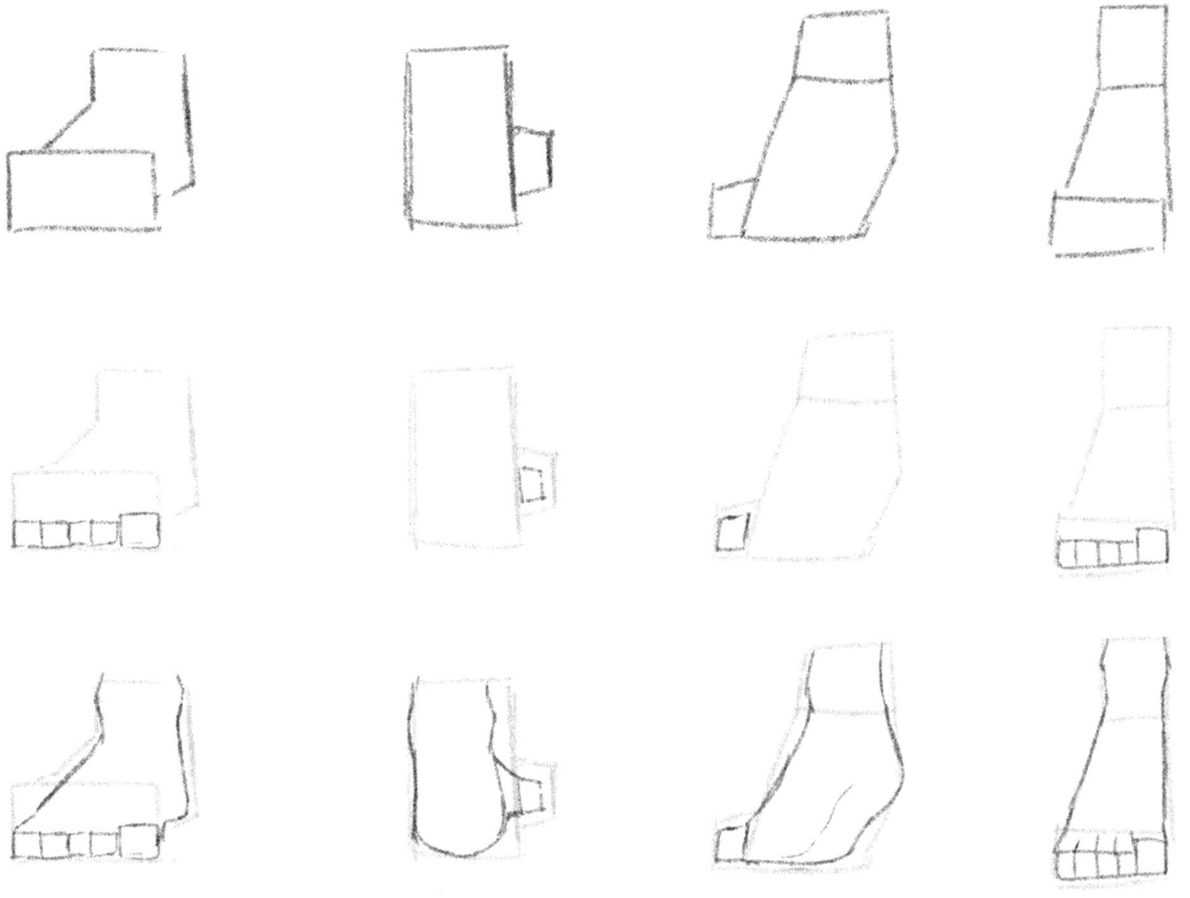

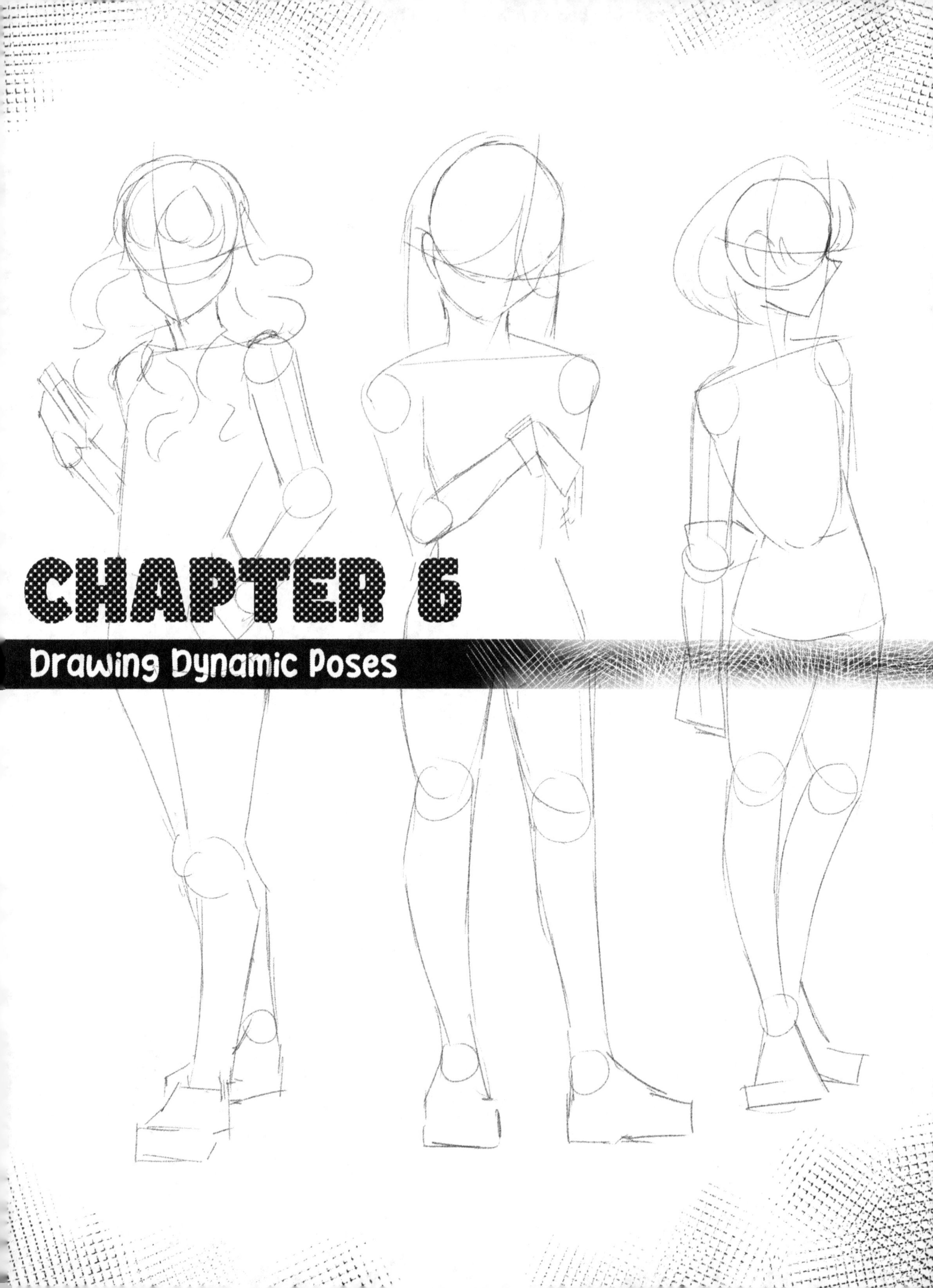

CHAPTER 6
Drawing Dynamic Poses

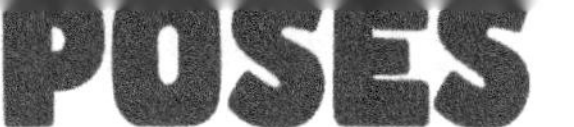

POSES

Drawing different poses is no cake walk, but I will say using references is very important For drawing the right pose you want. I still use references too.

If you're trying to draw a pose From a picture of someone, then I would suggest you outline the pose with shapes to make it easier.

Examples:

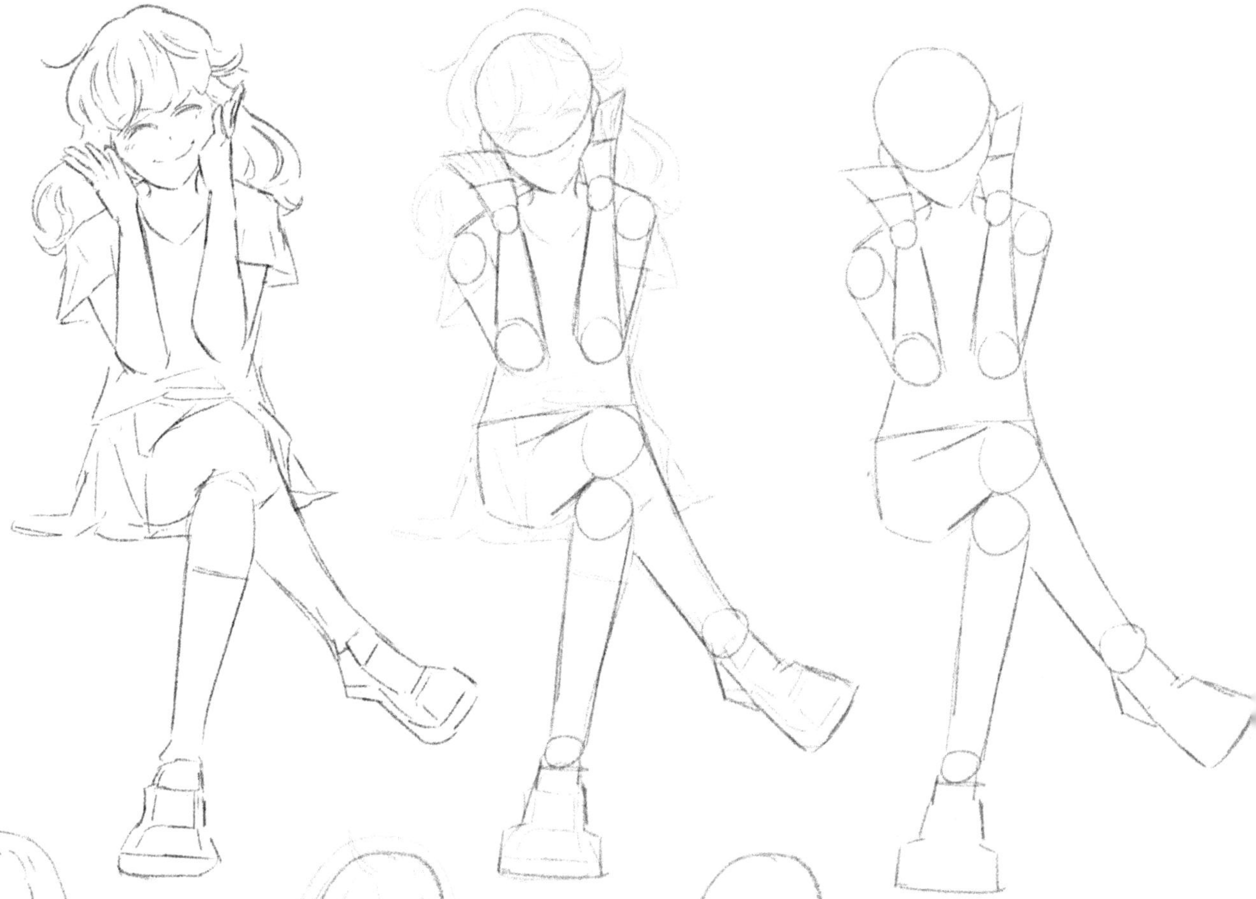

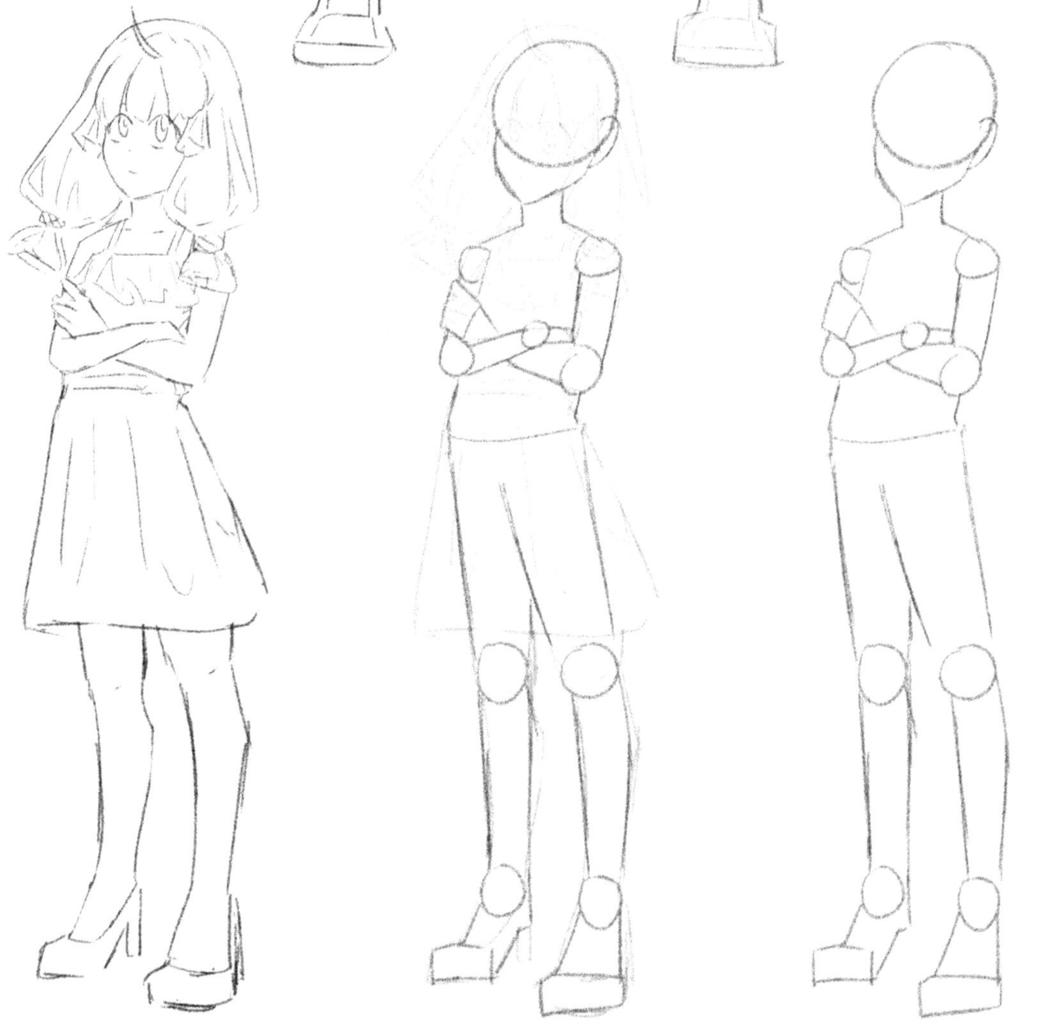

The more you practice, the more you will understand and the faster you'll be able to do it!

Now let's continue!

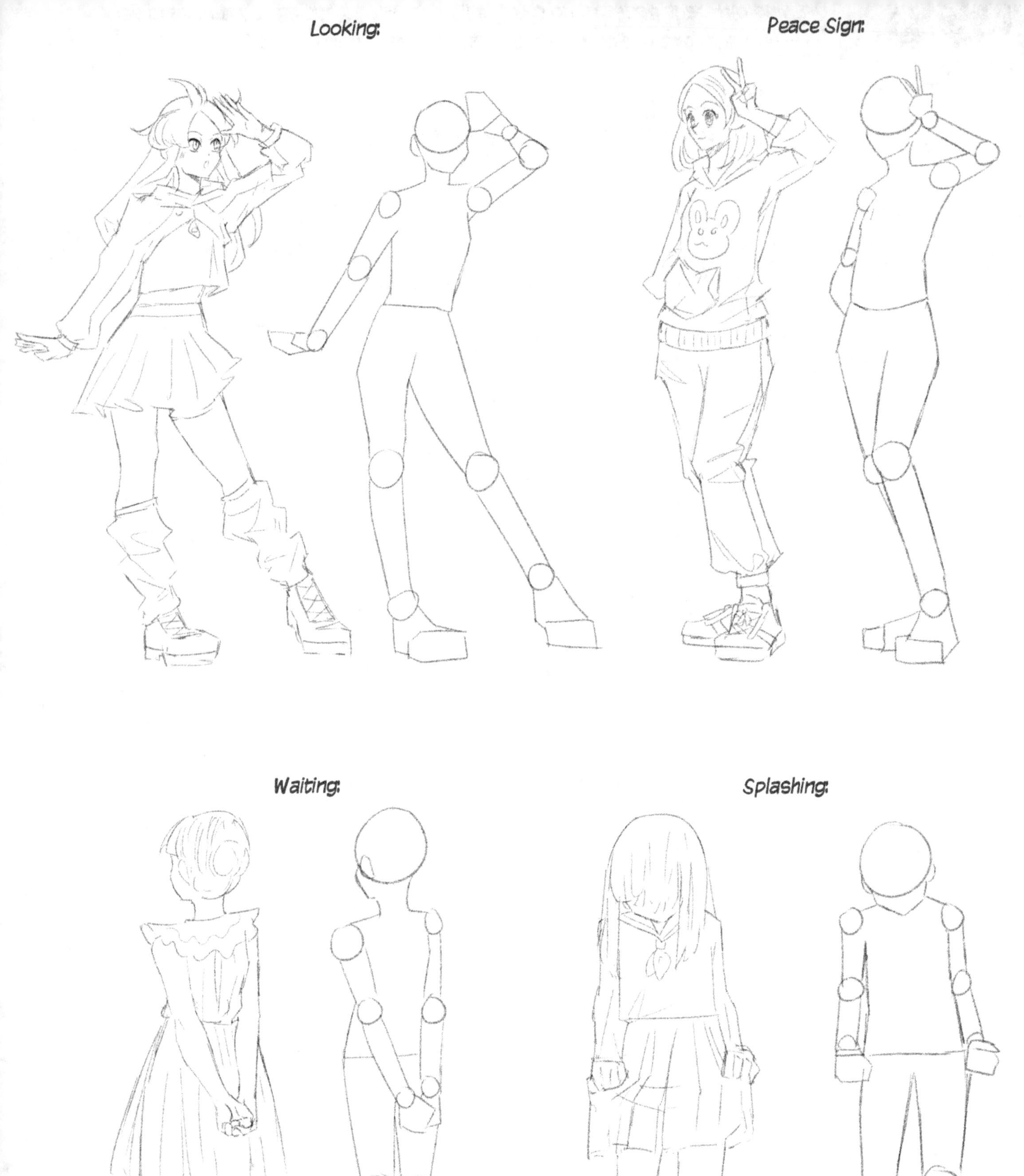

Looking:
Peace Sign:
Waiting:
Splashing:

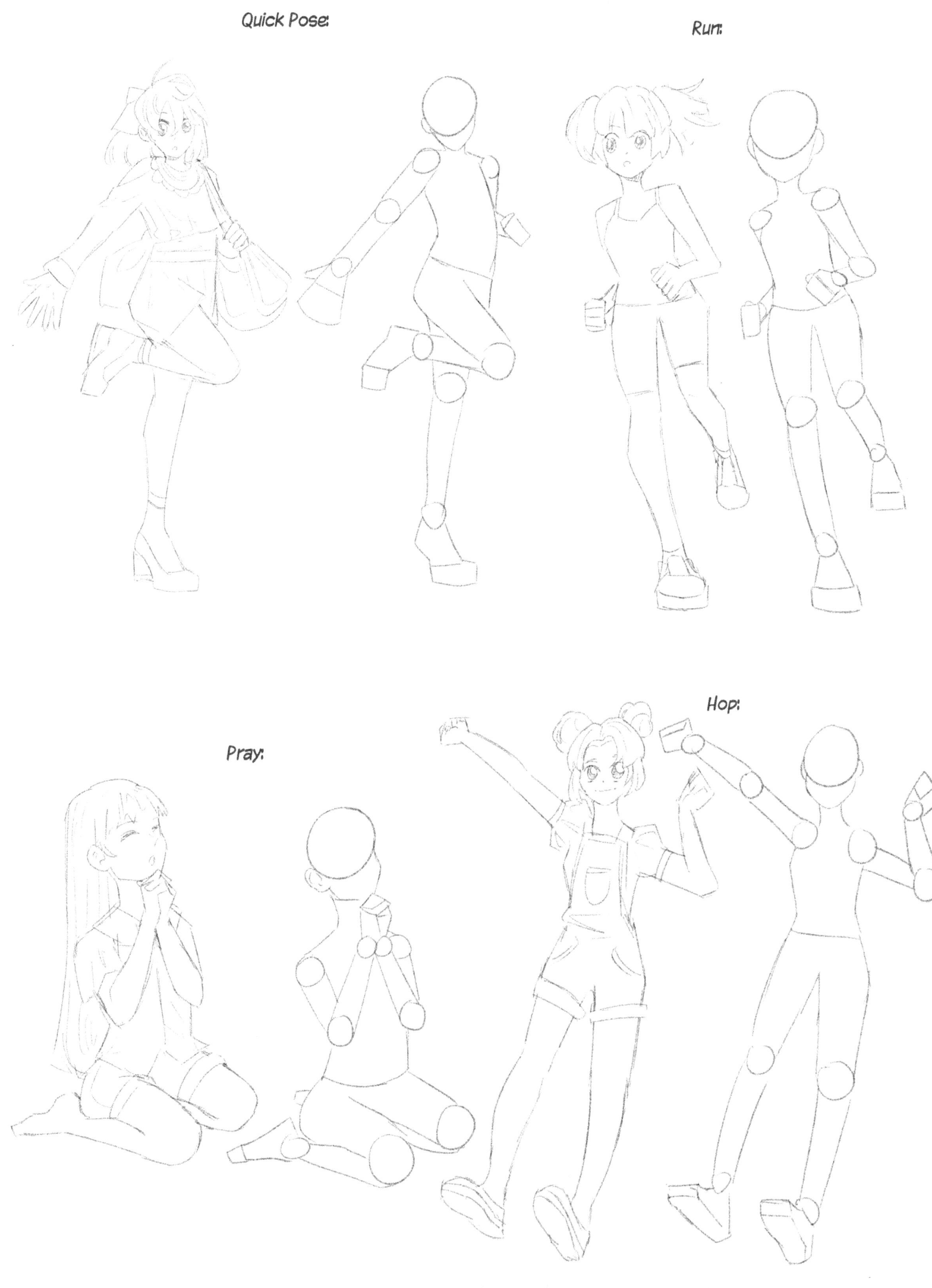

Quick Pose:
Run:
Pray:
Hop:

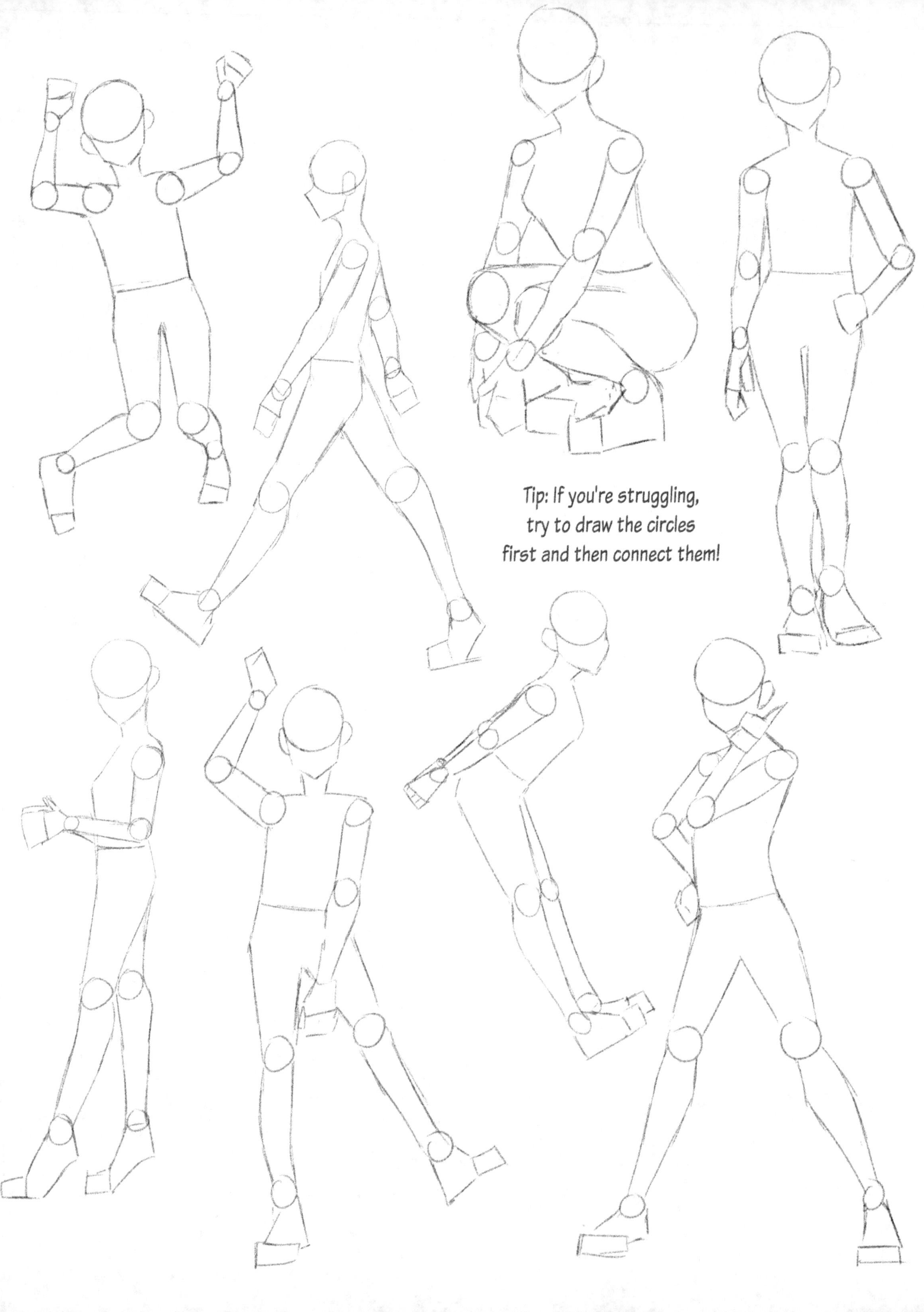

Tip: If you're struggling,
try to draw the circles
first and then connect them!

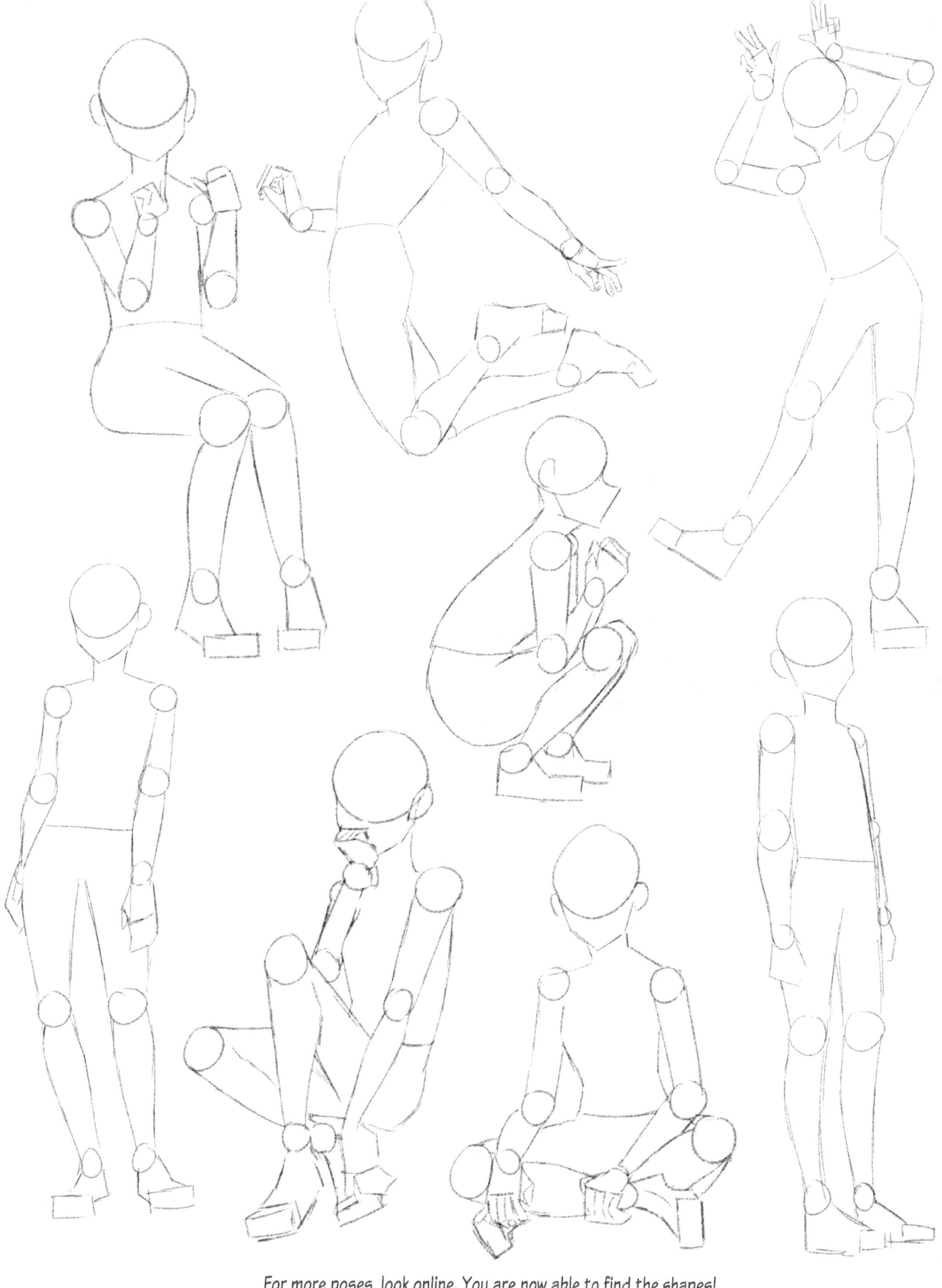

For more poses, look online. You are now able to find the shapes!
All you need to do is refine the body after the shape is made.

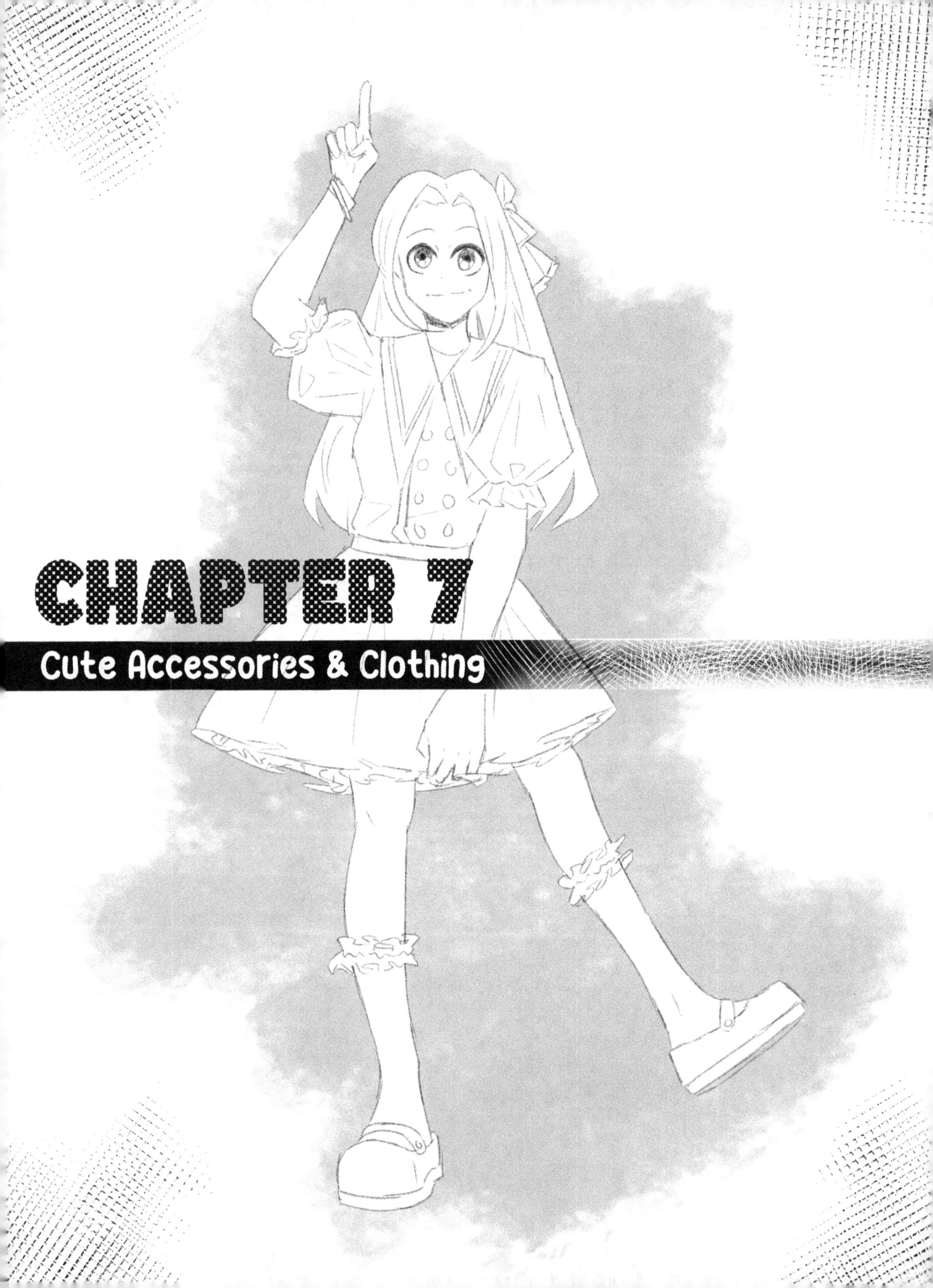

CHAPTER 7
Cute Accessories & Clothing

CLOTHING

Before we start drawing clothes, you should first learn
how gravity works for them!
This will help when you go to make clothing folds and wrinkles.

Here the tension is at the
top, causing everything
to flow loosely downwards.

The tension is at both sides,
causing more fold lines as the
fabric is stretched out.

Here there is no strong
tension as it's falling but
the heaviest part will fall faster,
causing a dip, so the edges
follow the heavy part down.

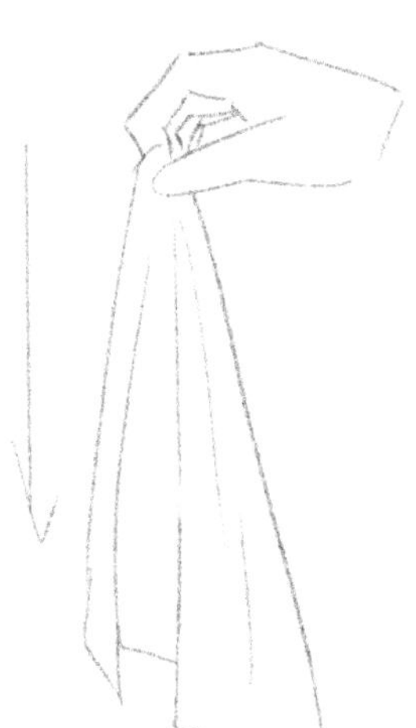

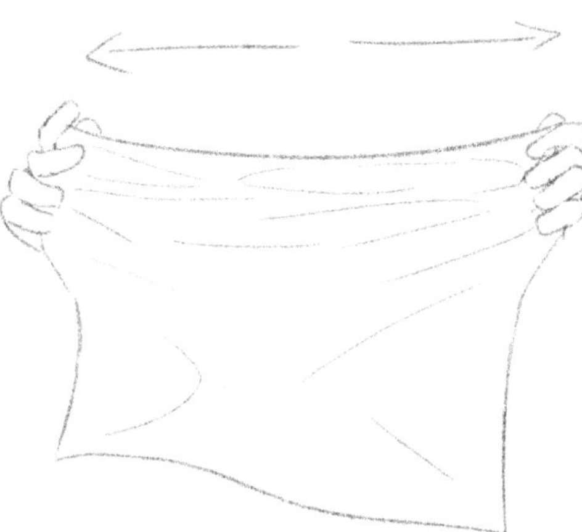

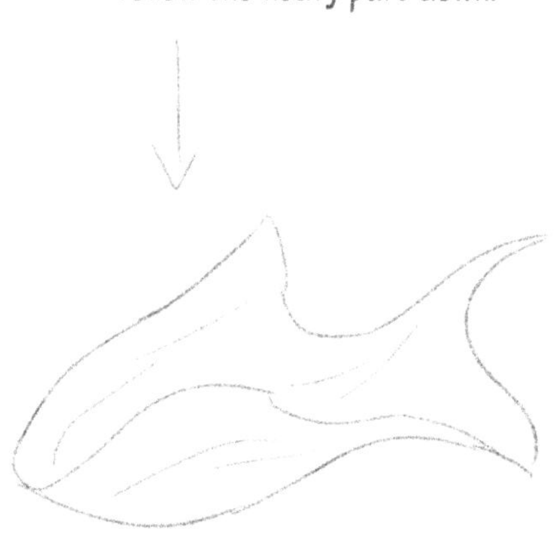

Example: Clothing is usually not too tight, so the lines will stay loose but suggest a tension area.
The shoulders here act as tension for the shirt, causing all the folds to be
directed downwards. The chest also causes the fabric to be pulled on both sides.

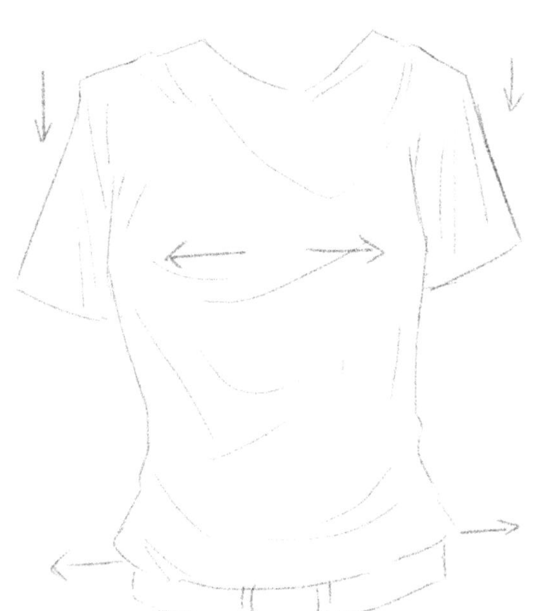

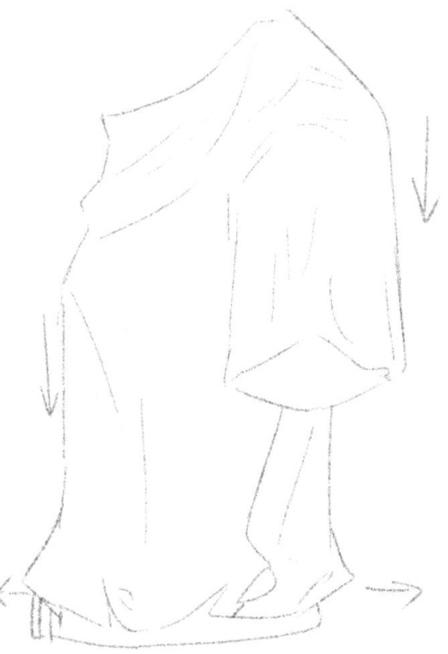

This bottom part folds out
because the belt is forcing
it to stop flowing down, so the
extra fabric just gathers and stays there.

So keep in mind where the fabric is being stretched and in what direction. Again, references
will help you spot that if you want more practice!

Let's talk about bunching areas where your limbs/body bends.
This is where folding lines are more visible (where the fabric gathers).
So let's see those areas!

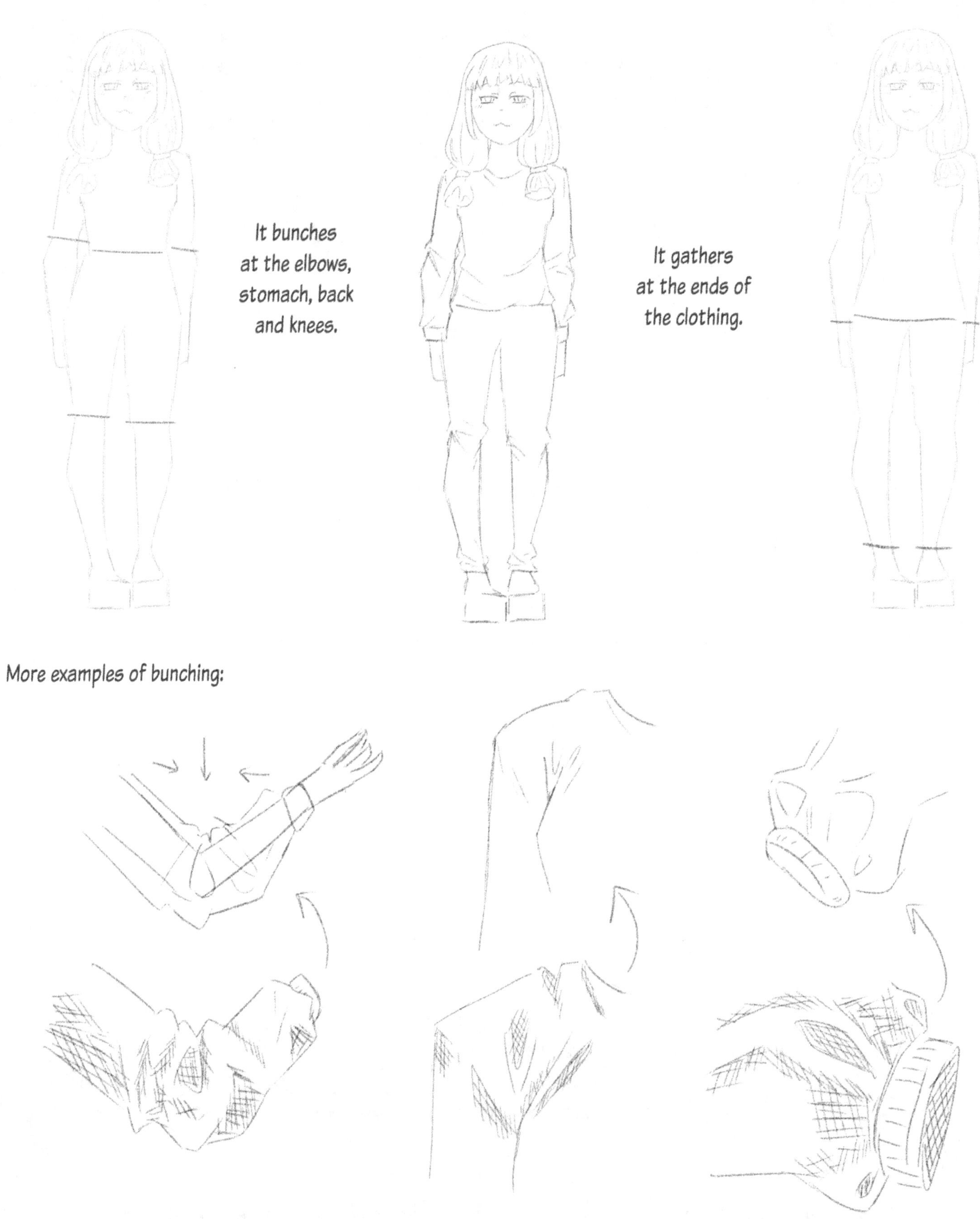

It bunches at the elbows, stomach, back and knees.

It gathers at the ends of the clothing.

More examples of bunching:

But again, it all varies with tight and loose clothing and also fabric type. Then stuff like wind and the pose you're in also play a part. Let's just do one step at a time.
Just think, where would tension come from?

Understanding fabric folds are very important to improving your clothing. I suggest looking at the lines first and then adding shadows.

Remember, the small lines should follow the larger shapes and then the shadows help it look better! You just really need to think, "If the light is coming from the top, where are the shadows sitting?"

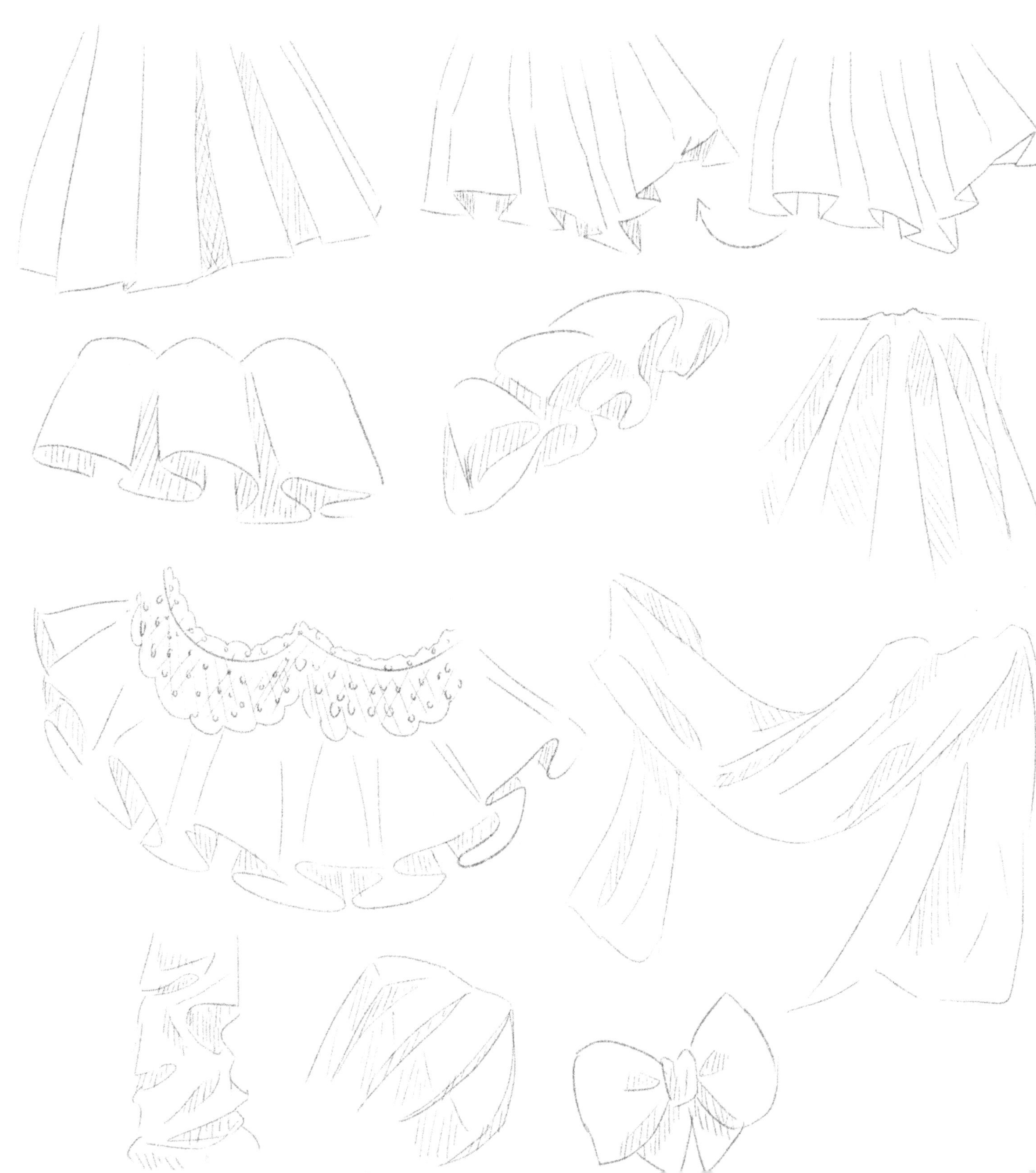

SHOES

One more thing. I draw shoes just outside the foot, like so:

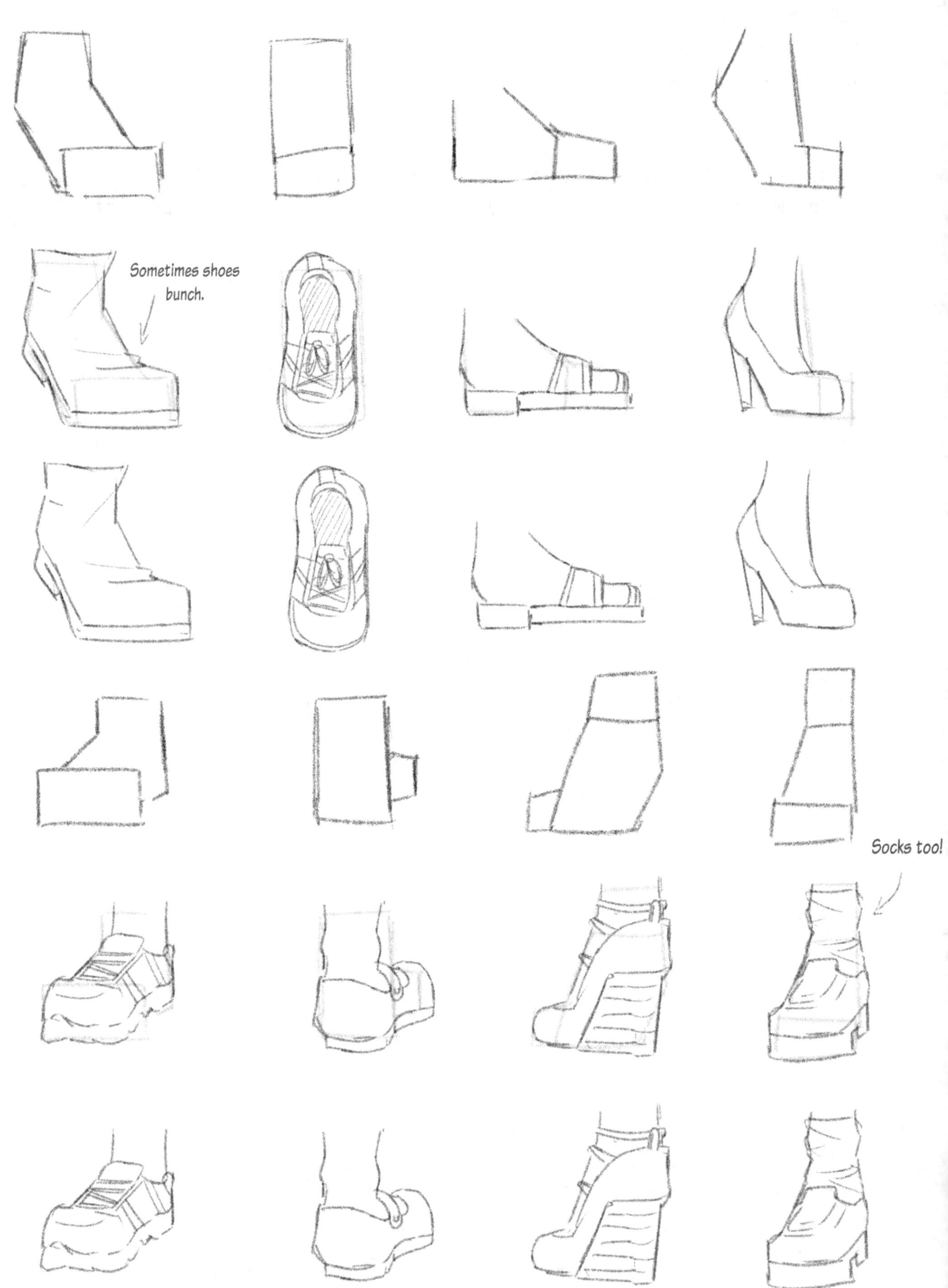

I would suggest referencing a pair of shoes you like from online.
They usually show different angles of the shoes, so that helps a lot!

Sometimes I draw clothes first and decide on the hair later.
Although, the other way is also perfectly fine.

This shirt is thick fabric like leather so it doesn't have
wrinkles in this pose because we're not giving it a lot of tension.

ACCESSORIES

Your accessories should match the character, and there are a wide range of different accessories you can use. For small accessories, you can just add them to the surface.

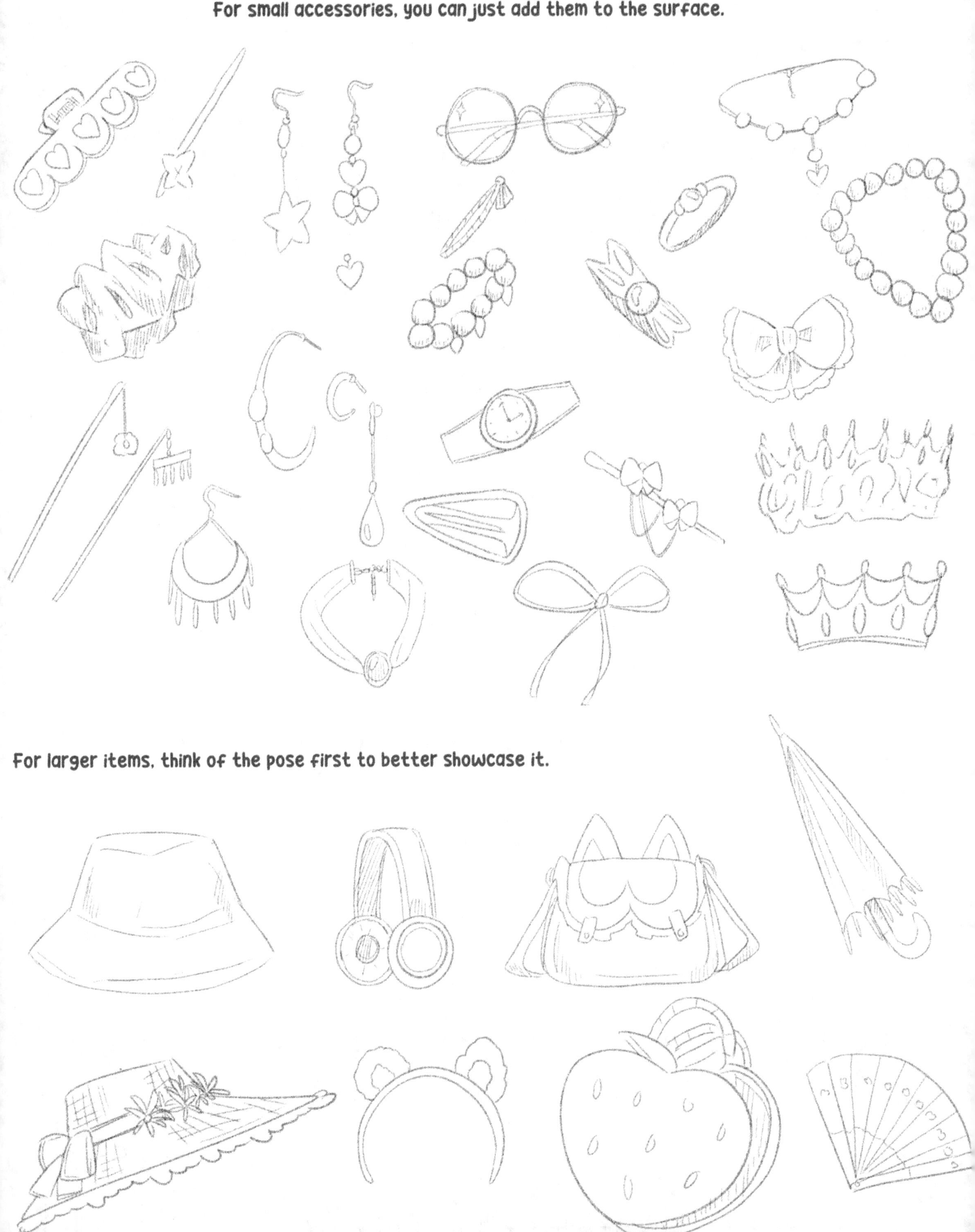

For larger items, think of the pose first to better showcase it.

Let's use some accessories to draw this next piece!

1.

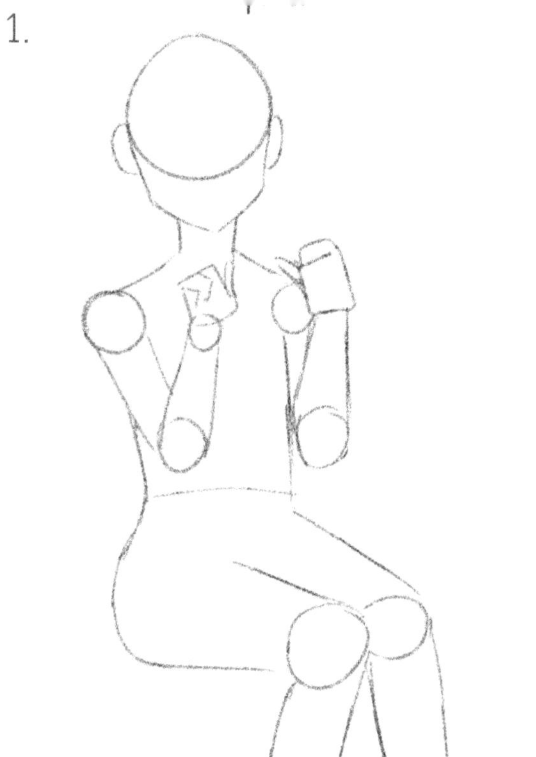

2.

I changed the hand
pose a bit because
I want to have
her hold an umbrella.

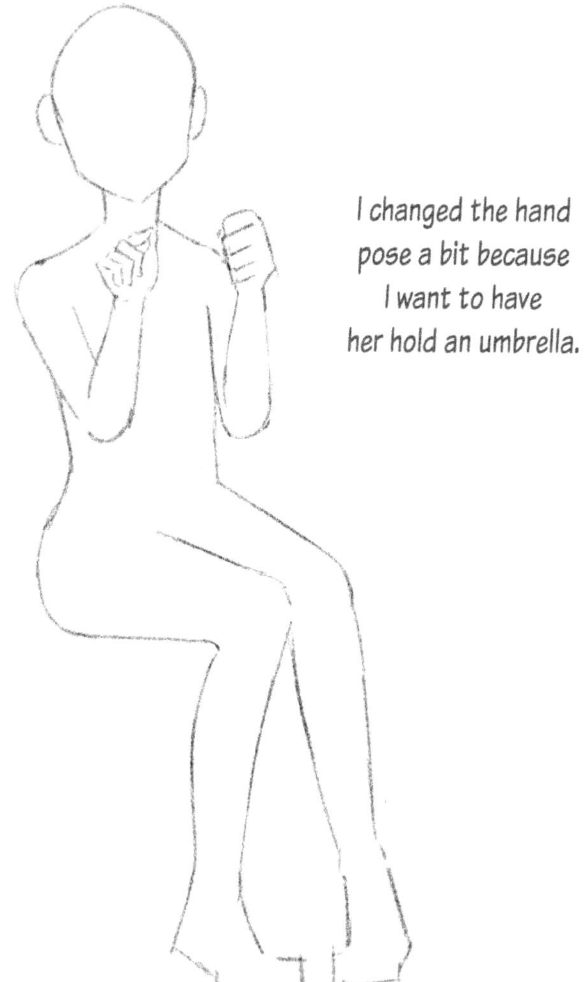

Add the silhouette of the clothes and shoes.

3.

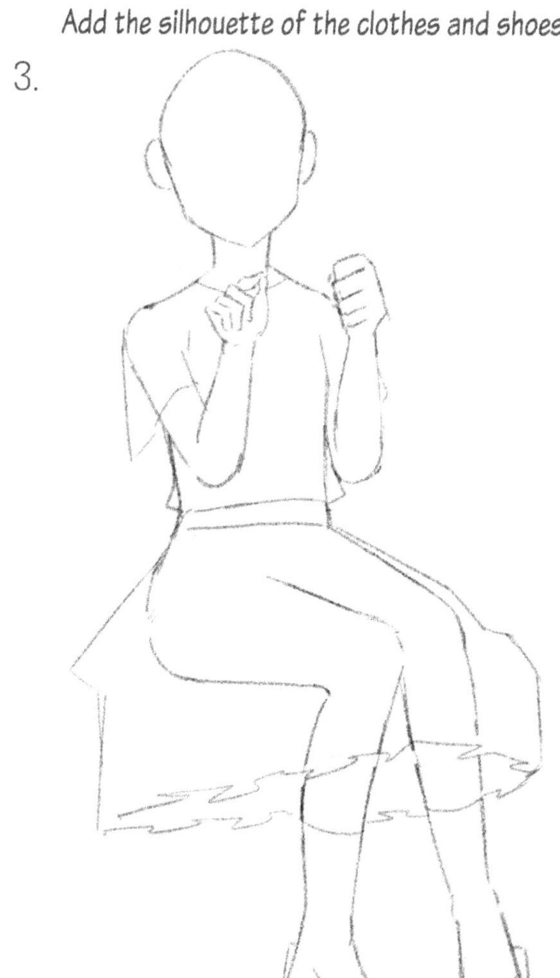

Draw the pleats, but remember she's sitting,
so the pleats have to look bigger
where her knees stick out!
Oh, and some more detail
for the shoes.

4.

Remember with
pleats you want to
match the line with its
bottom corner angle
so it makes sense.

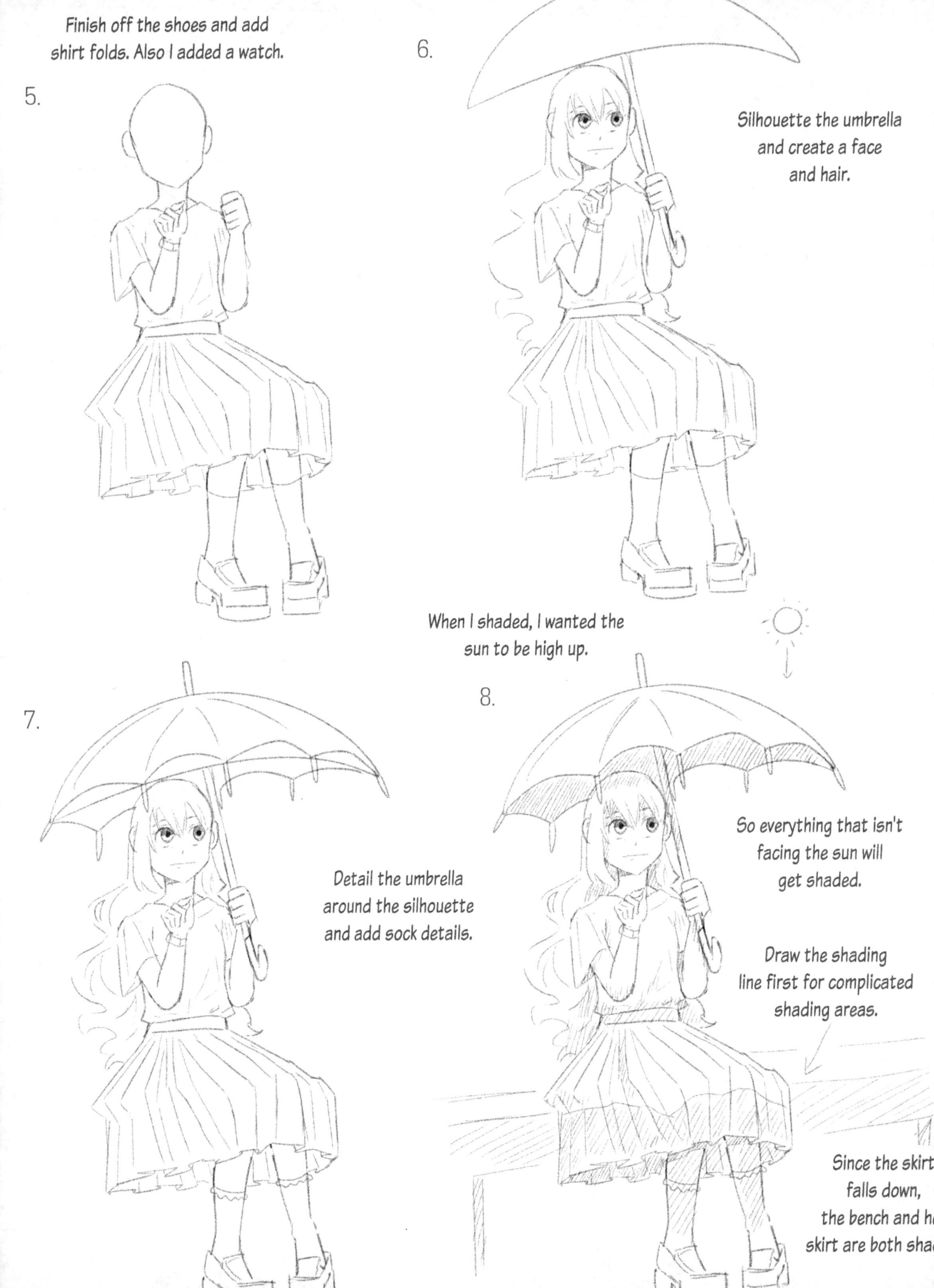

Finish off the shoes and add shirt folds. Also I added a watch.
5.
6.
Silhouette the umbrella and create a face and hair.
When I shaded, I wanted the sun to be high up.
7.
Detail the umbrella around the silhouette and add sock details.
8.
So everything that isn't facing the sun will get shaded.
Draw the shading line first for complicated shading areas.
Since the skirt falls down, the bench and he skirt are both shad

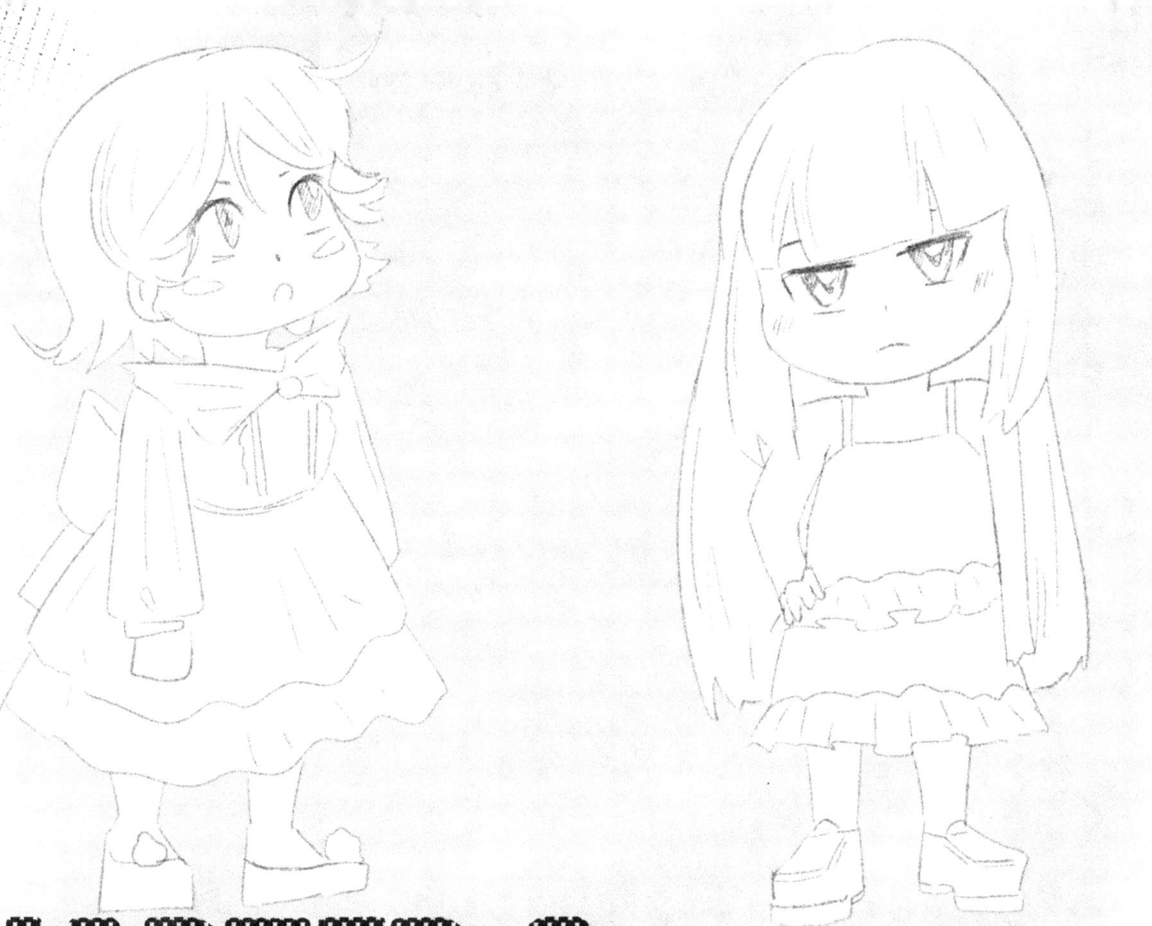

CHAPTER 8
Drawing Chibi

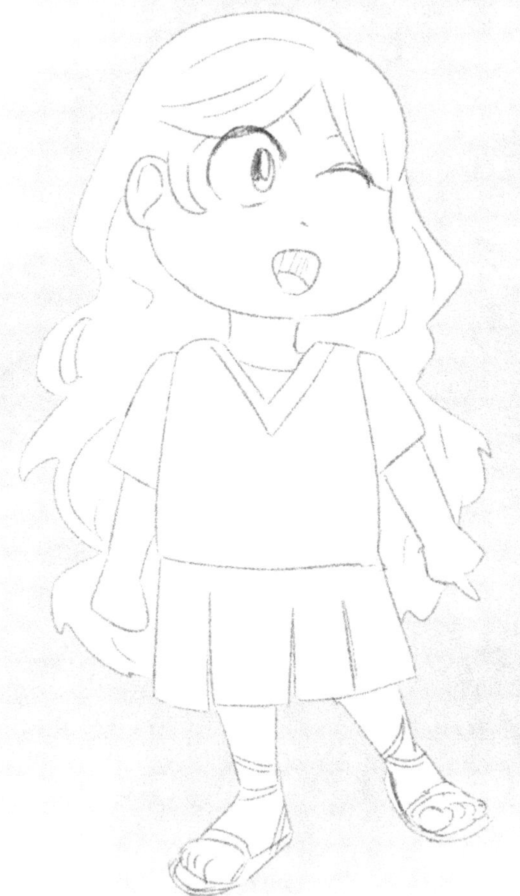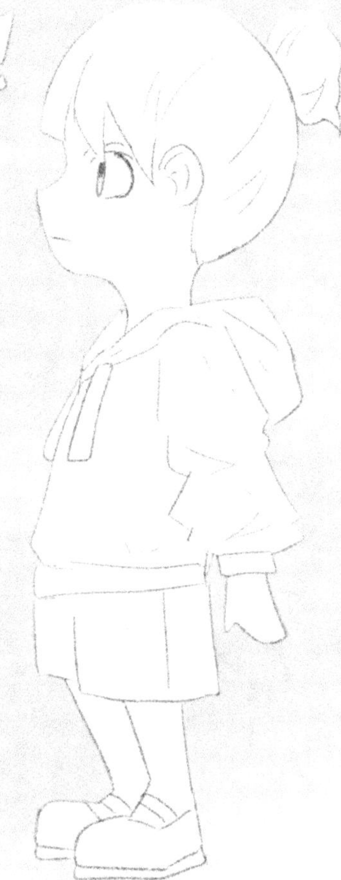

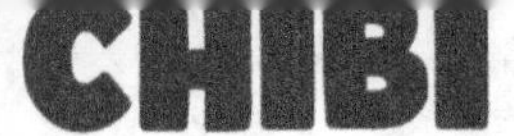

CHIBI

Chibi refers to a style of character design where characters are drawn with oversized heads and small, chubby bodies.
The style is often used to make characters appear more cute and childlike.

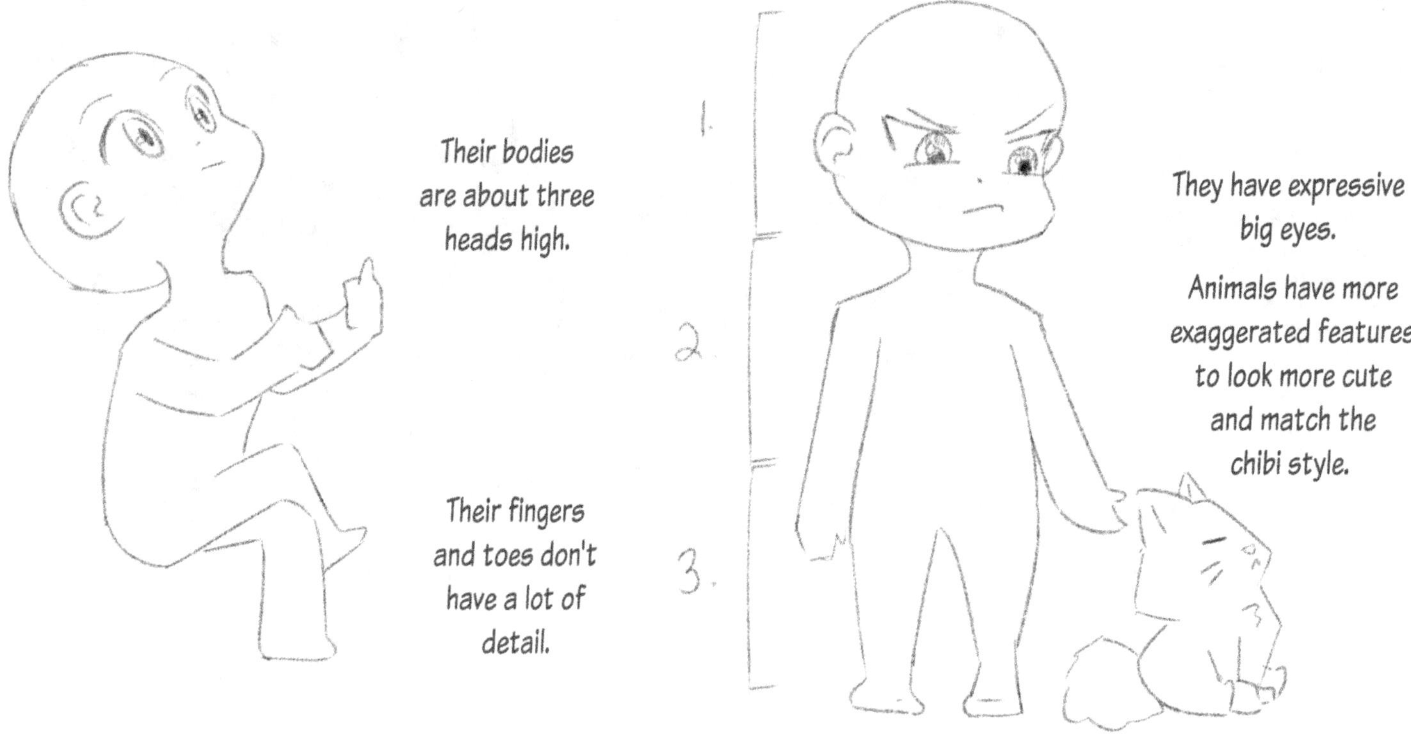

Their bodies are about three heads high.

Their fingers and toes don't have a lot of detail.

They have expressive big eyes.

Animals have more exaggerated features to look more cute and match the chibi style.

If you've learned how to draw anime figures, I know you can rock chibis!
Let's not waste any more time and dive right into it!

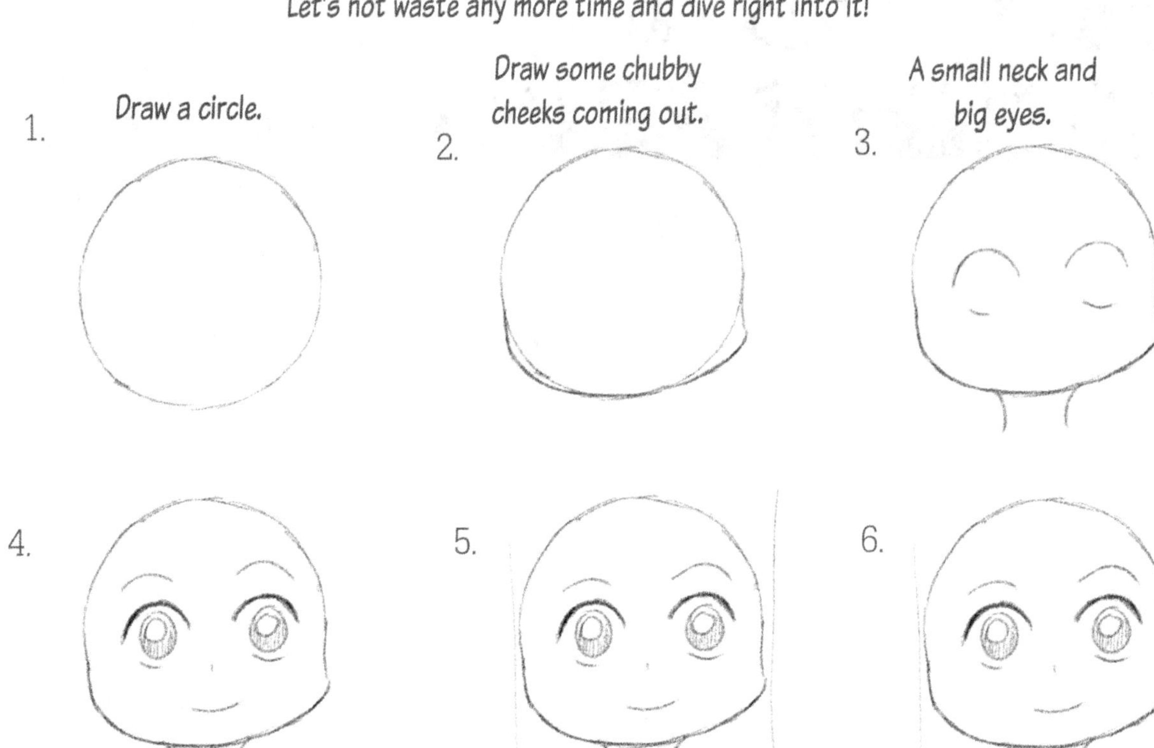

1. Draw a circle.

2. Draw some chubby cheeks coming out.

3. A small neck and big eyes.

4. Finish the face.

5. Now the shoulders. This size or smaller is fine but don't make them wider than the head.

6.

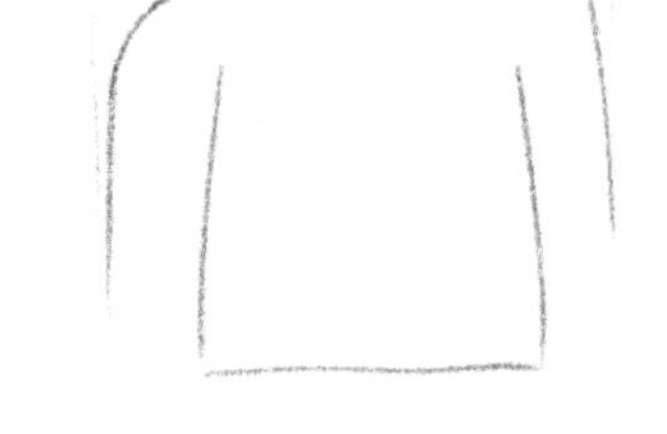

Remember, small body.

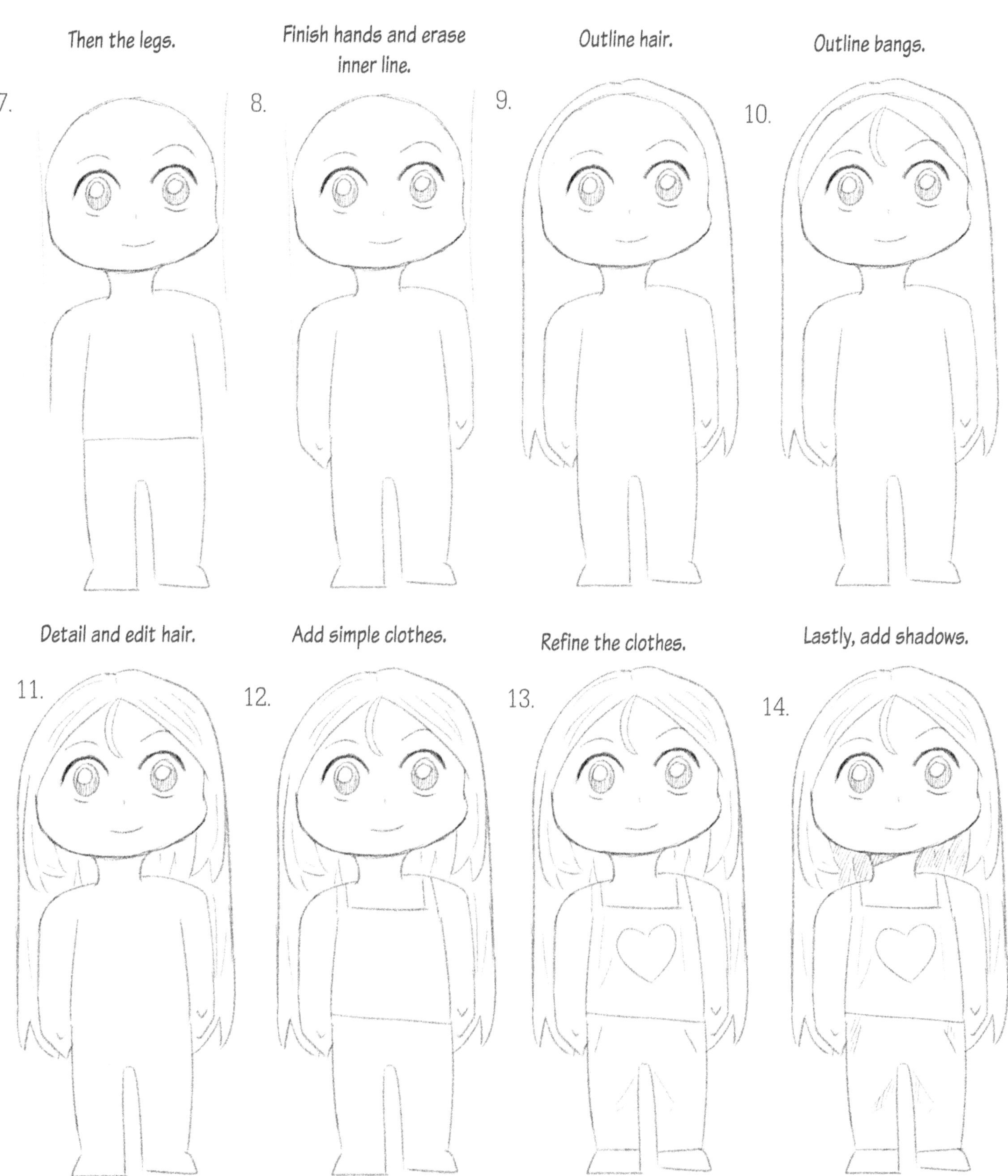

And you're done! That wasn't too hard, right?
Let's try some more!

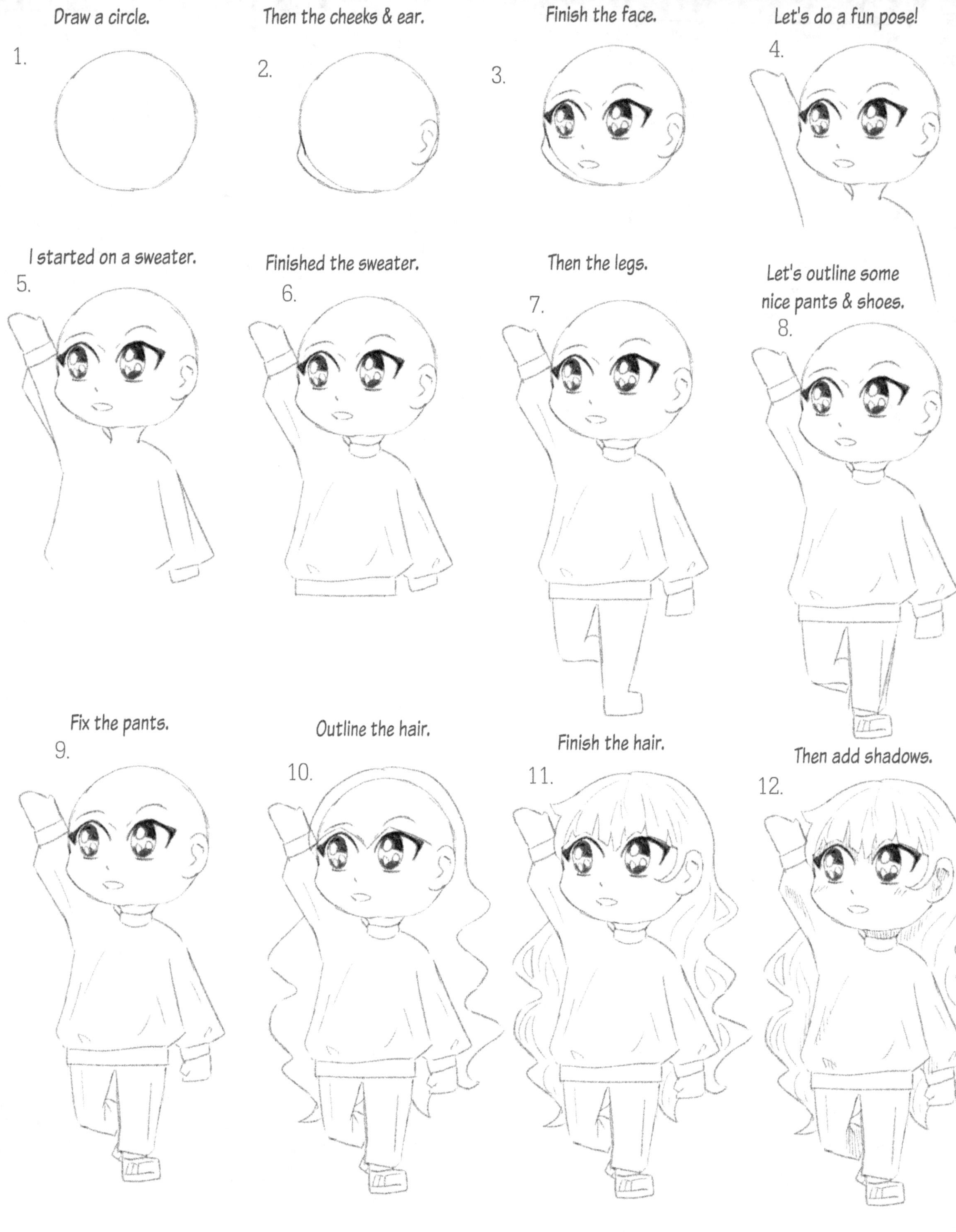

Let's do another one!

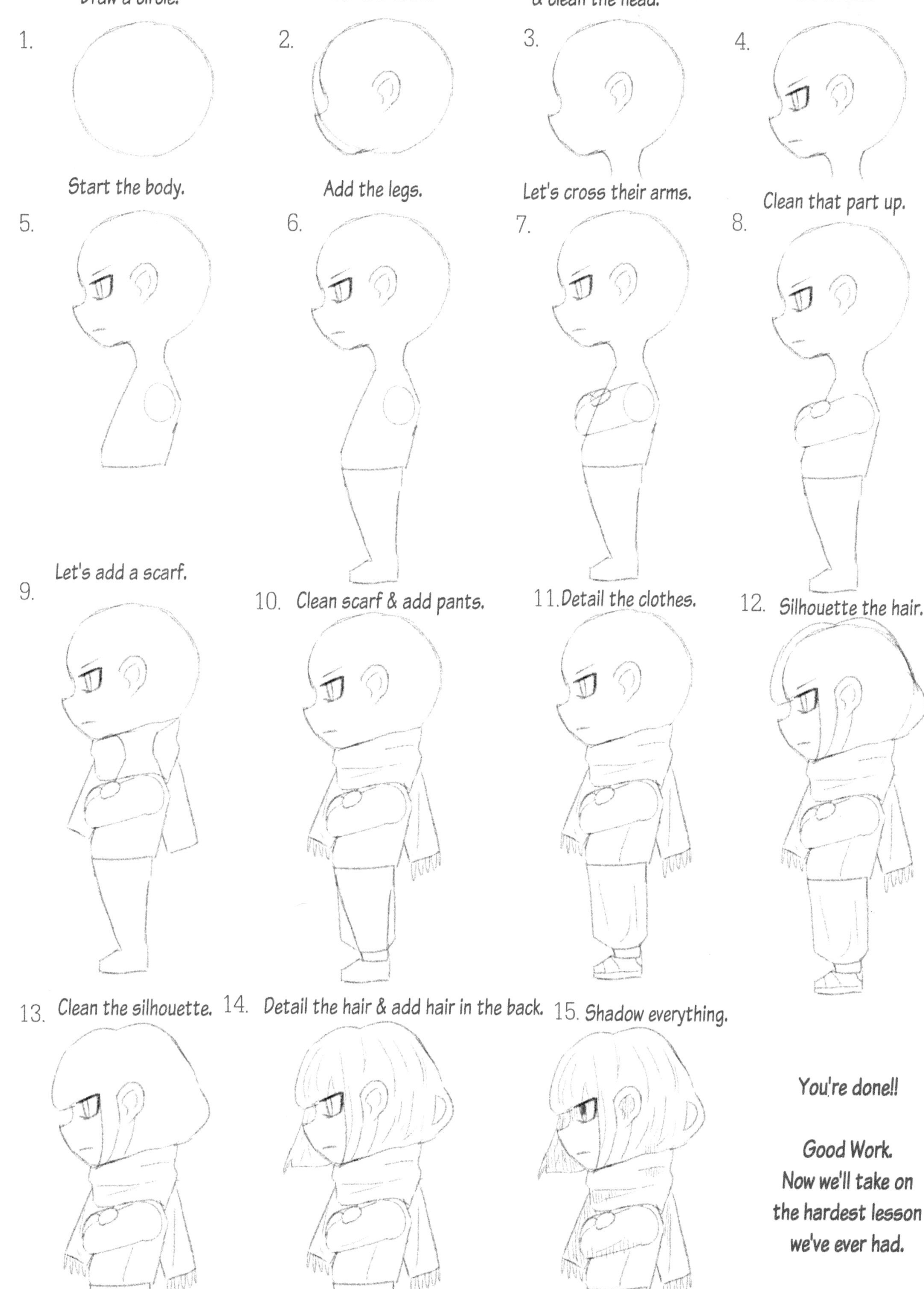

Draw a circle.
1.

Then the head.
2.

& clean the head.
3.

Add a face.
4.

Start the body.
5.

Add the legs.
6.

Let's cross their arms.
7.

Clean that part up.
8.

Let's add a scarf.
9.

10. Clean scarf & add pants.

11. Detail the clothes.

12. Silhouette the hair.

13. Clean the silhouette.

14. Detail the hair & add hair in the back.

15. Shadow everything.

You're done!!

Good Work.
Now we'll take on
the hardest lesson
we've ever had.

I wish you luck!

CHIBI ANIMALS

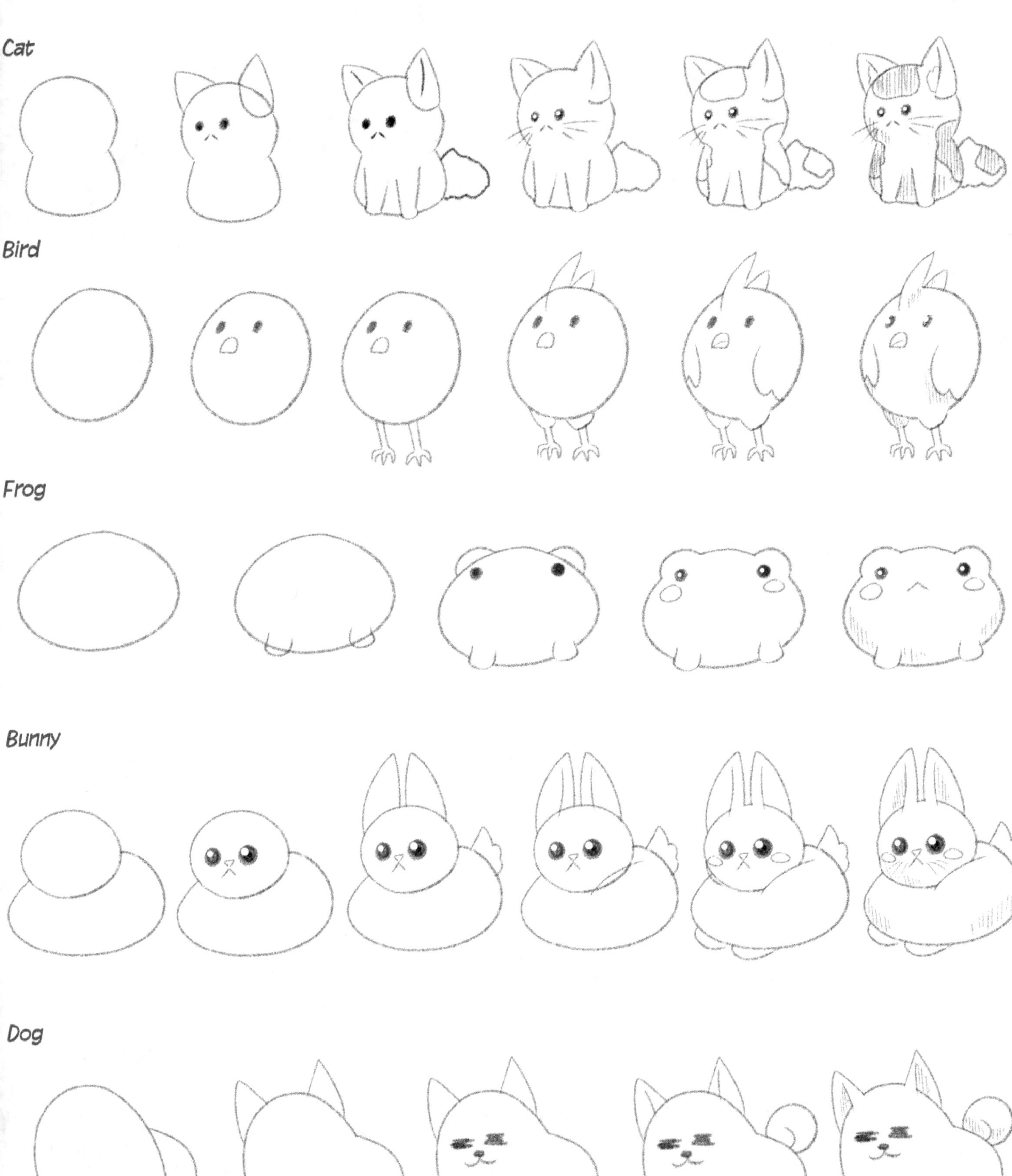

CHAPTER 9
kawaii characters & Stuff

KAWAII CHARACTERS

"Kawaii" is a Japanese word that means "cute," and is often used to describe a particular style of character design that features soft round shapes, big eyes, and generally innocent or youthful appearances.

It resembeles the "chibi" style and the "anime" style together.

The heads look more chibi-like but

the body has more detail and is more like the anime style with the proportions being less exaggerated.

There are many ways to draw these characters but here is my style. I also helped you out and made my character's hands to be less difficult.

I call it the mitten hand! You can draw these characters with less worry about getting everything right.

Now that you know more about kawaii characters. Let's have some fun and dive into drawing some!

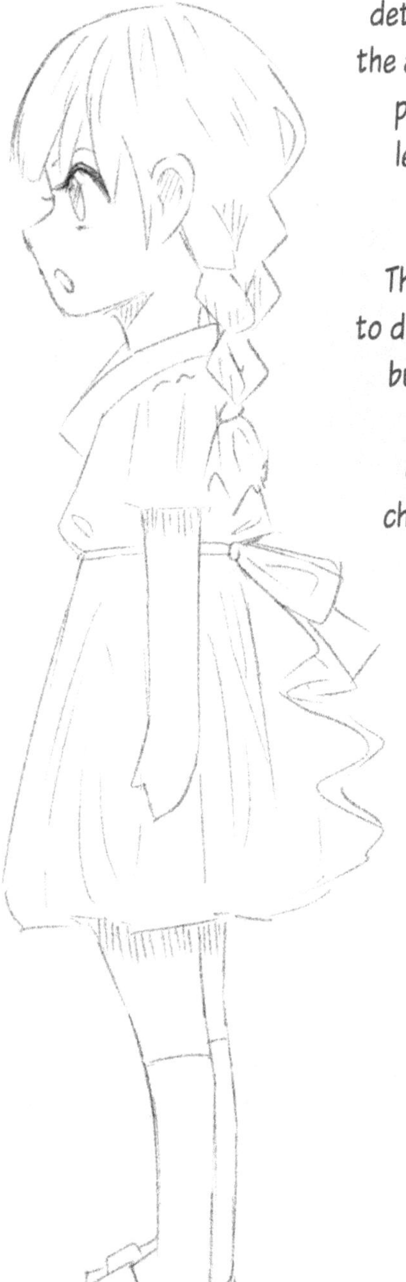

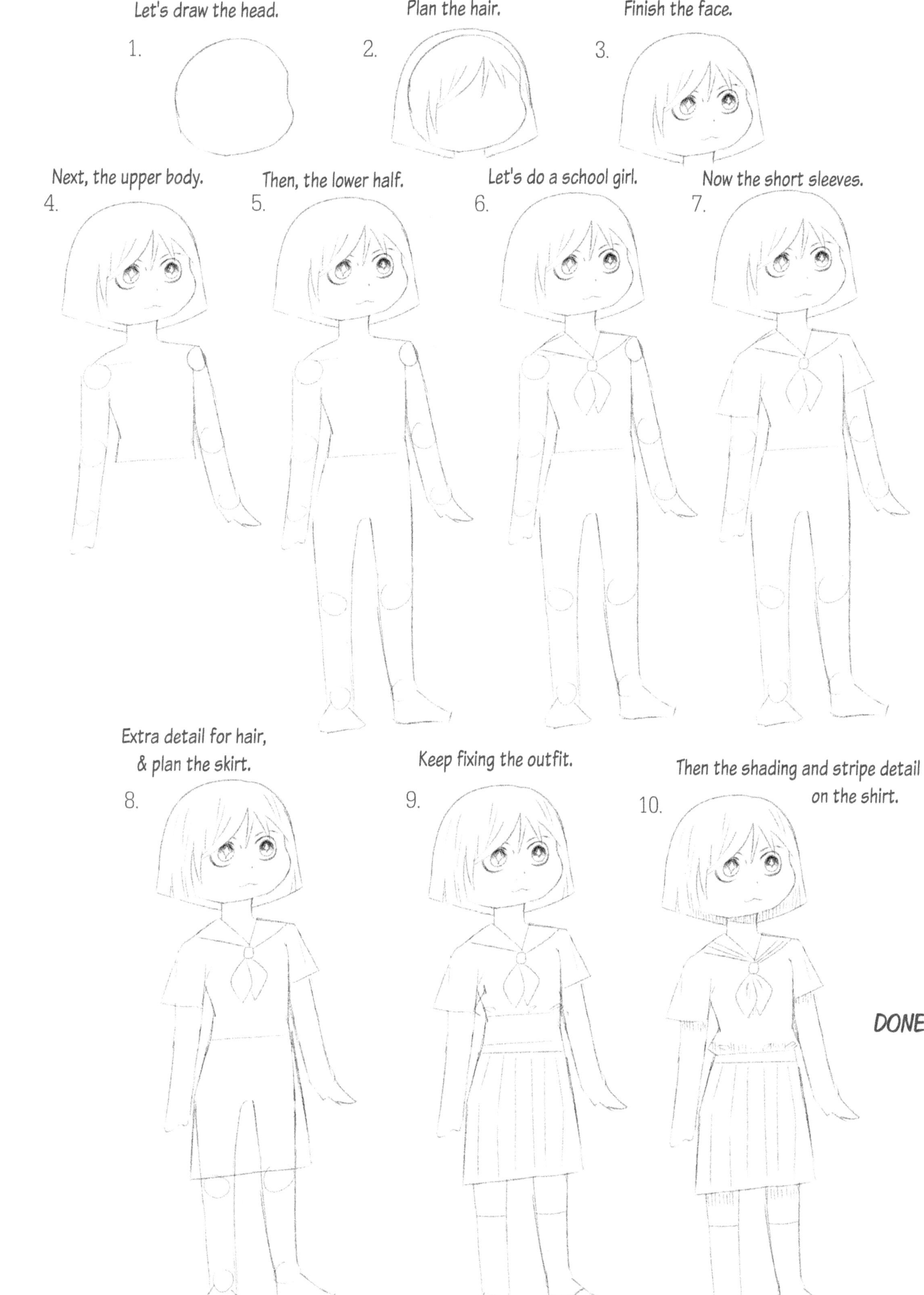

Let's draw the head.
1.
Plan the hair.
2.
Finish the face.
3.
Next, the upper body.
4.
Then, the lower half.
5.
Let's do a school girl.
6.
Now the short sleeves.
7.
Extra detail for hair, & plan the skirt.
8.
Keep fixing the outfit.
9.
Then the shading and stripe detail on the shirt.
10.
DONE!

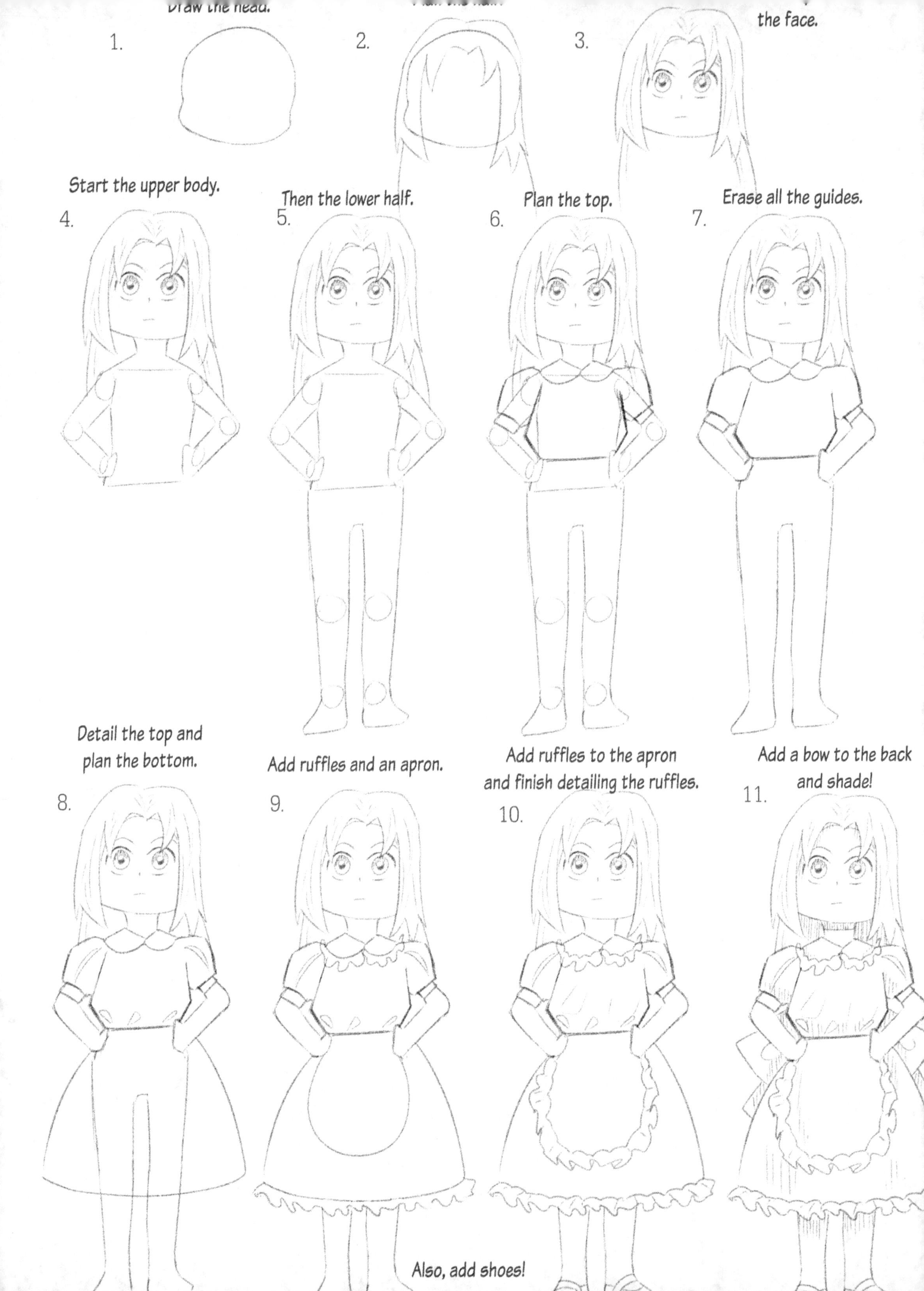

Draw the head.
1.
Plan the hair.
2.
the face.
3.
Start the upper body.
4.
Then the lower half.
5.
Plan the top.
6.
Erase all the guides.
7.
Detail the top and
plan the bottom.
8.
Add ruffles and an apron.
9.
Add ruffles to the apron
and finish detailing the ruffles.
10.
Add a bow to the back
and shade!
11.
Also, add shoes!

CUTE ANIMALS

These are more proportional &
more detailed than the chibi animals.

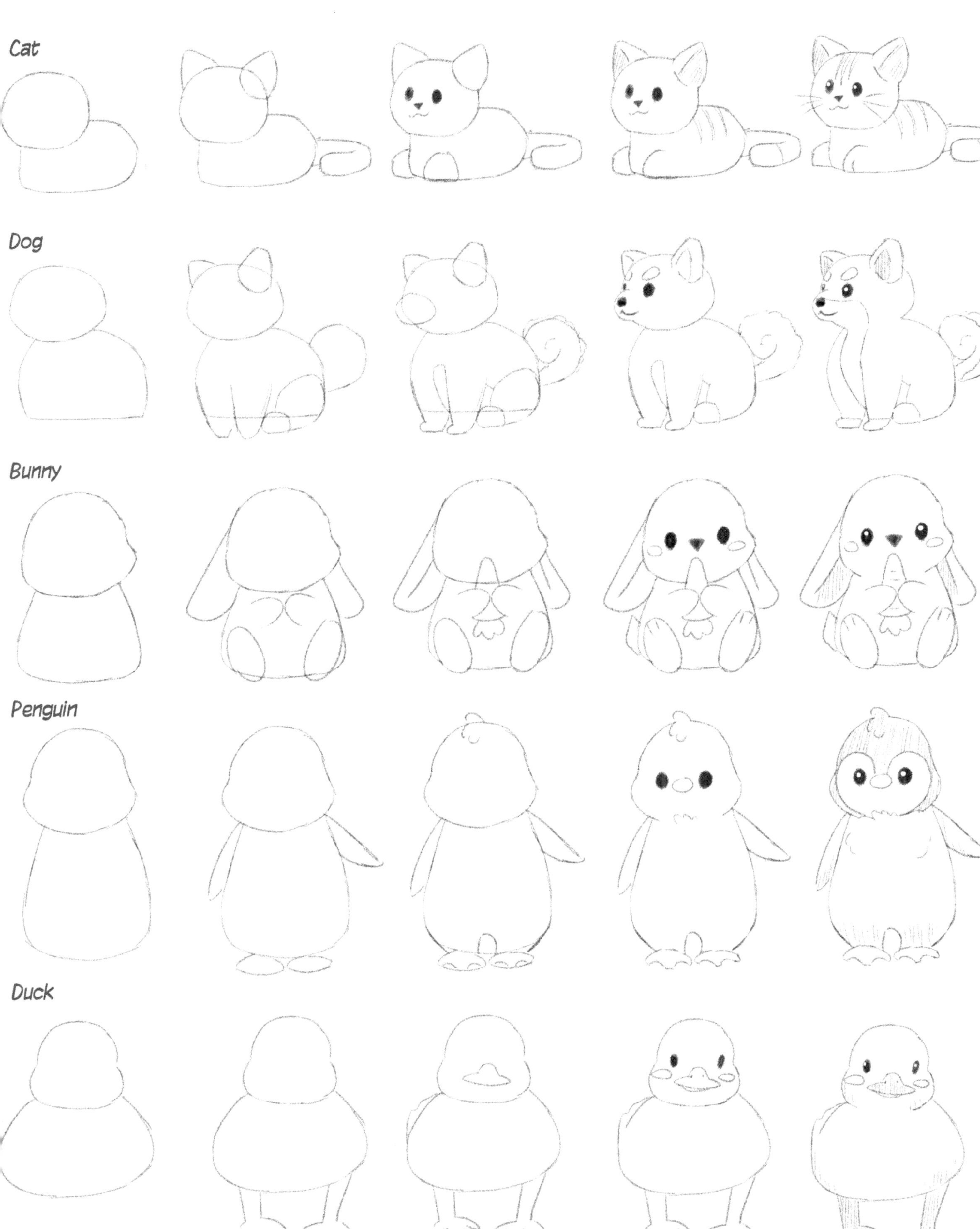

CUTE FOOD

There are many types of "cute food" you can draw.
I am here to go over some of the more popular types.
Now let's get to drawing!

 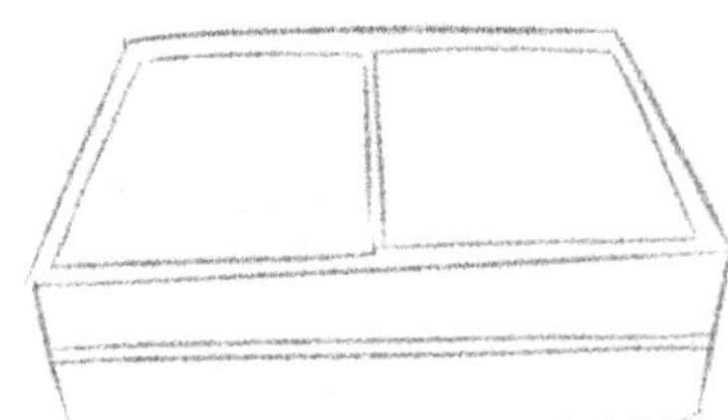 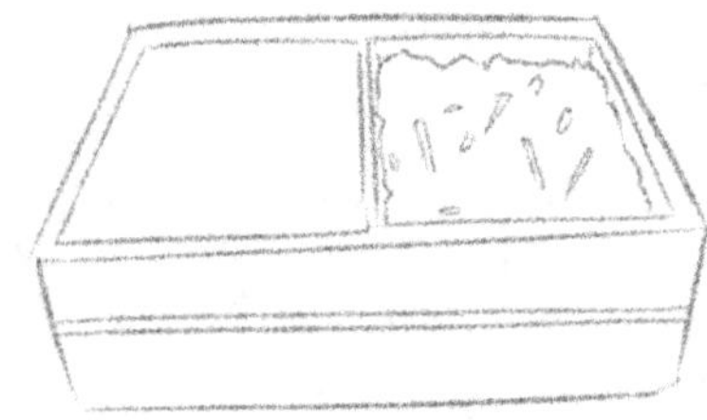

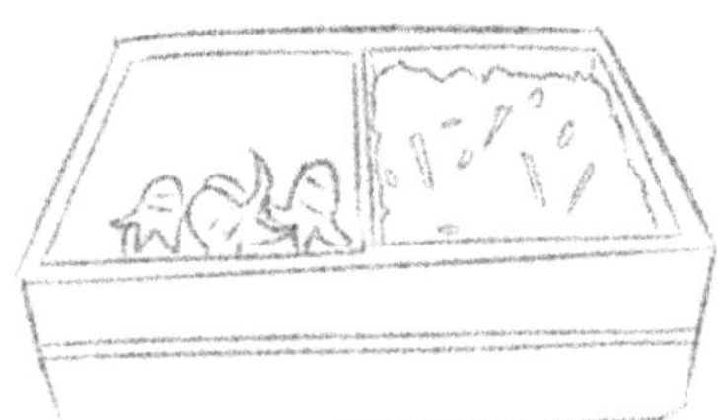 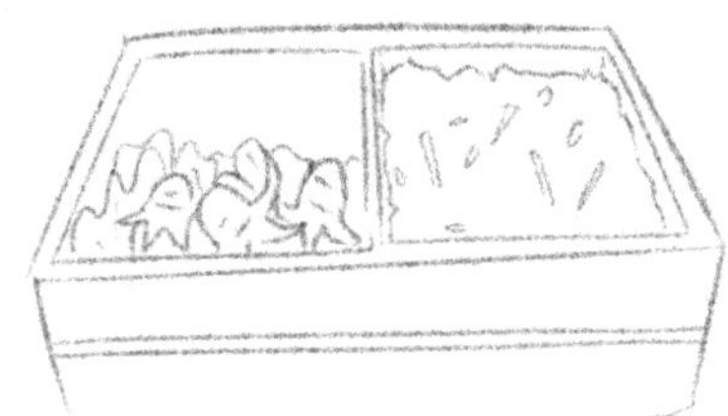 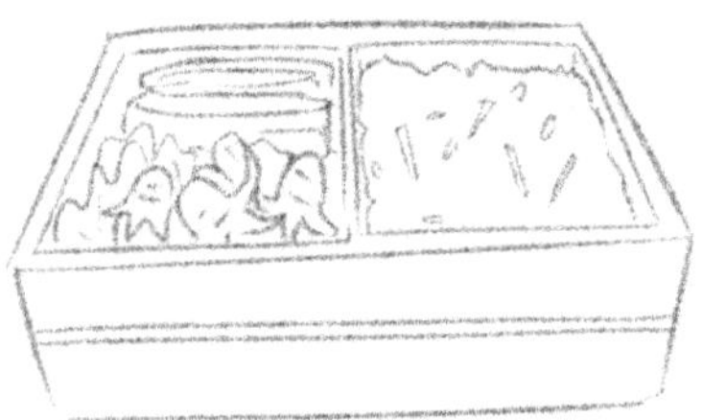

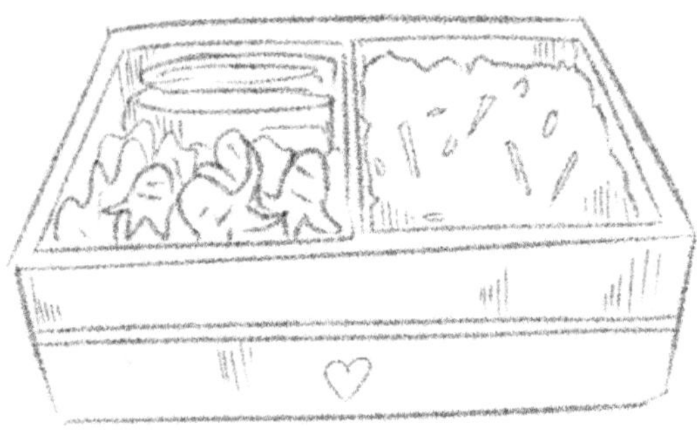

"Bento Box"- This boxed lunch can be organized in many ways. I just added the standard version but you can mix and match in any way.

"Rice Ball"

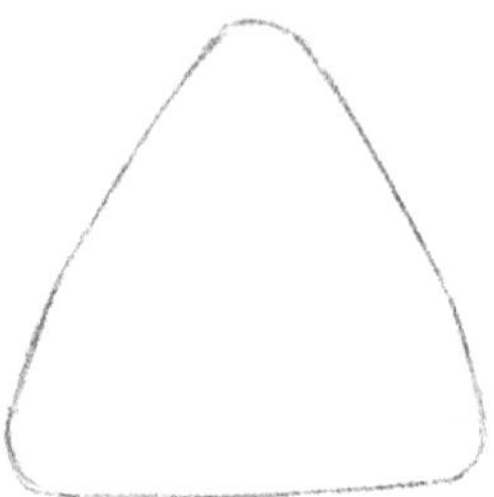 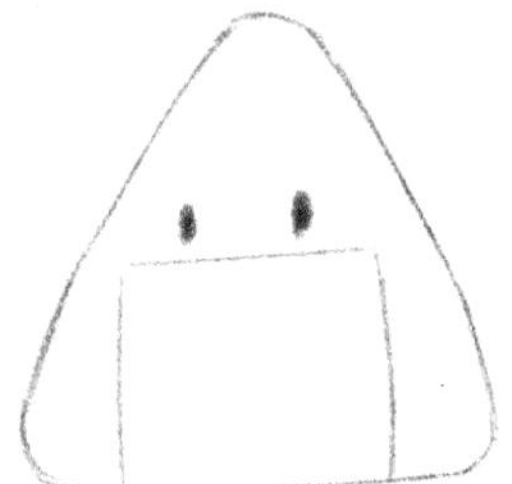 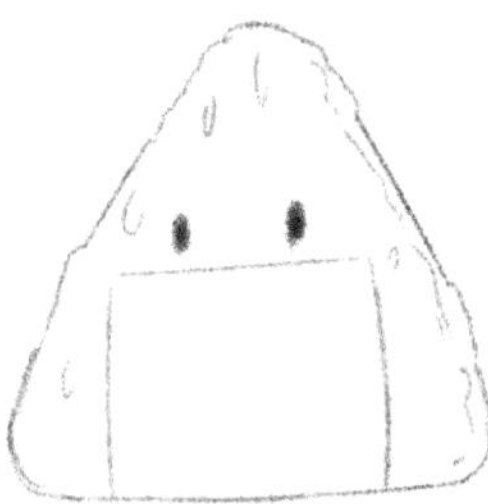 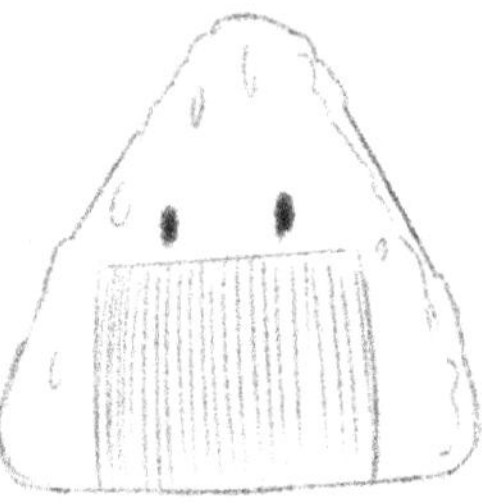

"Pancakes"

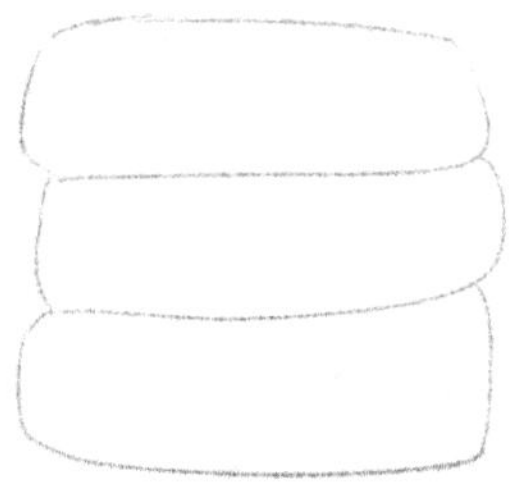 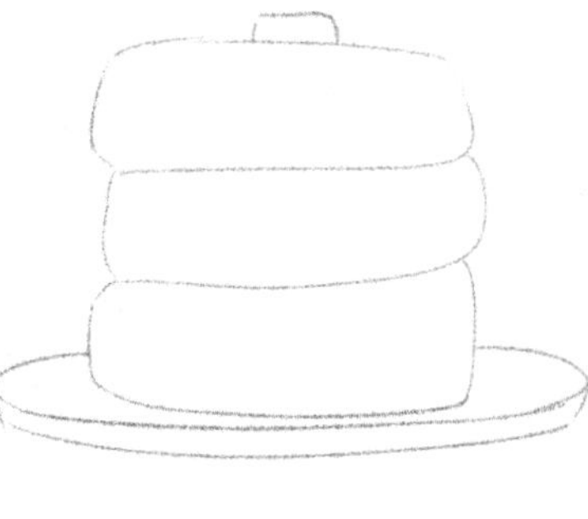 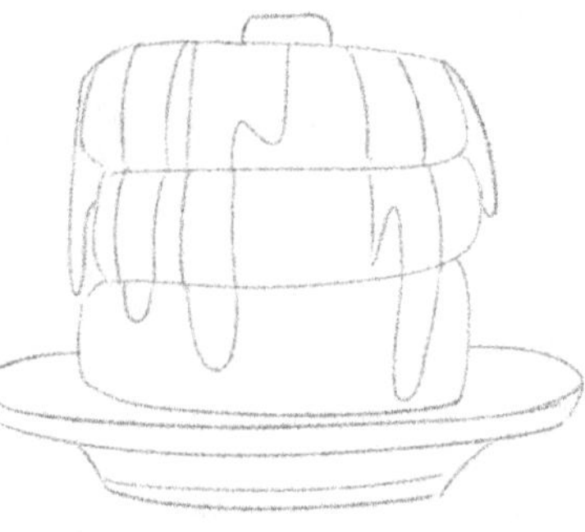 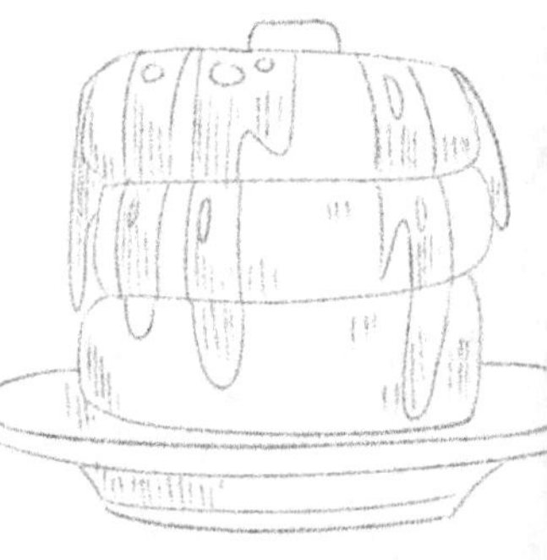

"Cupcake"

"Ice Cream"

"Dango"

"Boba"

"Sushi"

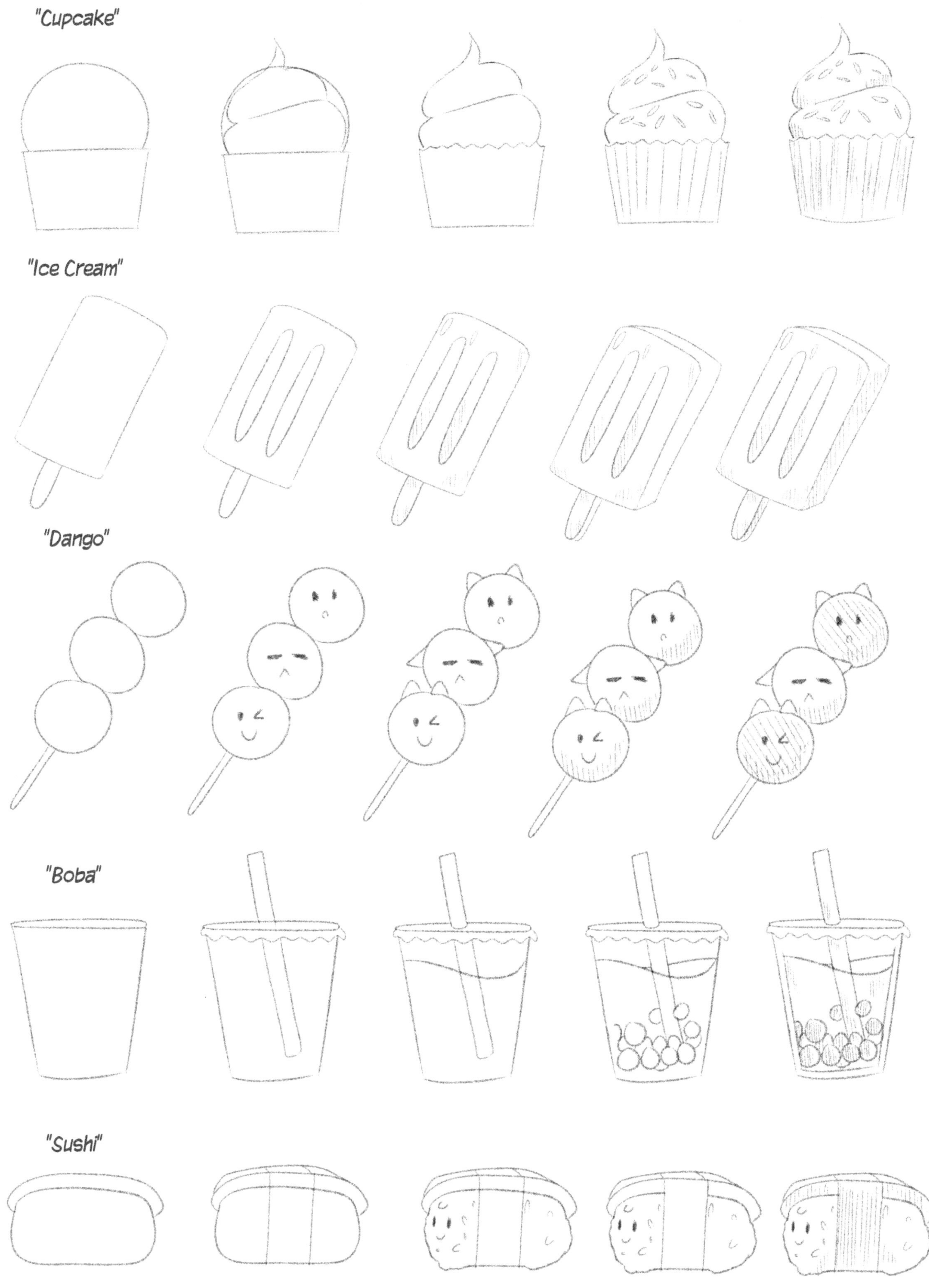

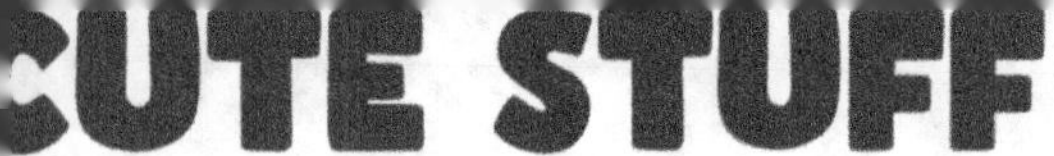

CUTE STUFF

This portion involves many cute iconic symbols that scream a "cute" aesthetic!

Let's dive in to this cuteness!

Hearts

Yes, you have your standard hearts but there are a few ways to incorporate them into your drawing in a different way!

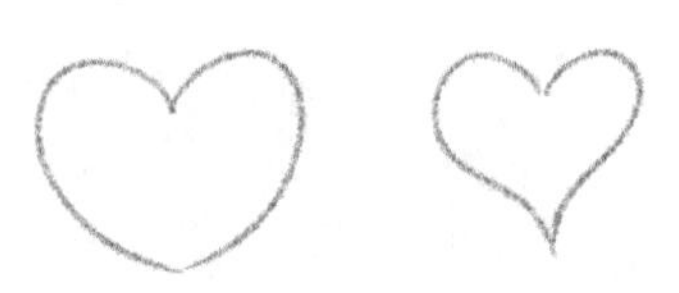

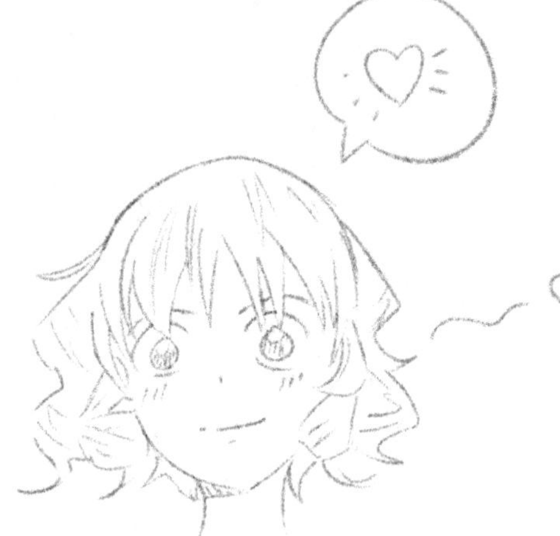

Speech bubble heart.

Heart bangs!

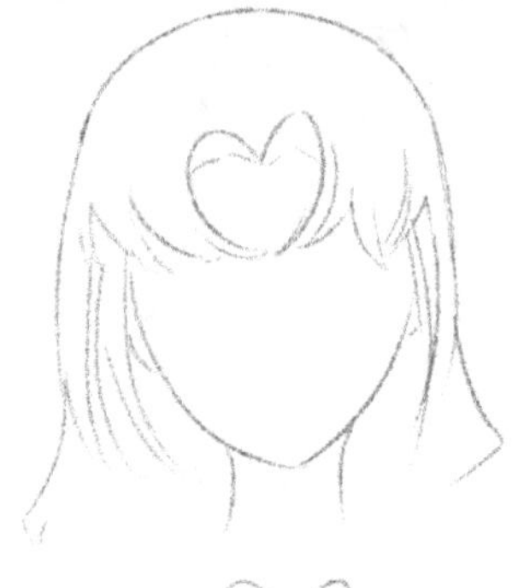

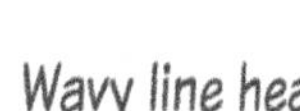 Wavy line heart.

Heart hair curl.

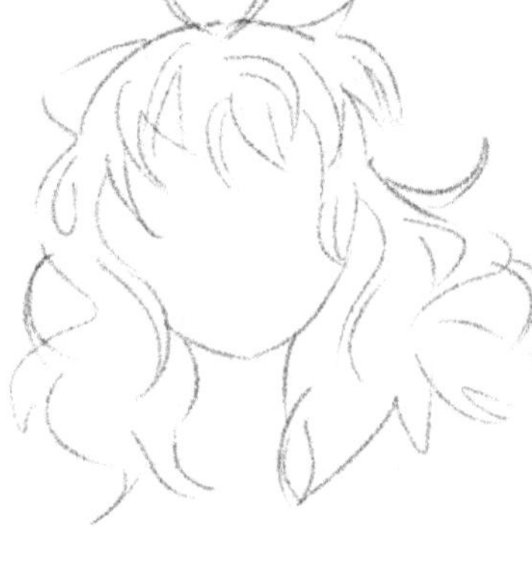

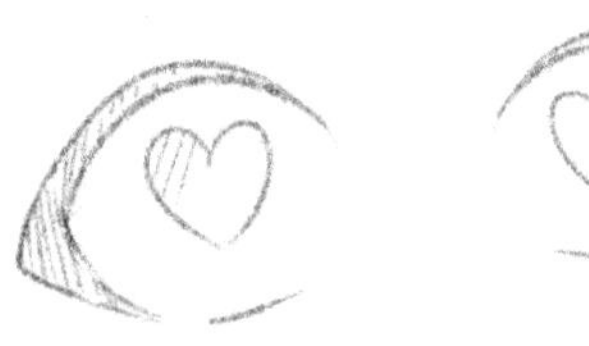 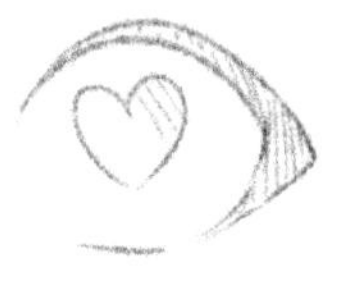

Heart in the eyes.

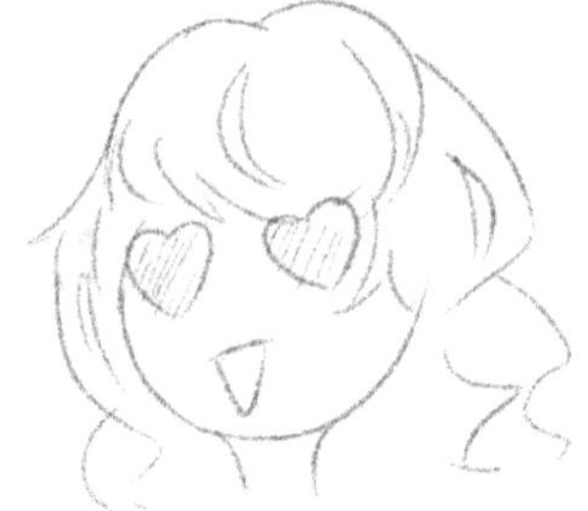

Heart eyes for chibi characters.

Flowers

Roses:

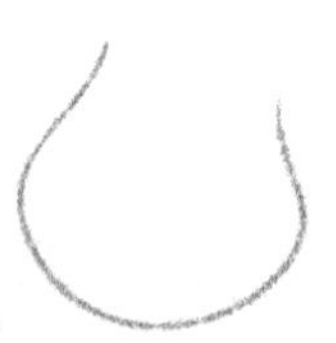 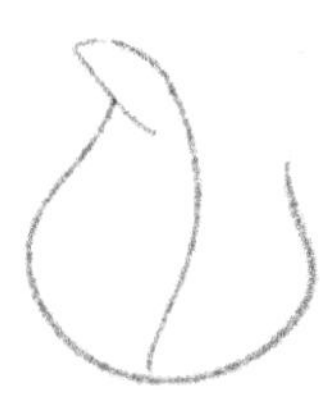 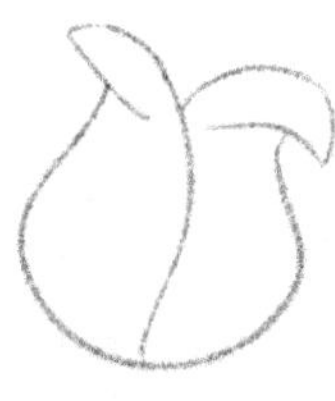 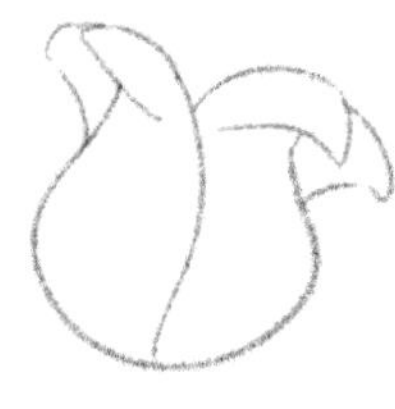 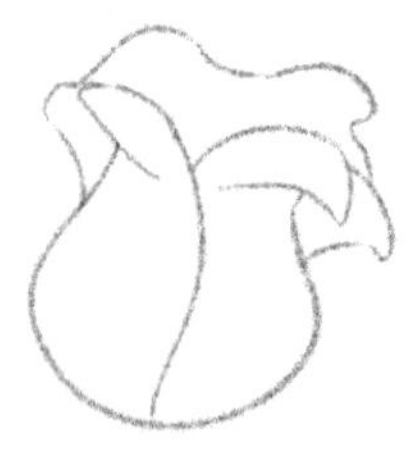 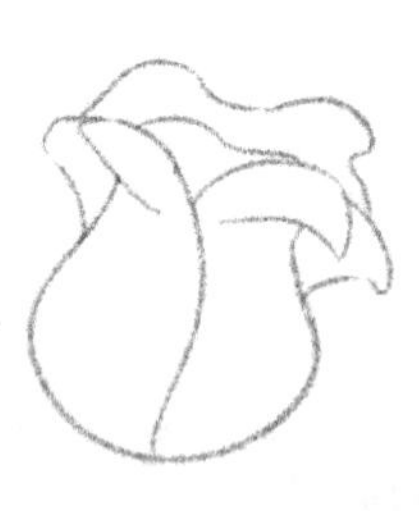 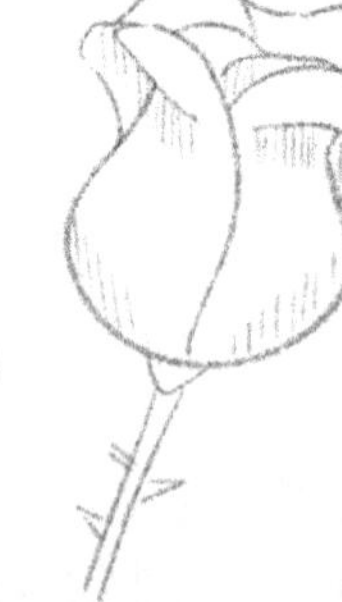

They are all about building up the petals over time!

 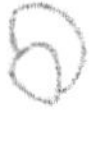 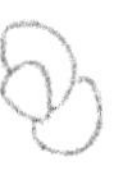 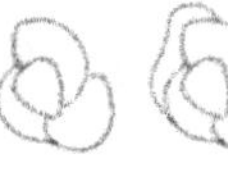 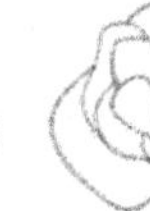 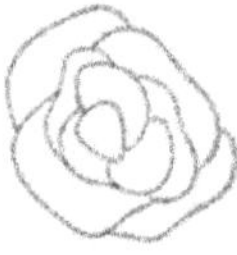 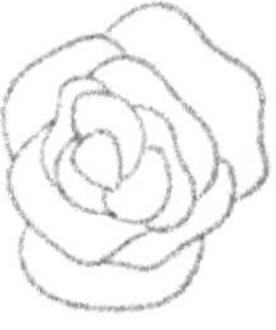 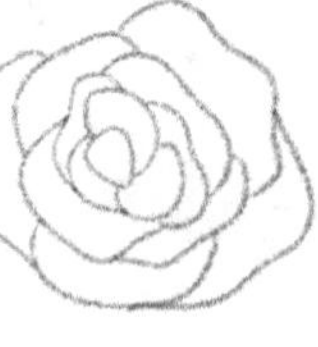 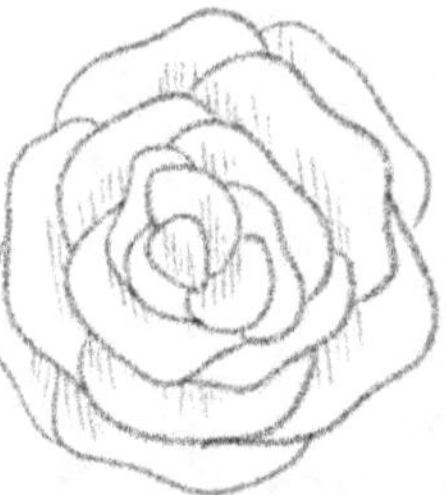

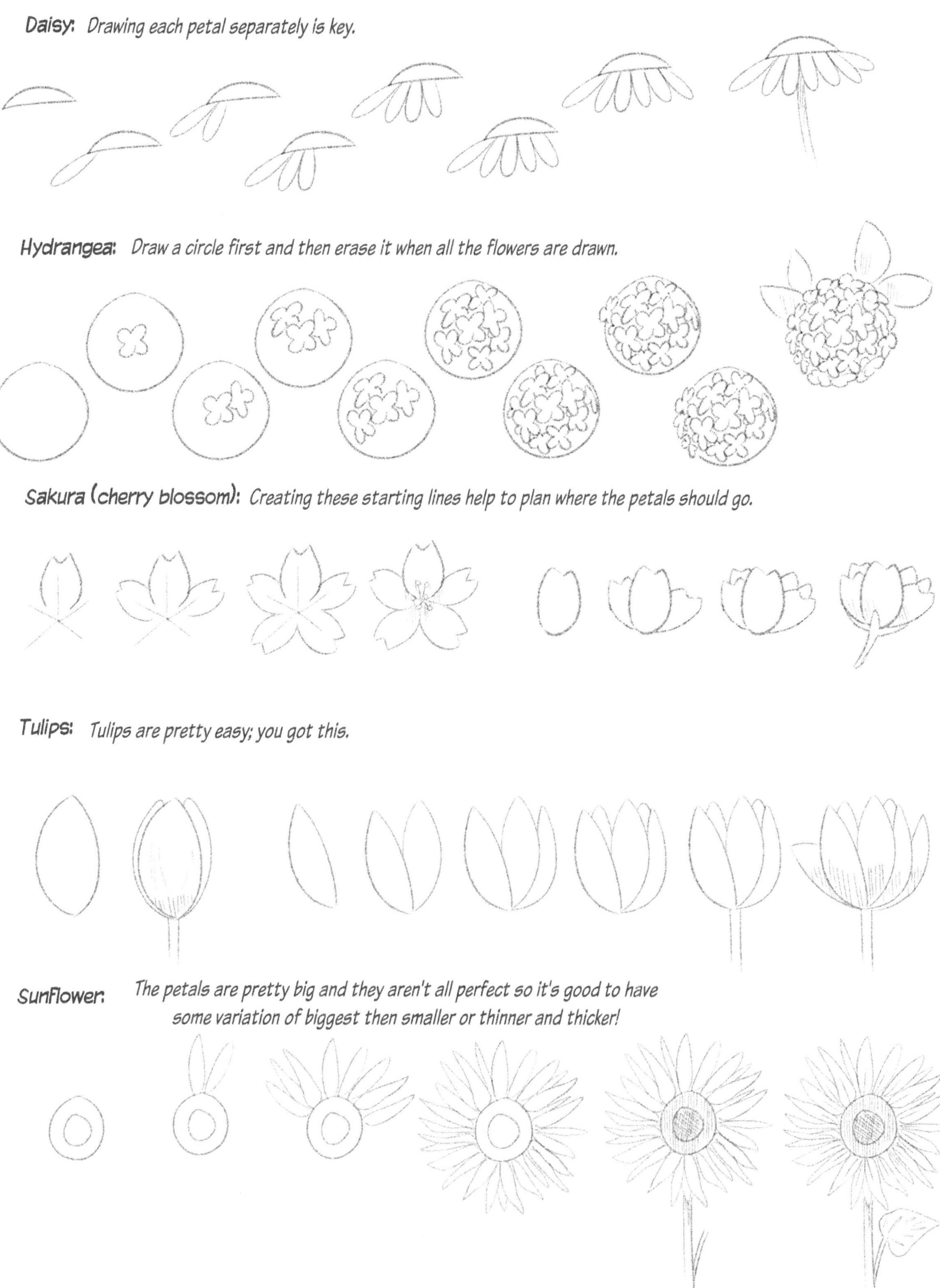

Daisy: Drawing each petal separately is key.

Hydrangea: Draw a circle first and then erase it when all the flowers are drawn.

Sakura (cherry blossom): Creating these starting lines help to plan where the petals should go.

Tulips: Tulips are pretty easy; you got this.

Sunflower: The petals are pretty big and they aren't all perfect so it's good to have
some variation of biggest then smaller or thinner and thicker!

Clouds

Clouds are pretty random but remember to shade them. The shades are random too; just think about which part you want shaded.

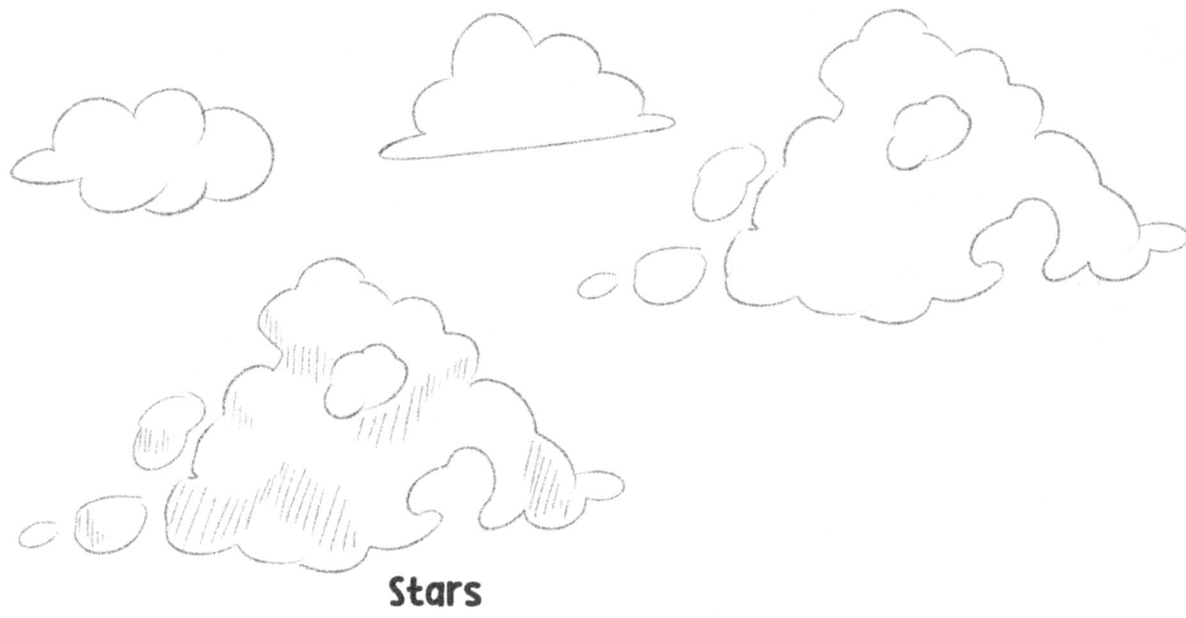

Stars

Here are some standard stars but there are a few ways to incorporate them into your drawing in a different way!

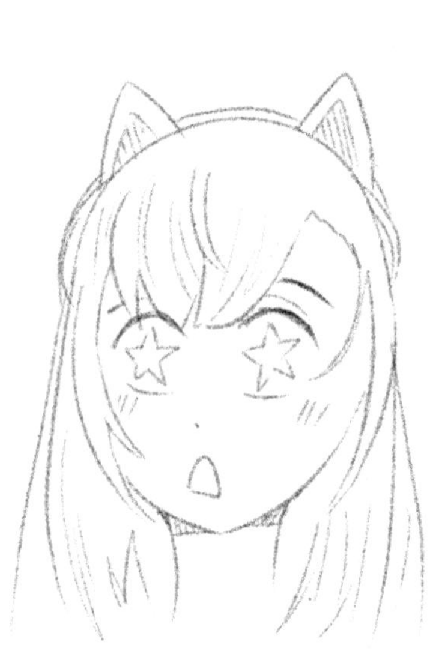

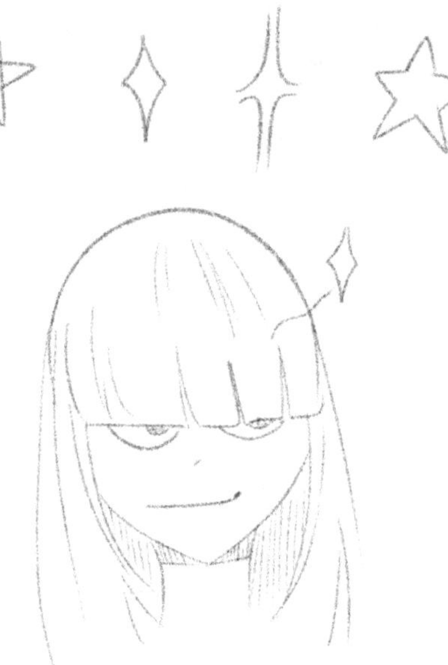

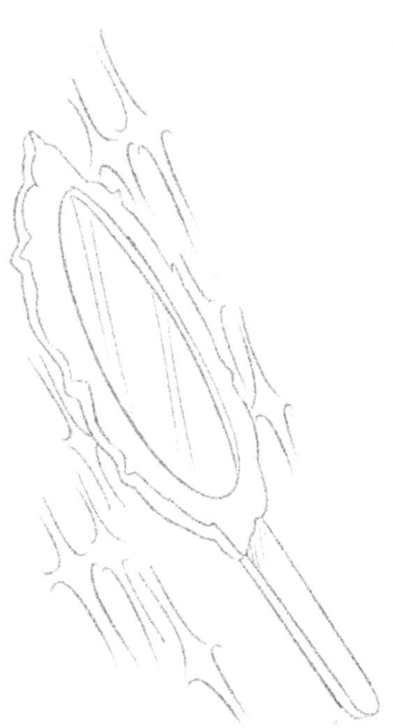

Stars can be in the eyes to show wonder.

Stars can show up when your character is being sneaky or plotting. A smirking face.

These type of stars usually show up when something is shiny or clean.

Fruit

Strawberry:

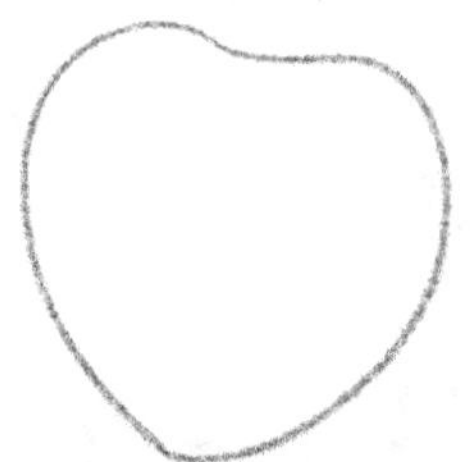
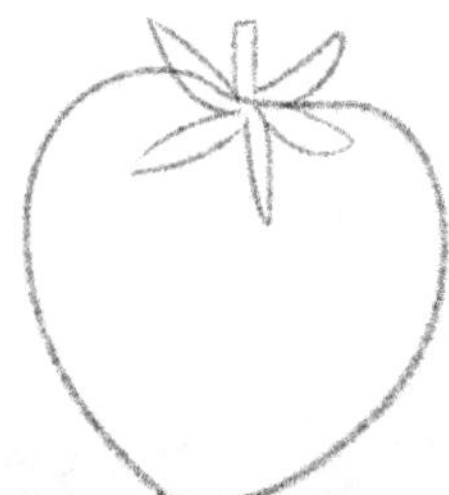
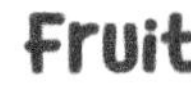

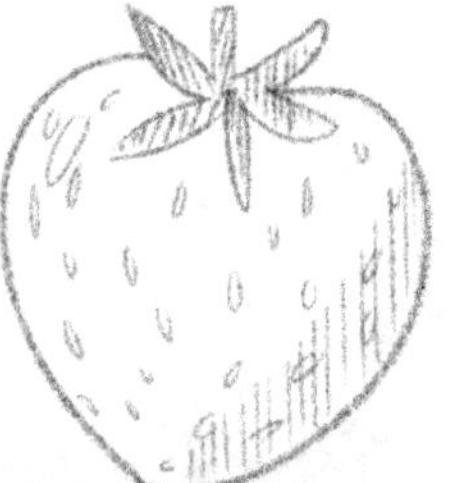

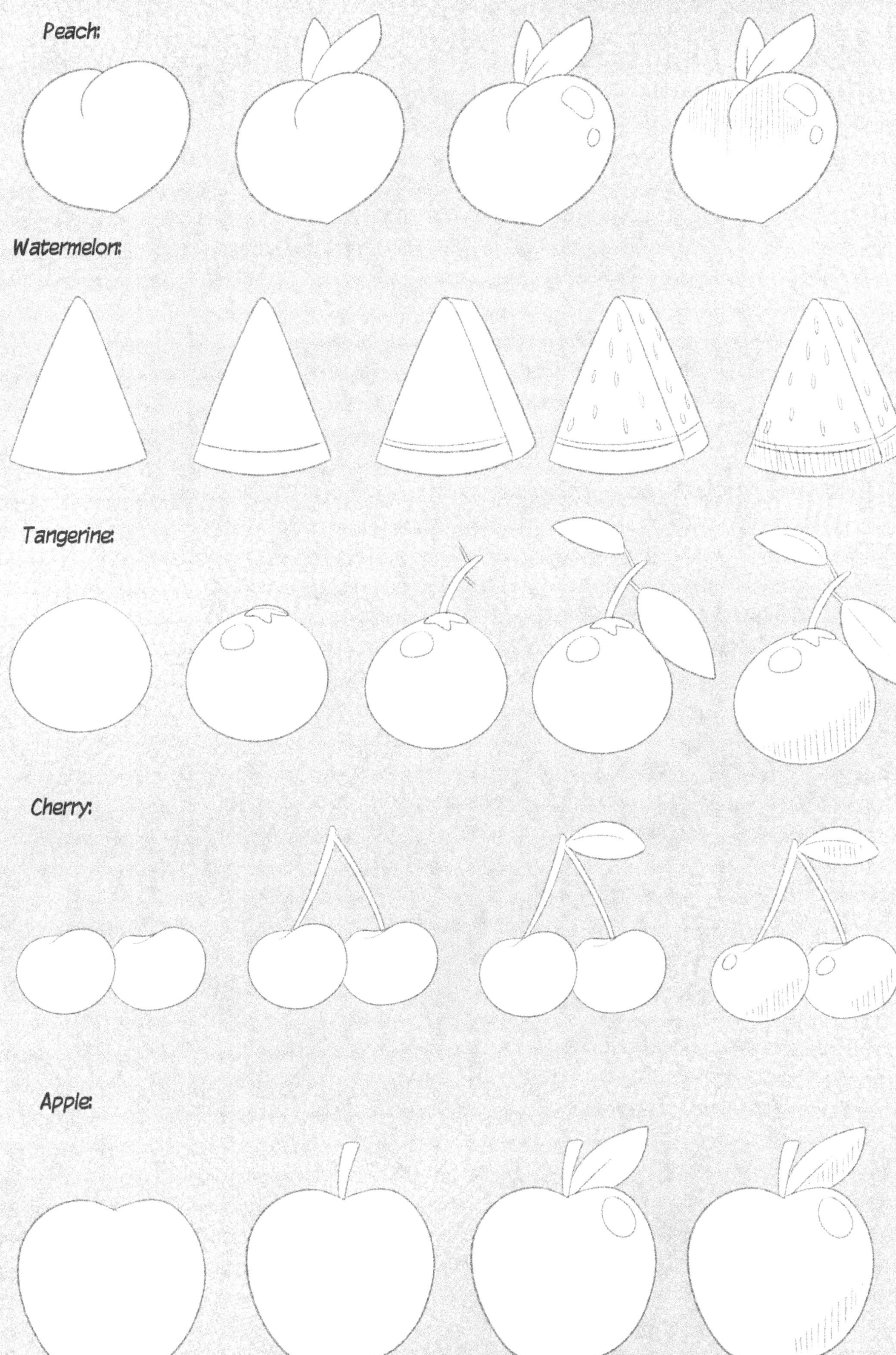

Peach:
Watermelon:
Tangerine:
Cherry:
Apple:

Rainbows

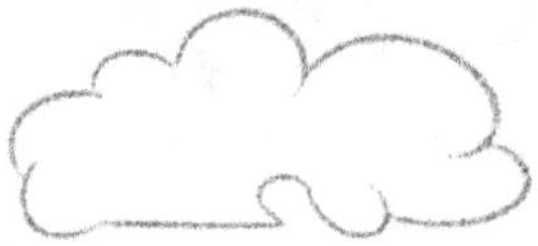

*Rainbows can be used not only for
the background but also for
clothing patterns or sun glares!*

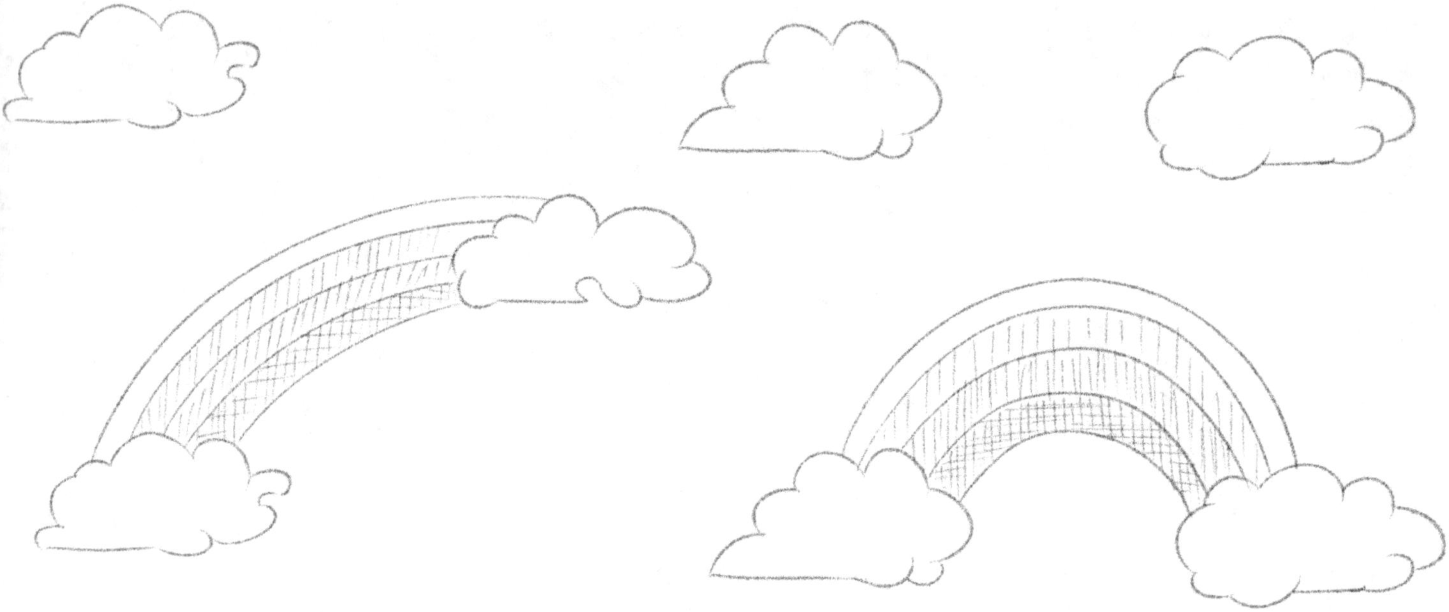

Bows

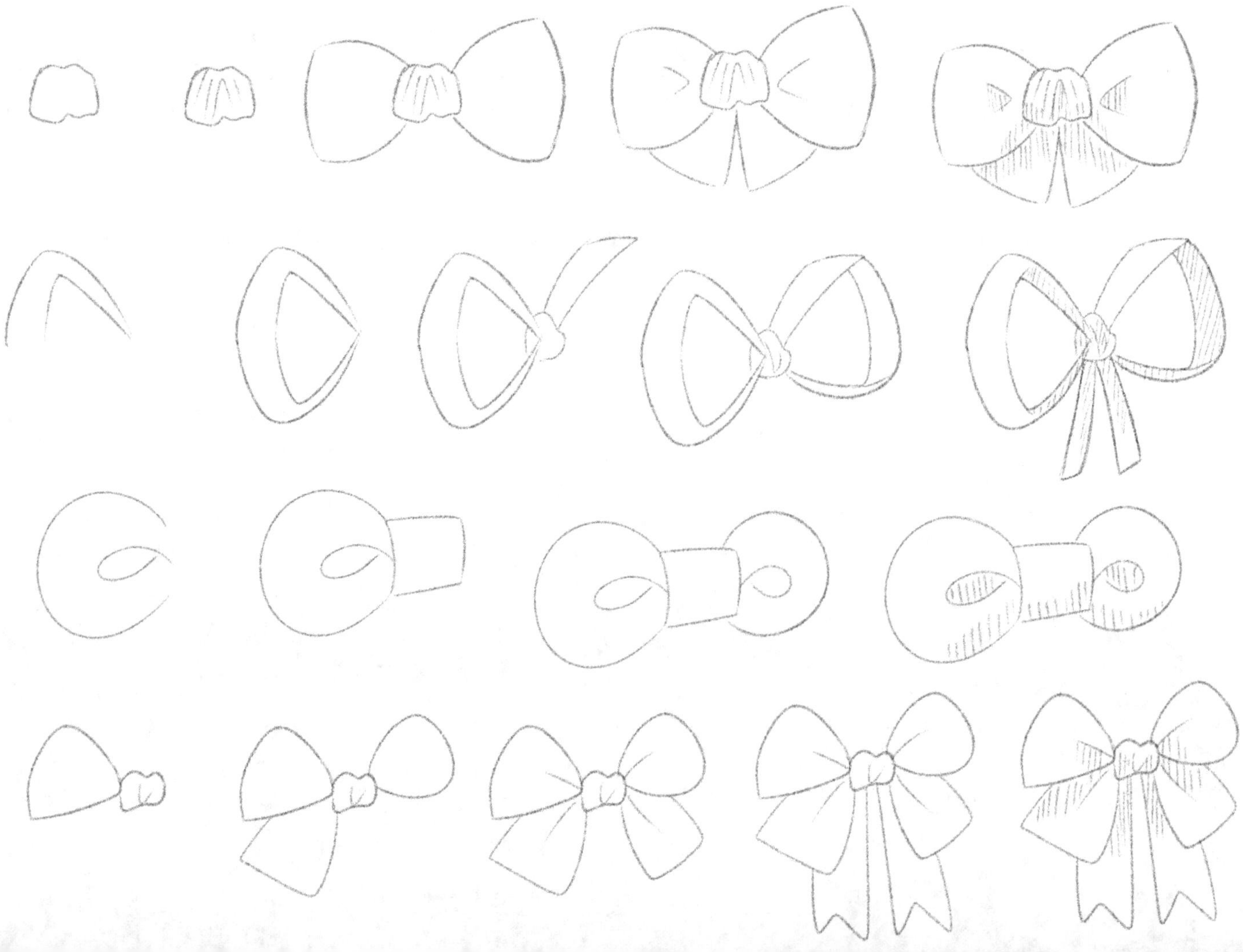

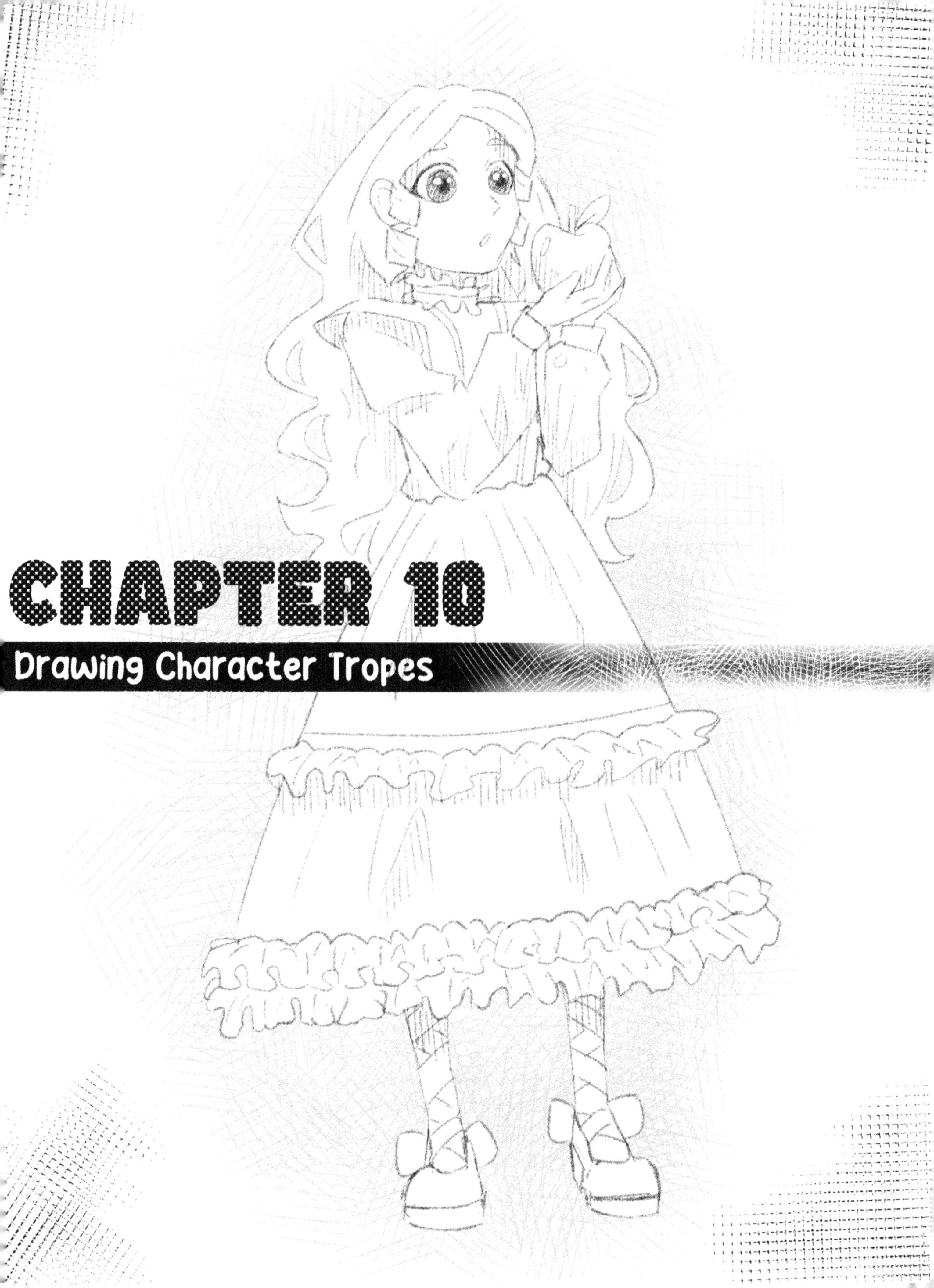

CHAPTER 10
Drawing Character Tropes

THE MAGICAL GIRL

The magical girl is a classic trope in anime and manga that involves a young girl who transforms into a powerful heroine with magical abilities. This character type often features a cute and colorful outfit, as well as a cheerful and optimistic personality.

Let's draw the head shape.

1.

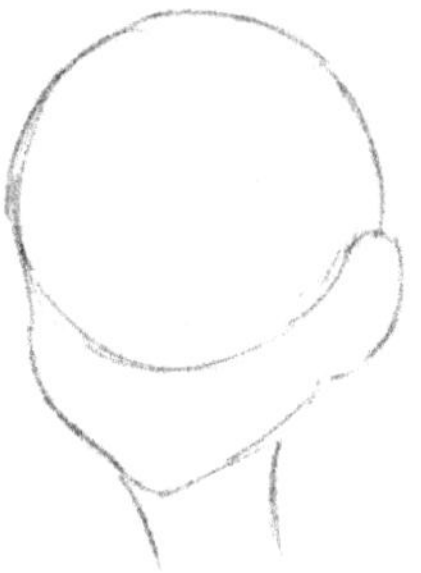

I found a reference of a pose I liked so now comes finding the shapes in the pose.

2.

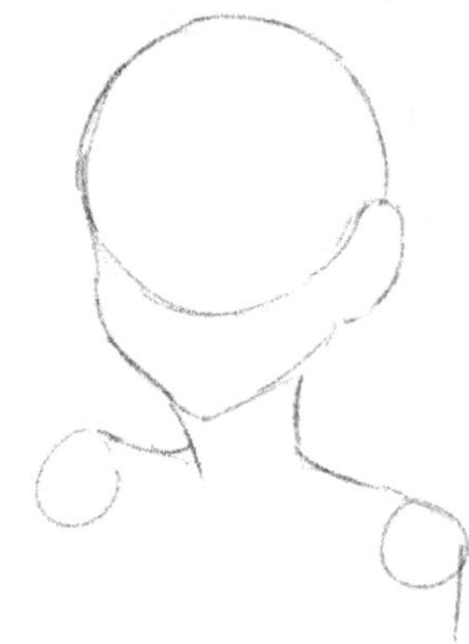

Drawing the joint circles ahead of time can really help to make sure your proportions are right.

3.

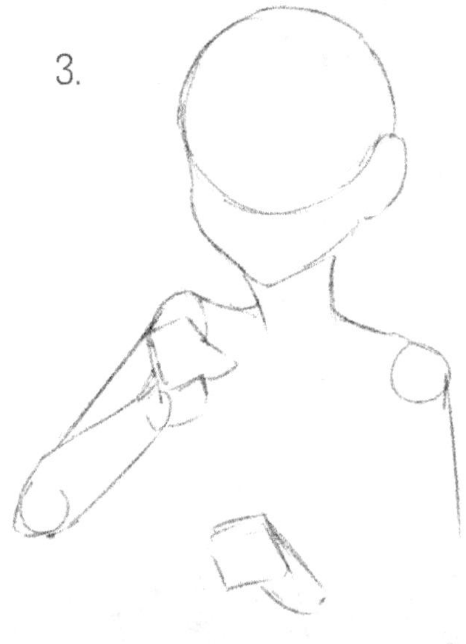

4.

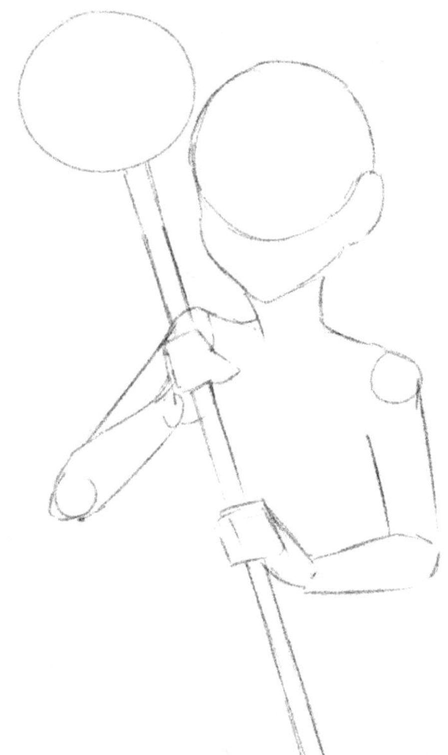

I want this magical girl to hold a magical staff. Now it'll be a magical sign, until we decide what we want it to look like.

5.

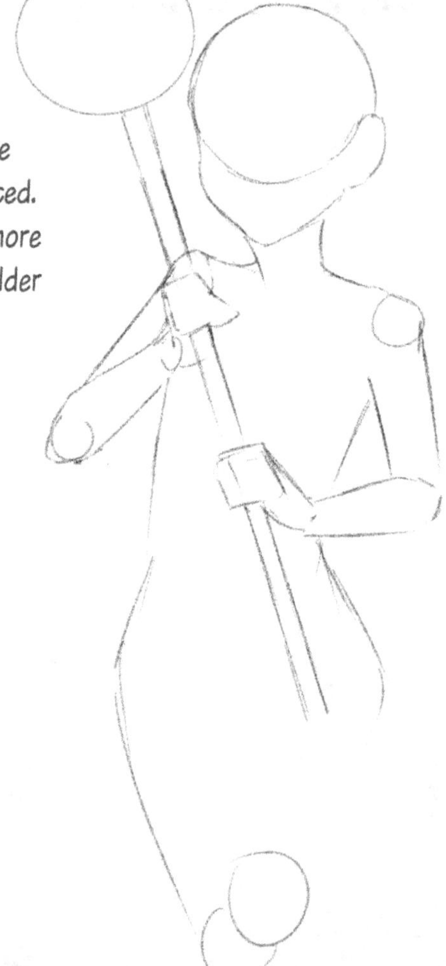

Keep in mind where these joints are placed. The knee joints are more below the right shoulder joint.

6.

Let's finish off the
legs. Again, if your
character doesn't
seem to be standing
right, you can use
these draft lines
I drew to see where
the joints sit.

7.

Now let's erase
all the guide lines
and draw a face.

8.

Let's outline the
hair and draw in
the shoes!
Remember your hair
doesn't have to look
exactly like mine.
You can be as
creative as you want.

9.

Now I outlined
an outfit I thought
would go well.
I also tried a moon-
shaped staff with
a star inside.

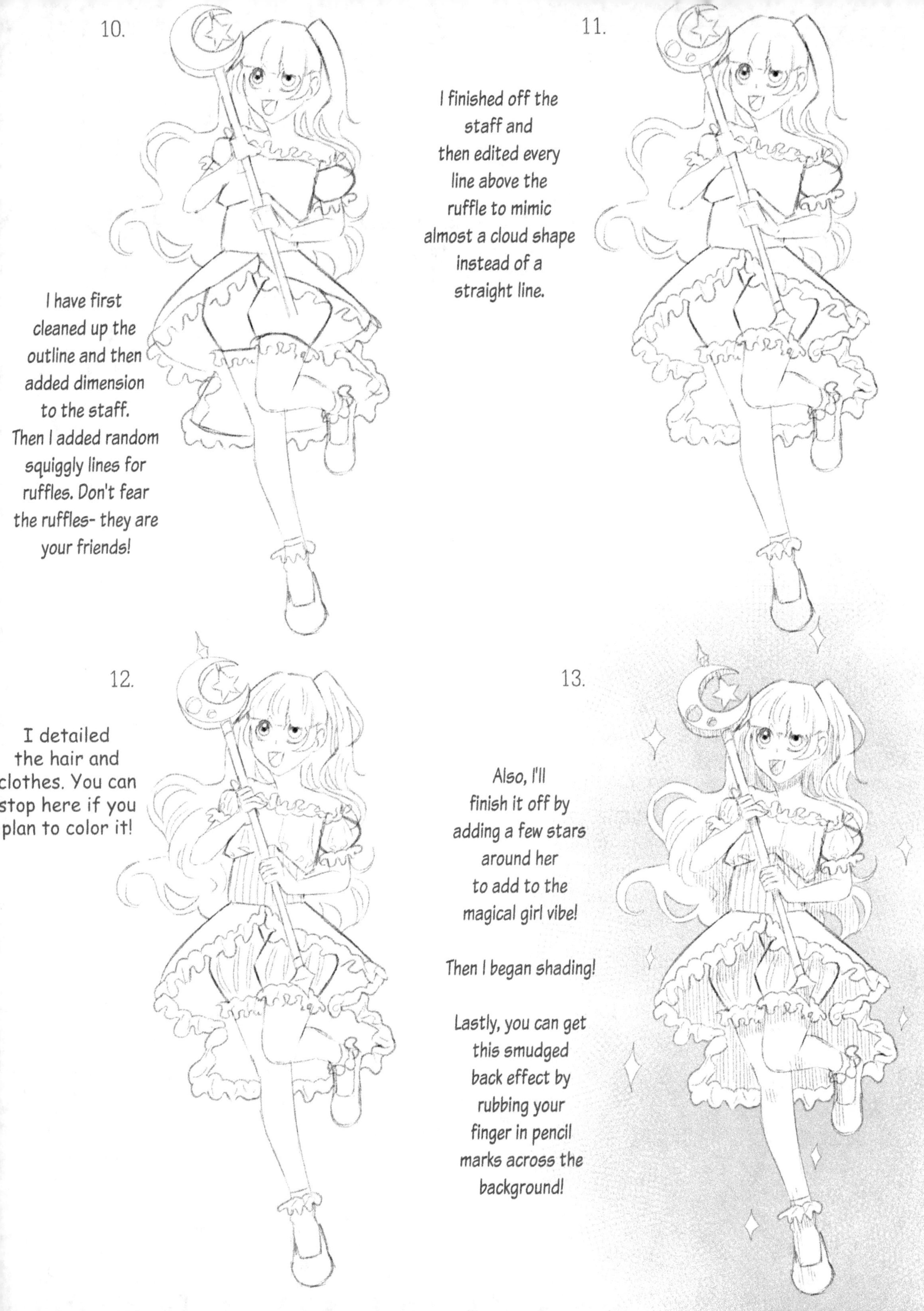

10.

I have first
cleaned up the
outline and then
added dimension
to the staff.
Then I added random
squiggly lines for
ruffles. Don't fear
the ruffles- they are
your friends!

11.

I finished off the
staff and
then edited every
line above the
ruffle to mimic
almost a cloud shape
instead of a
straight line.

12.

I detailed
the hair and
clothes. You can
stop here if you
plan to color it!

13.

Also, I'll
finish it off by
adding a few stars
around her
to add to the
magical girl vibe!

Then I began shading!

Lastly, you can get
this smudged
back effect by
rubbing your
finger in pencil
marks across the
background!

THE SCHOOL GIRL

The school girl is another classic character trope in anime and manga. These characters are often depicted in school uniform, and may have a cute and innocent appearance that emphasizes their youthfulness.

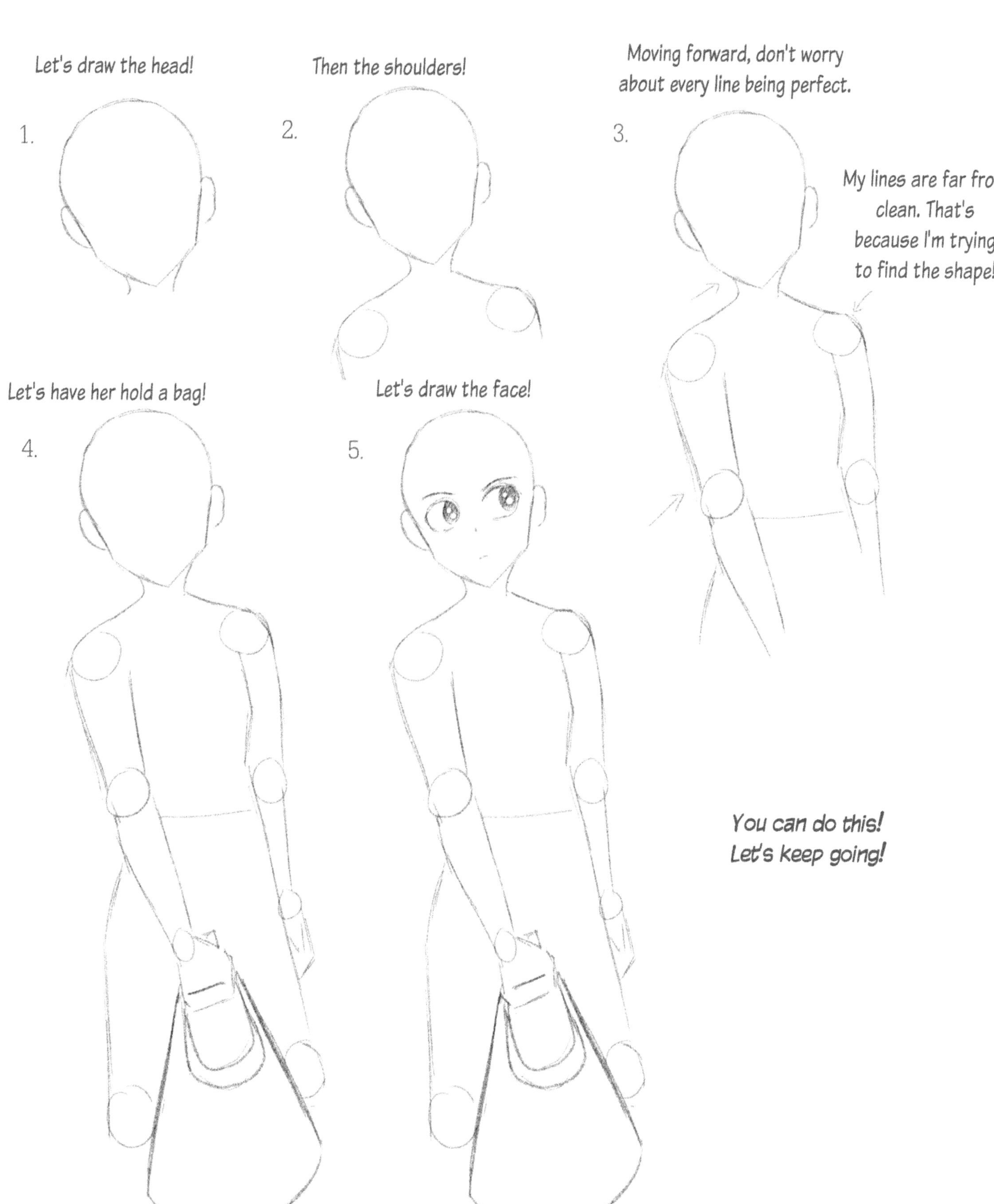

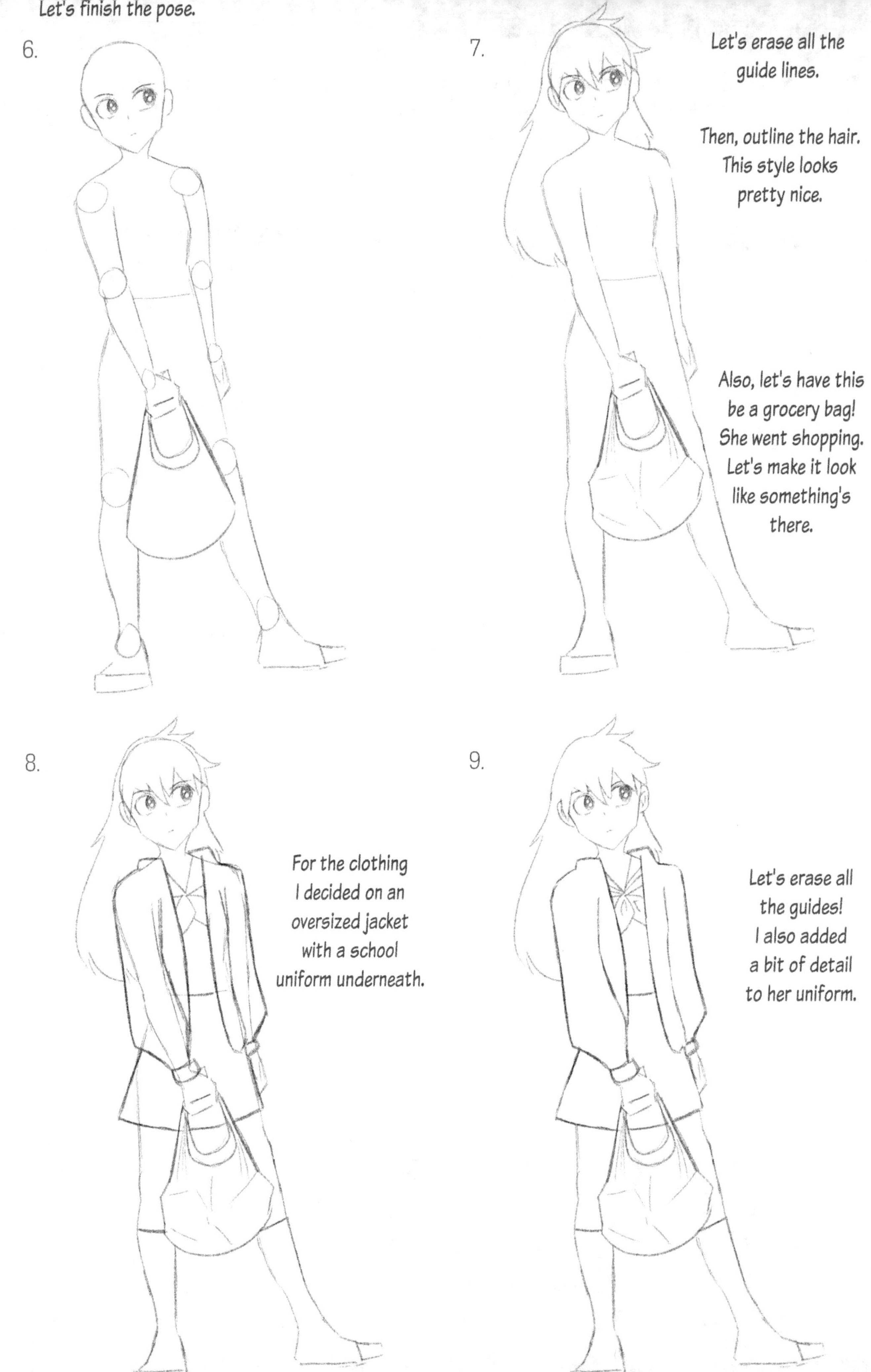

Let's finish the pose.

6.

7. Let's erase all the guide lines.

Then, outline the hair. This style looks pretty nice.

Also, let's have this be a grocery bag! She went shopping. Let's make it look like something's there.

8. For the clothing I decided on an oversized jacket with a school uniform underneath.

9. Let's erase all the guides! I also added a bit of detail to her uniform.

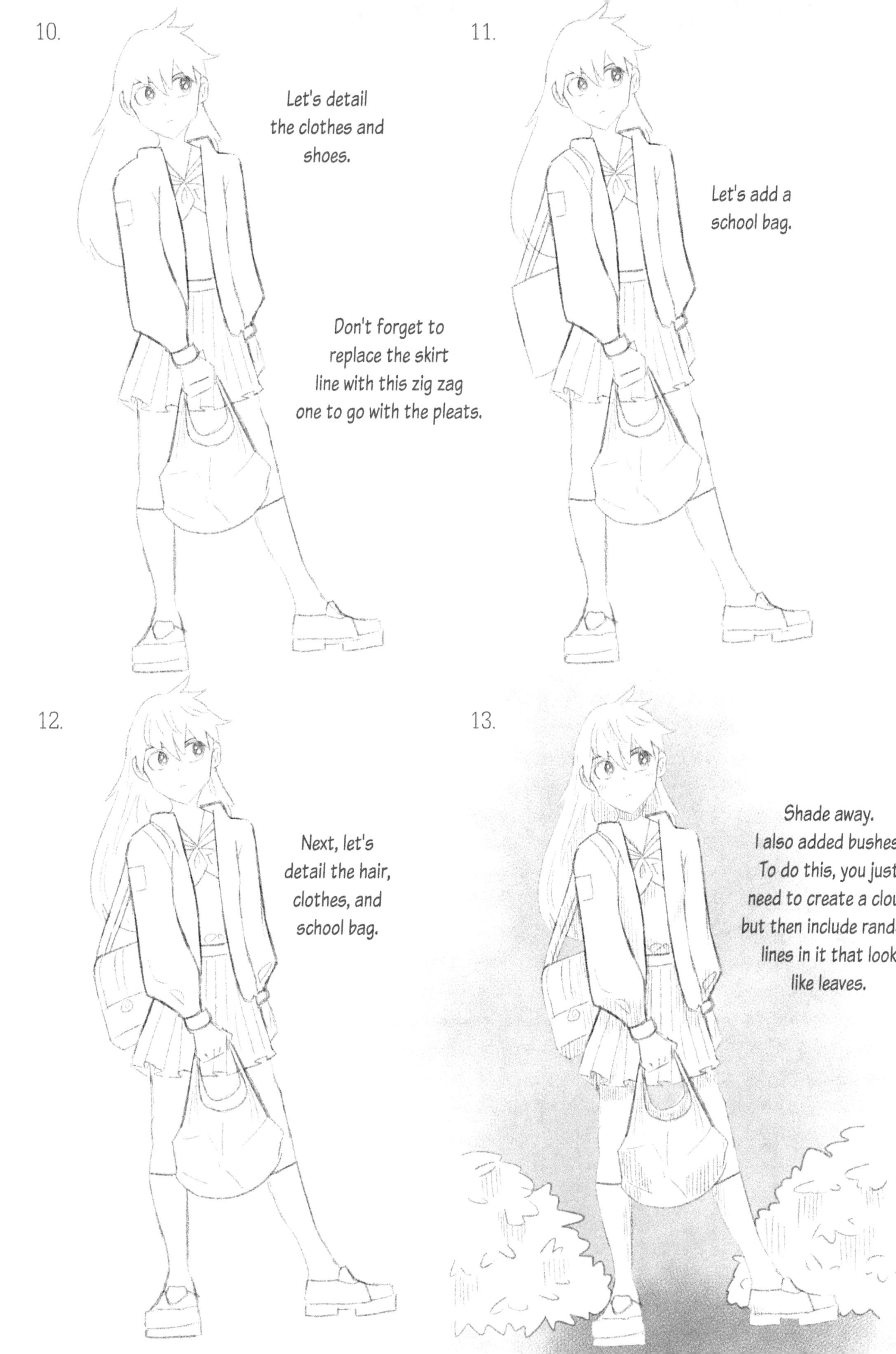

10.

Let's detail
the clothes and
shoes.

Don't forget to
replace the skirt
line with this zig zag
one to go with the pleats.

11.

Let's add a
school bag.

12.

Next, let's
detail the hair,
clothes, and
school bag.

13.

Shade away.
I also added bushes.
To do this, you just
need to create a clou.
but then include rando
lines in it that look
like leaves.

THE ANIMAL COMPANION

Many cute anime characters have animal companions, such as a small pet or talking animal. These companions are often designed to be adorable and endearing, and may provide comic relief or emotional support for the main character.

Let's do a portrait drawing for this piece.

1. 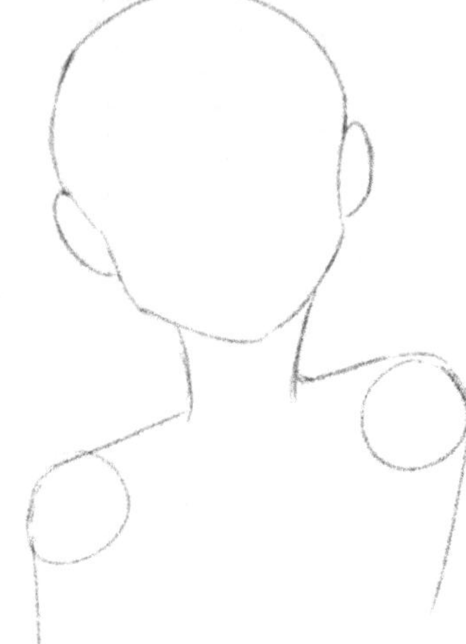

Let's outline the rabbit.

2. 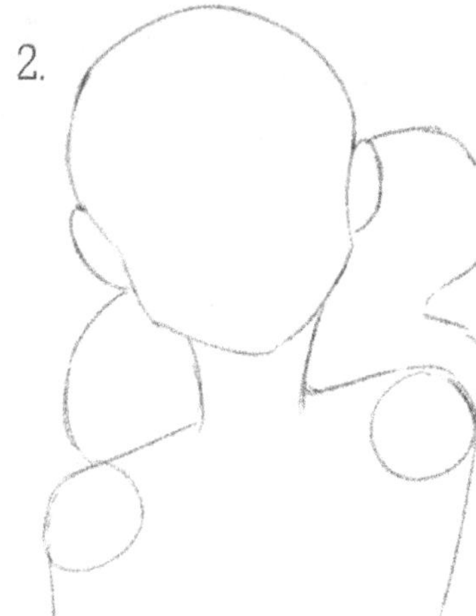

Add in the ears, paws, & tail.

3. 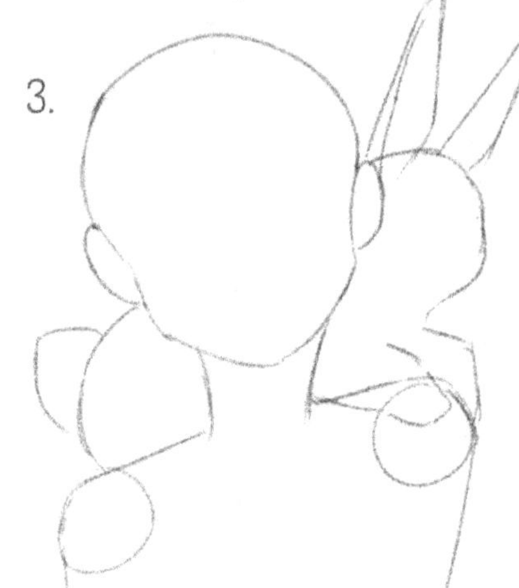

Draw in her face.

4. 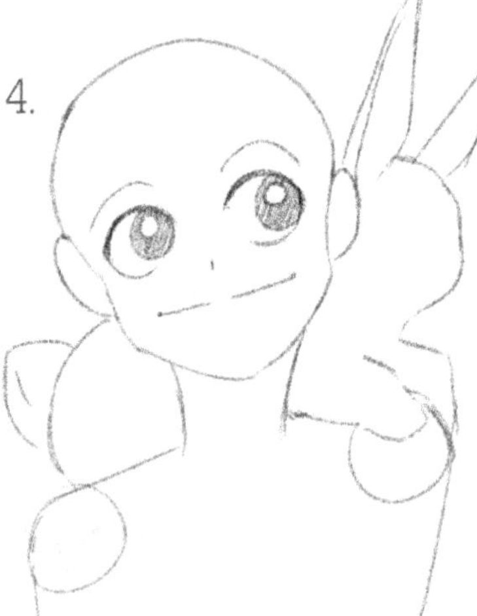

Let's draw the arms & the rabbit's face.

5. 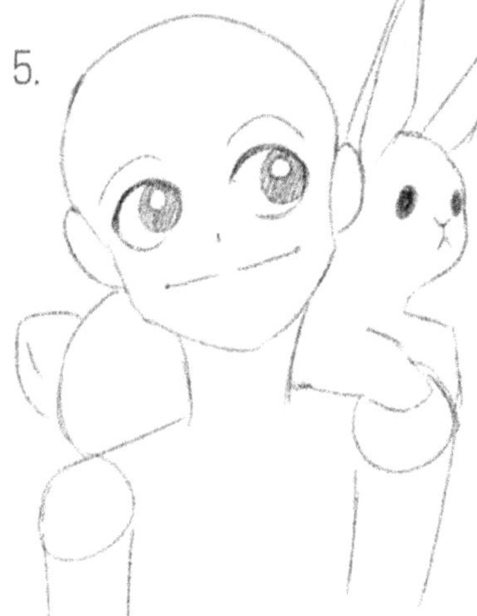

Clear the guides and outline her hair.

6. 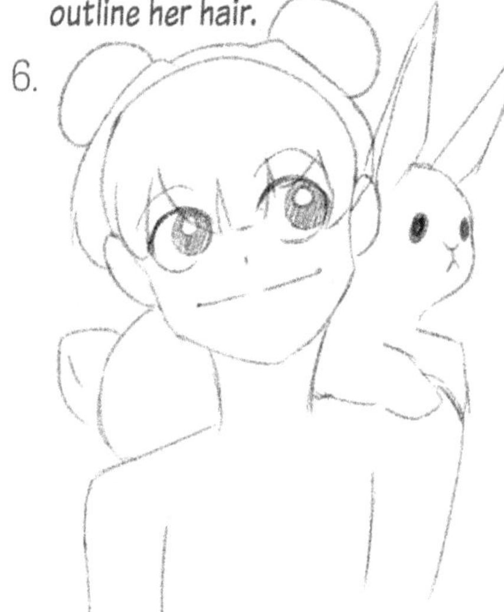

Erase everything under the hair, & detail it.

7. 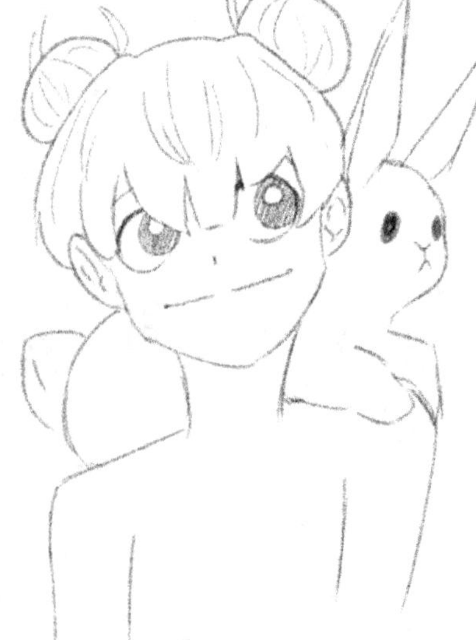

Draw a simple top and detail the bunny.

8. 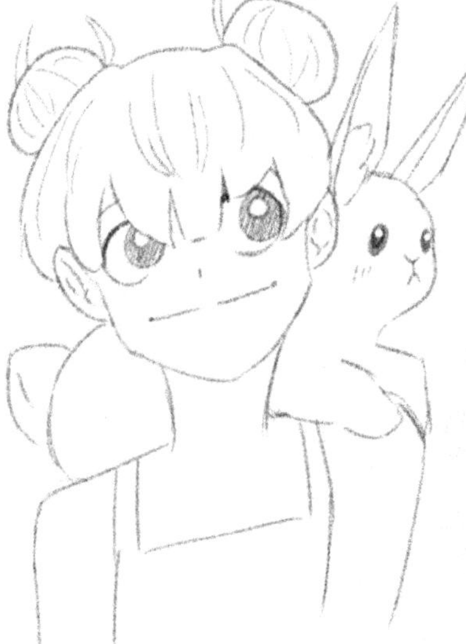

Shade! I also added a line under the lip. It seemed empty.

9. 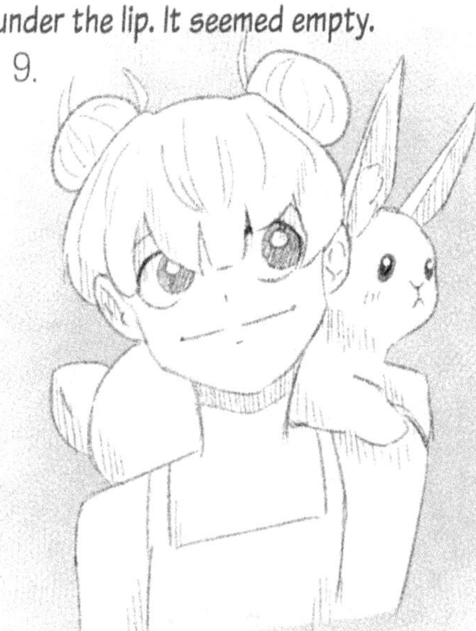

THE MOE GIRL

"Moe" is a term used in anime and manga to describe a character who is cute, innocent, and lovable. Moe characters often have a youthful appearance and a sweet, gentle personality that makes them endearing to viewers.

Let's draw the head!

1.

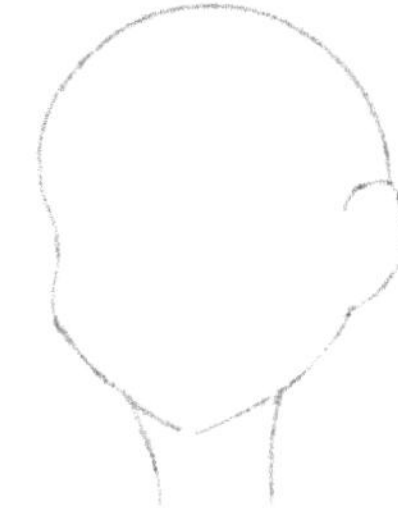

Start on the arms.

2.

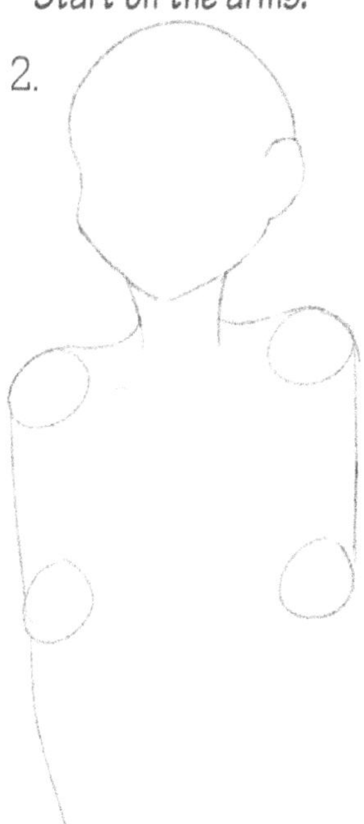

Let's give her a shy pose.

3.

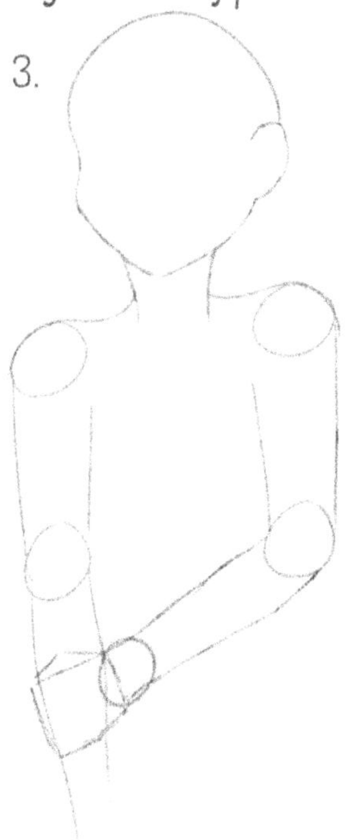

Next, to the knees!

4.

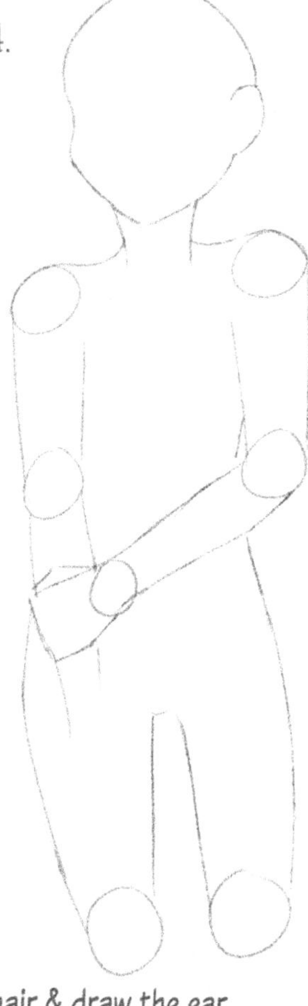

Let's finish the body.

5.

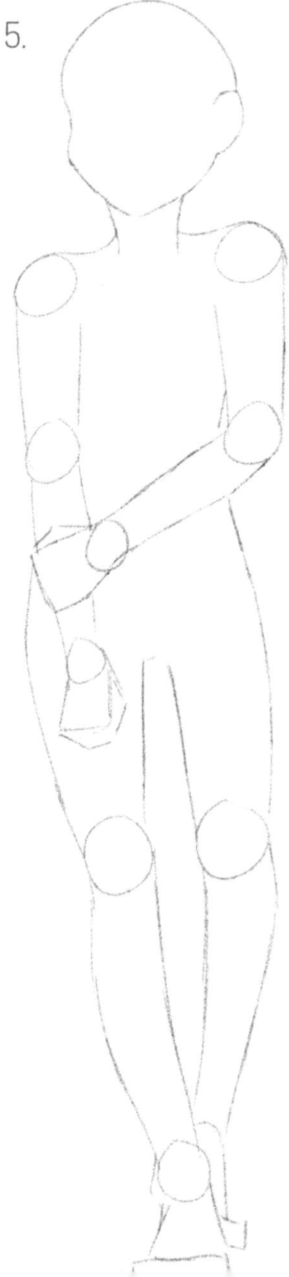

On to the face!

6.

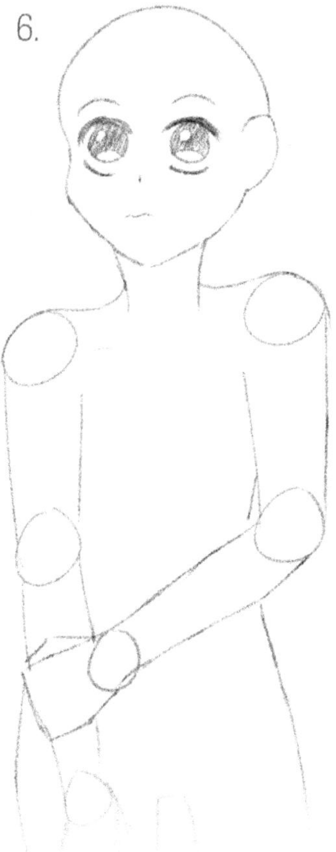

Outline the hair & draw the ear.

7.

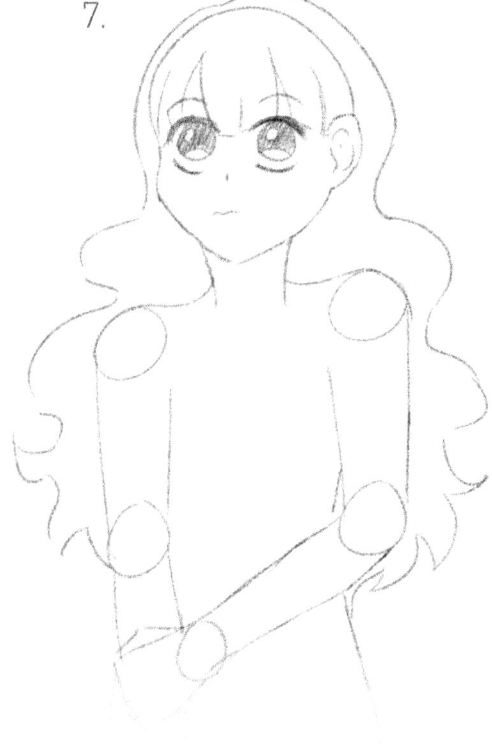

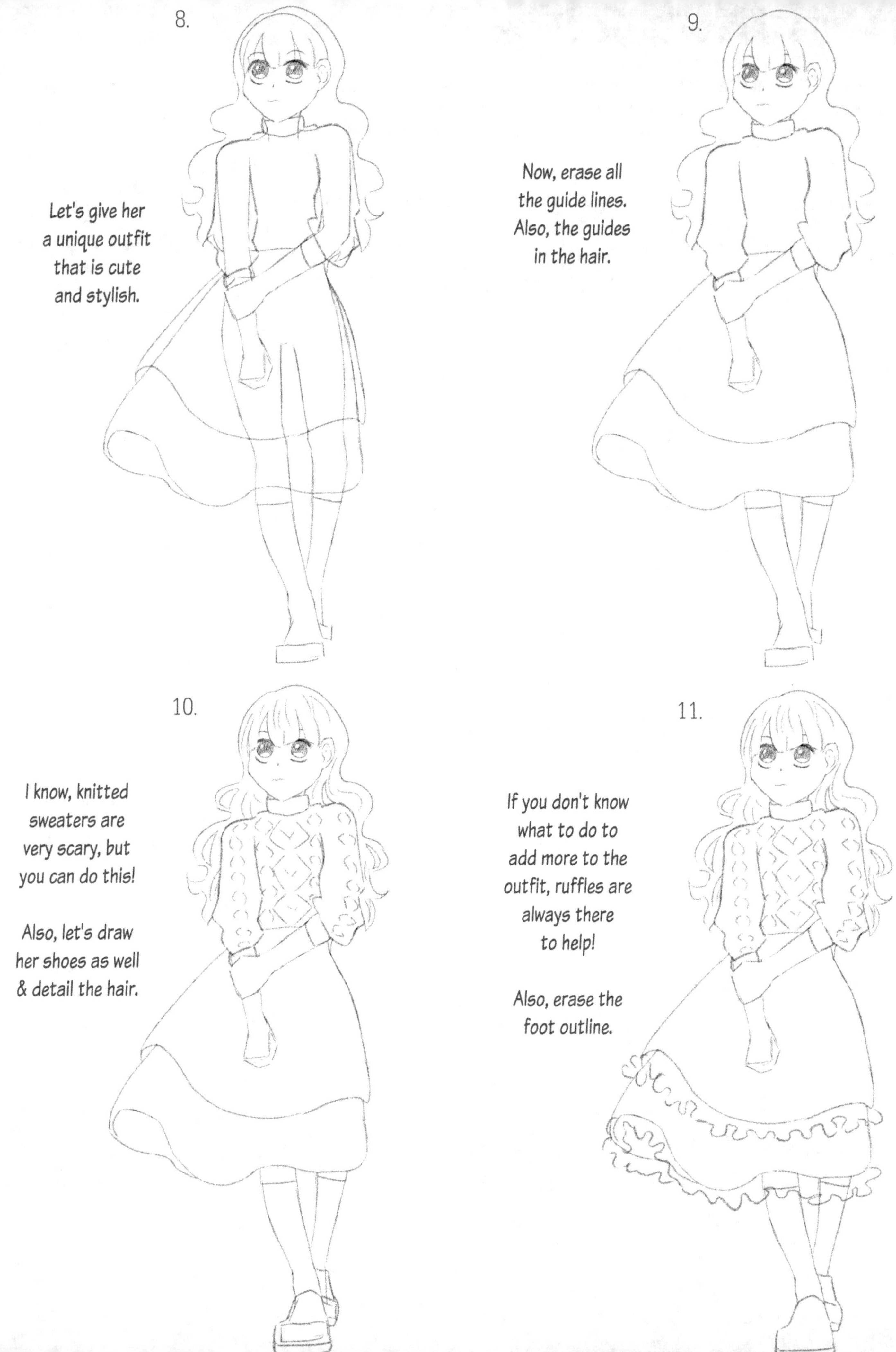

8.

Let's give her
a unique outfit
that is cute
and stylish.

9.

Now, erase all
the guide lines.
Also, the guides
in the hair.

10.

I know, knitted
sweaters are
very scary, but
you can do this!

Also, let's draw
her shoes as well
& detail the hair.

11.

If you don't know
what to do to
add more to the
outfit, ruffles are
always there
to help!

Also, erase the
foot outline.

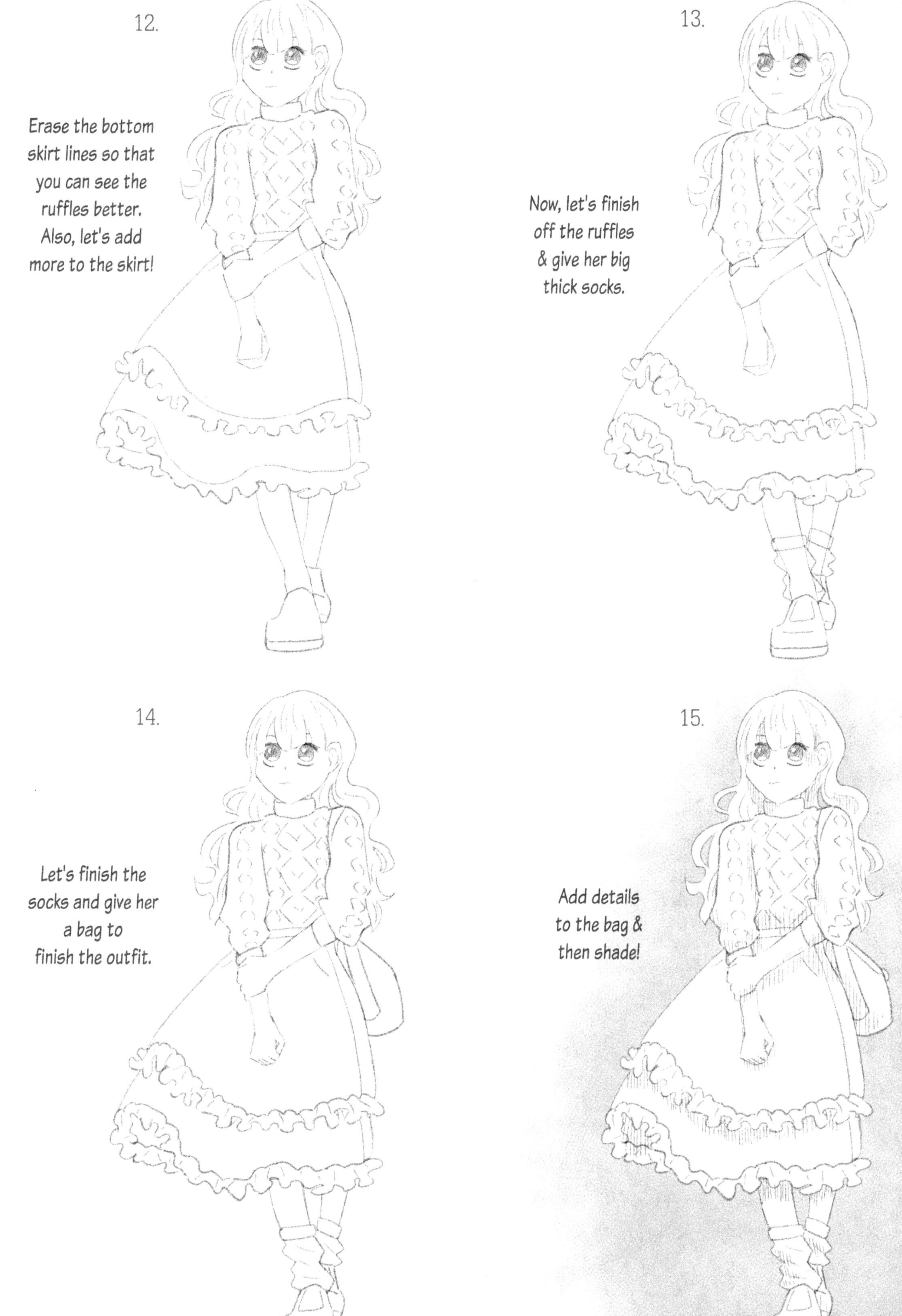

12.
Erase the bottom skirt lines so that you can see the ruffles better. Also, let's add more to the skirt!
13.
Now, let's finish off the ruffles & give her big thick socks.
14.
Let's finish the socks and give her a bag to finish the outfit.
15.
Add details to the bag & then shade!

THE CUTE MONSTER

Some anime and manga feature cute monsters, such as small creatures with big eyes and playful personalities. These characters are often designed to be both adorable and approachable, and may serve as mascots or companions for the main characters.

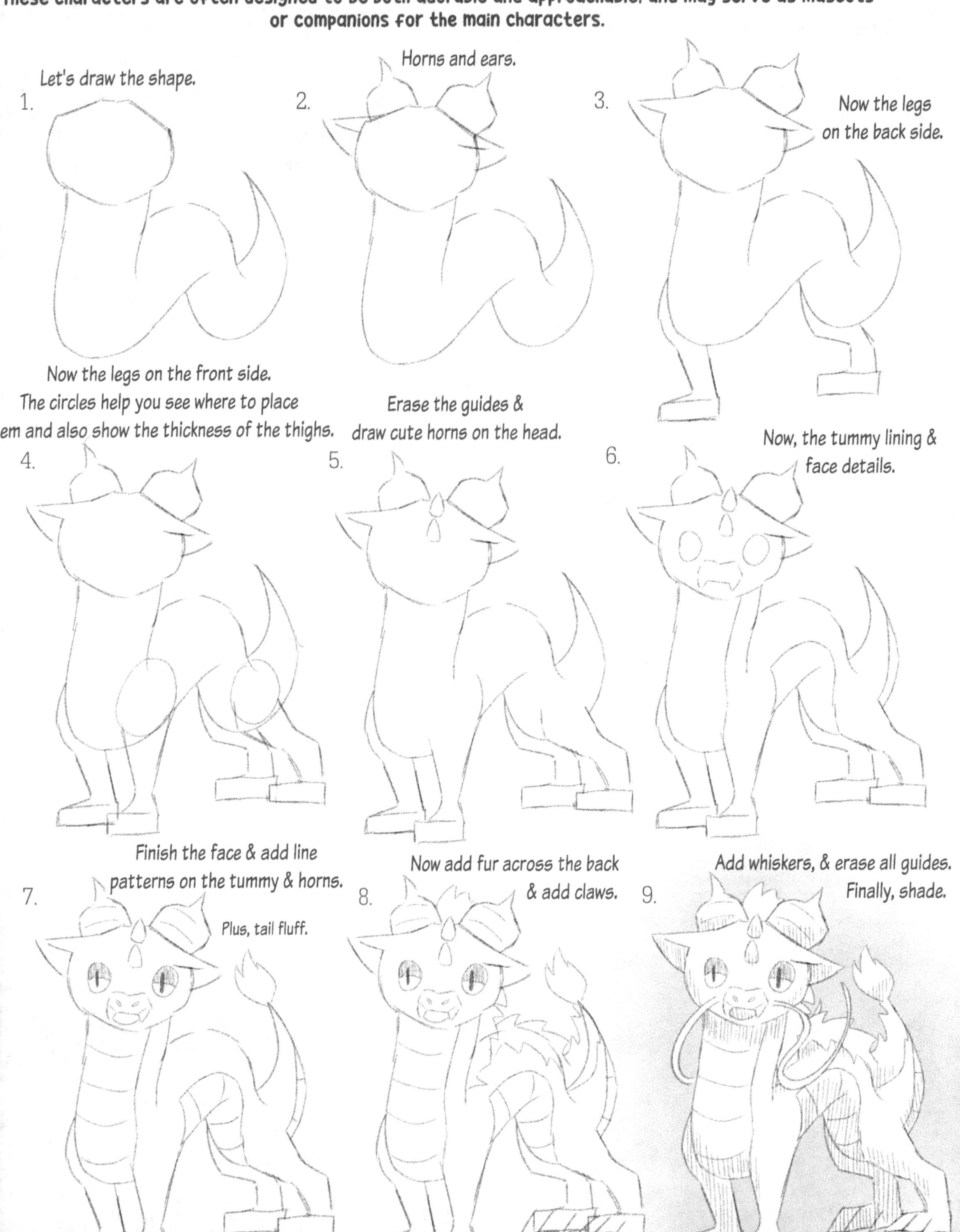

1. Let's draw the shape.

Now the legs on the front side. The circles help you see where to place them and also show the thickness of the thighs.

2. Horns and ears.

Erase the guides & draw cute horns on the head.

3. Now the legs on the back side.

Now, the tummy lining & face details.

4.

5.

6.

7. Finish the face & add line patterns on the tummy & horns. Plus, tail fluff.

8. Now add fur across the back & add claws.

9. Add whiskers, & erase all guides. Finally, shade.

THE ROBOT OR ANDROID

Robots and androids are common in anime and manga, and may be designed to have a cute and childlike appearance. These characters often have a childlike innocence and a desire to learn about the world around them, which can make them endearing to viewers.

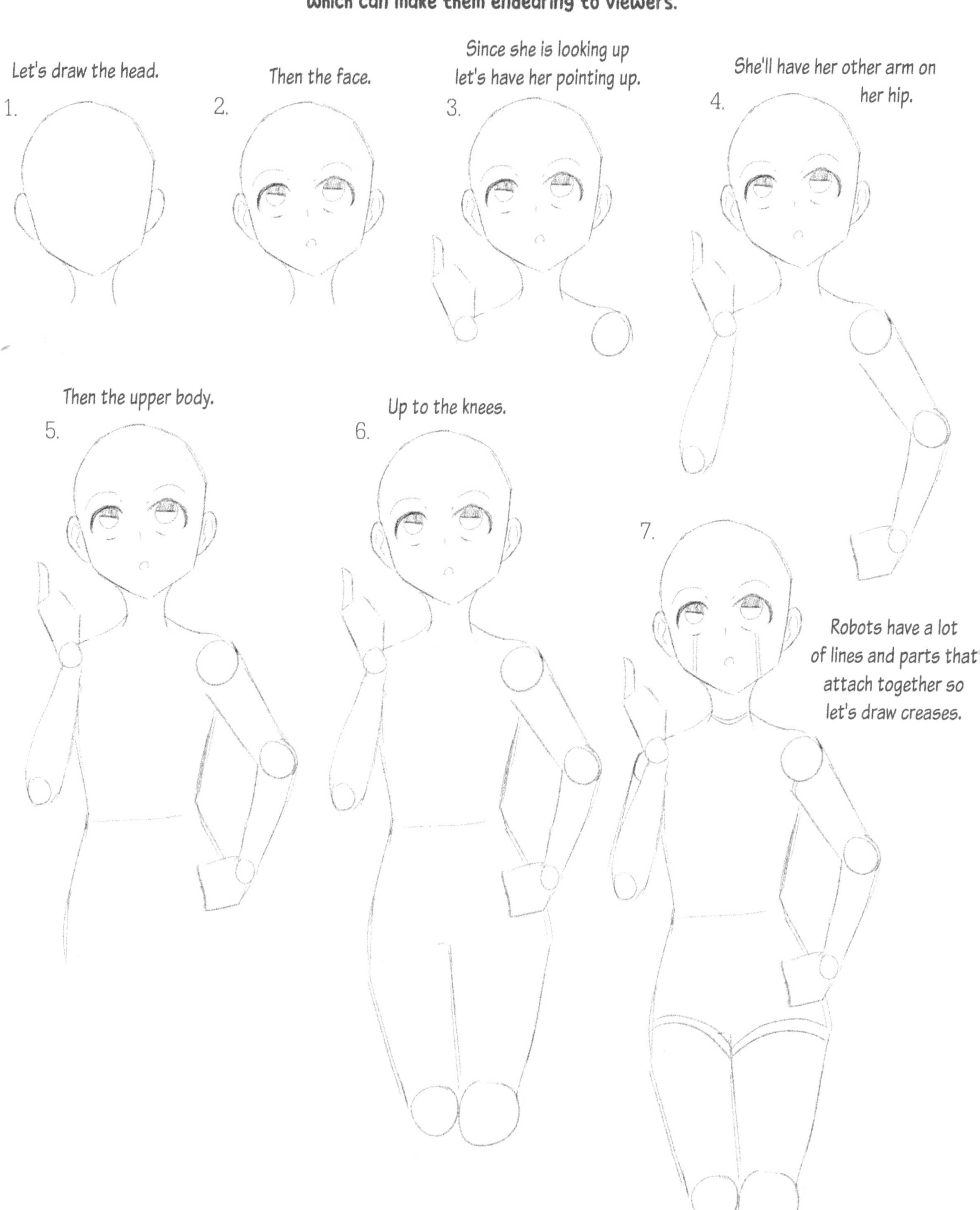

8.

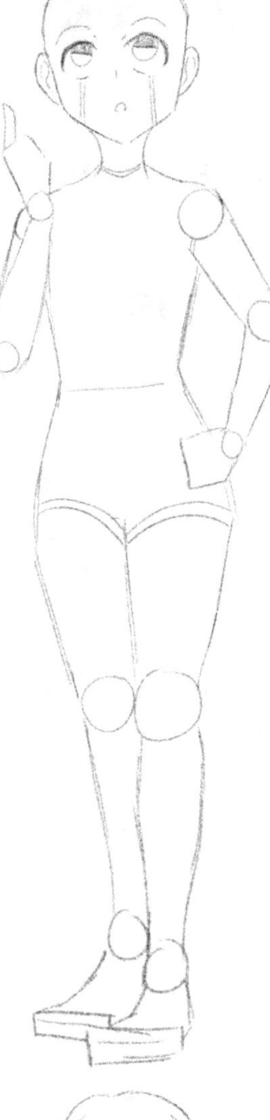

Let's finish up
the pose.

9.

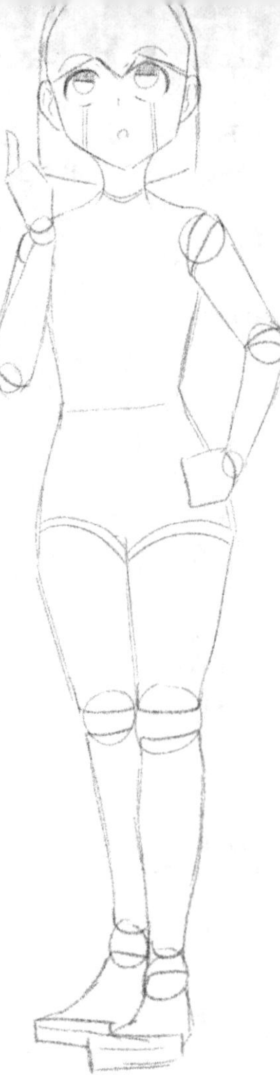

Let's outline
the hair style.

Also, since she's
a robot/android,
let's let the joint
circles peak out
& we'll connect
the parts together.

10.

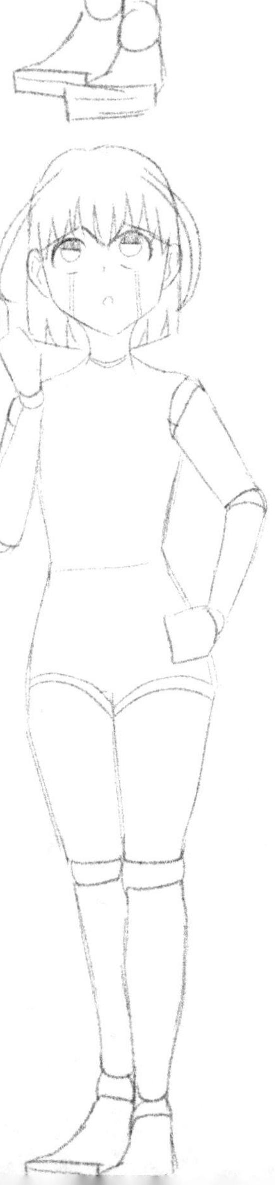

Erase what's
overlapping
& fix up her hair.
I added these hair
strands sticking
out because I thought
they made her look
more interesting.

11.

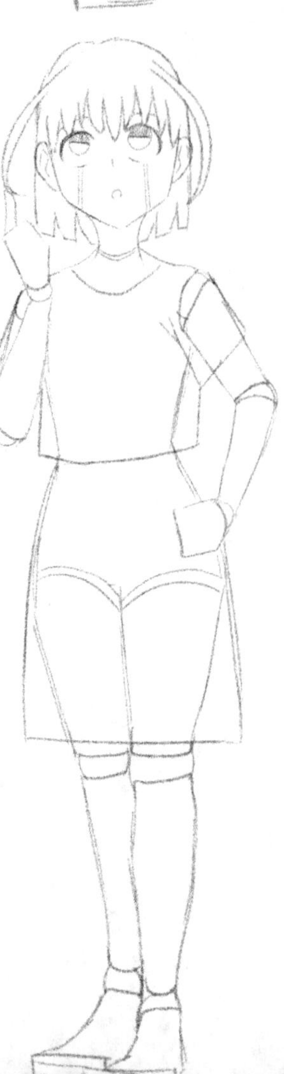

I've outlined
some simple
clothing, but
you can decide
how you want
the clothing to look.

12.

Let's detail
the clothing.

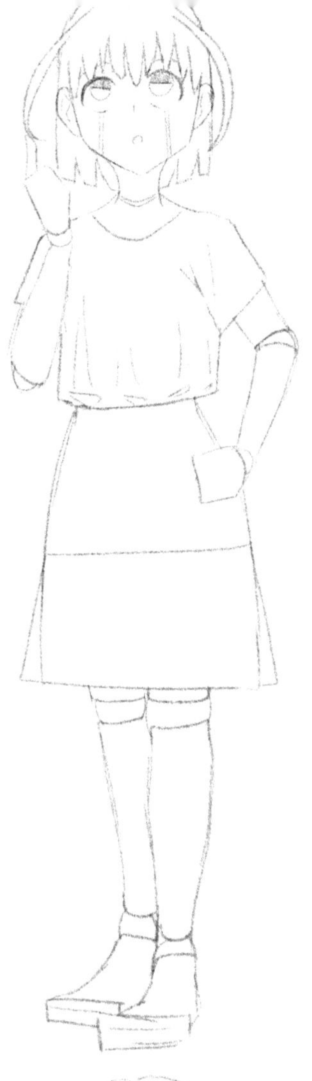

13.

I fixed the
skirt by adding
a pocket for her
hand.

Also, I added a
lose big ruffle
halfway through
the skirt.

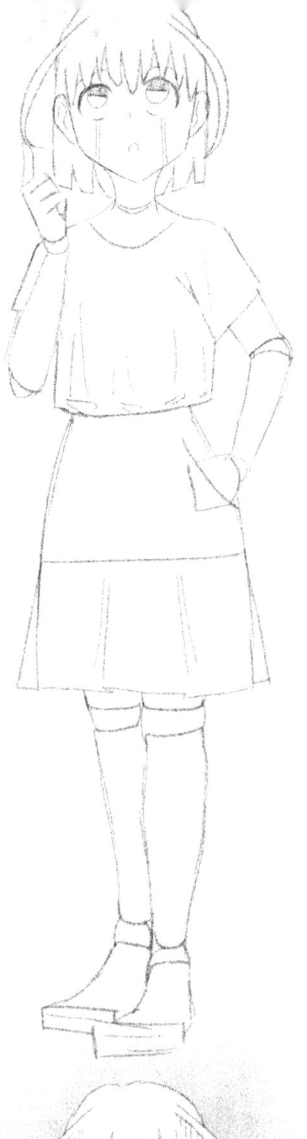

14.

Some more
detail for the
outfit & erase
the part of the
hand that's
in the pocket.

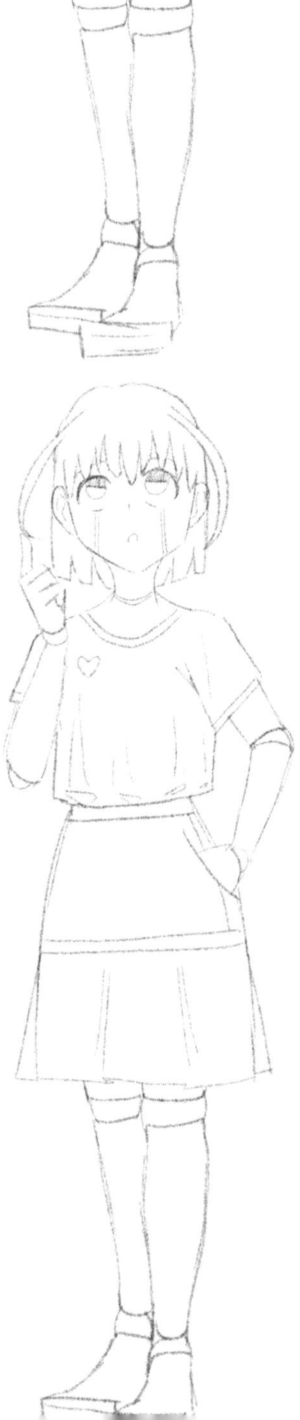

15.

Then shade.
You are done!

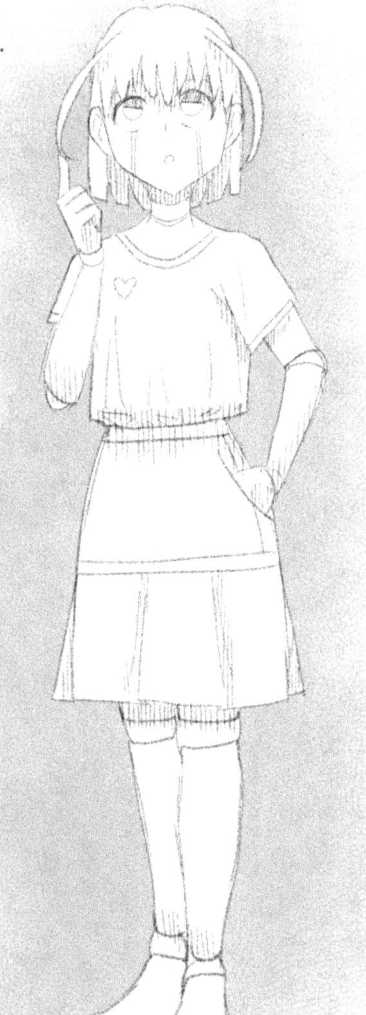

THE TSUNDERE

The tsundere is a character trope that involves a character who is initially cold and aloof, but gradually becomes warmer and more affectionate as they form deeper relationships with other characters. These characters often have a cute and spunky appearance, and may be designed to have a fiery, or tsundere, personality.

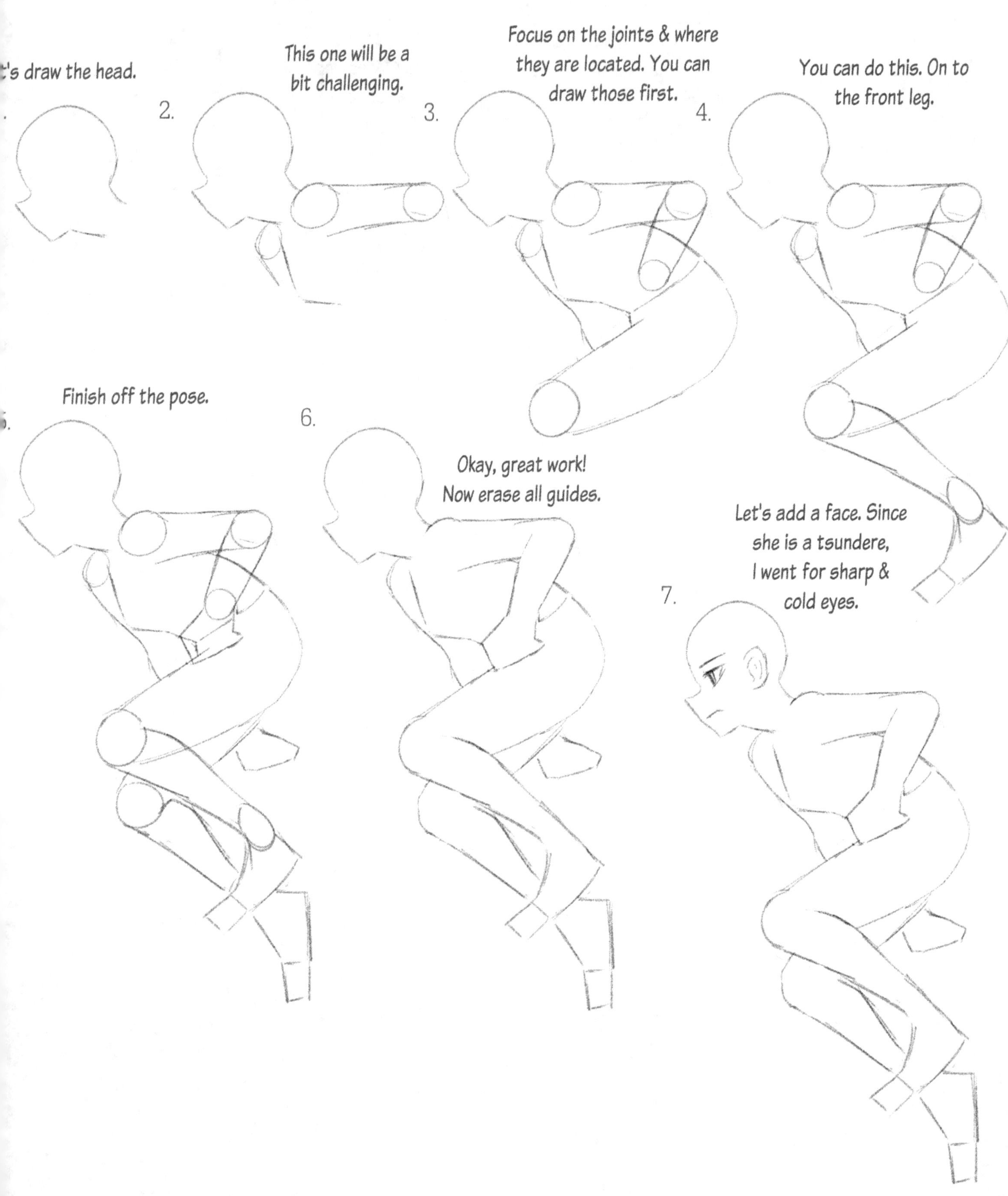

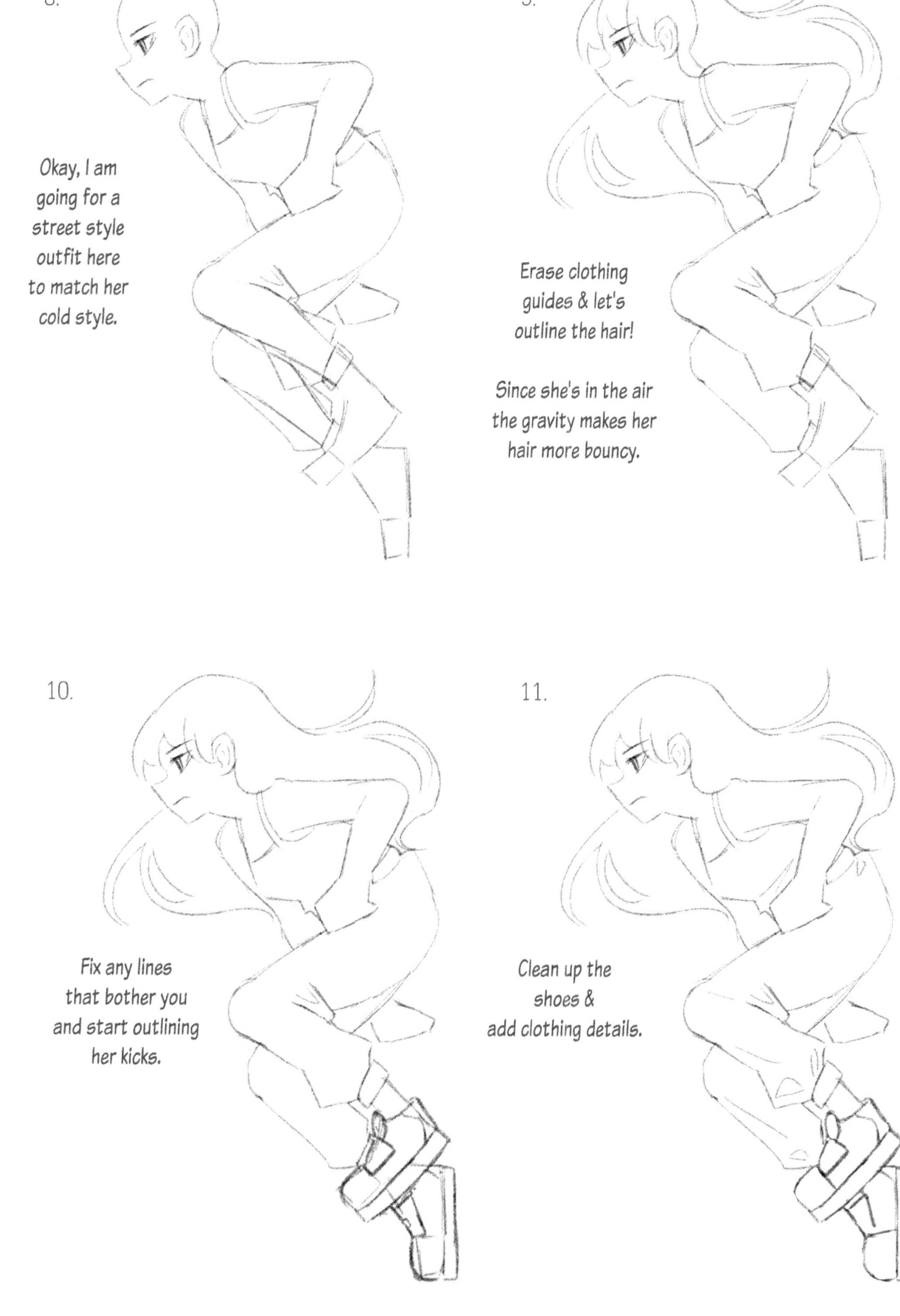

8.

Okay, I am
going for a
street style
outfit here
to match her
cold style.

9.

Erase clothing
guides & let's
outline the hair!

Since she's in the air
the gravity makes her
hair more bouncy.

10.

Fix any lines
that bother you
and start outlining
her kicks.

11.

Clean up the
shoes &
add clothing details.

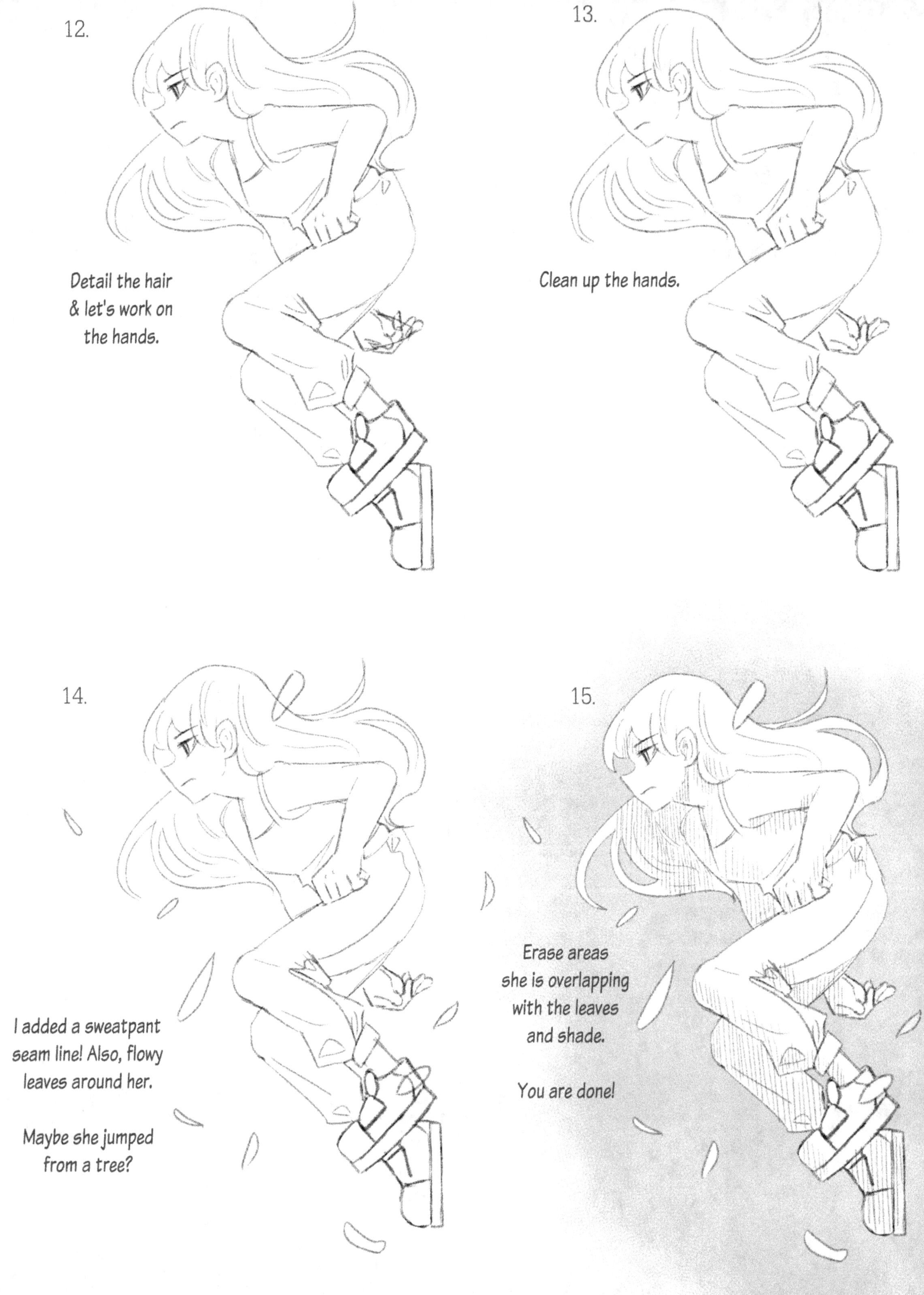

12.
Detail the hair & let's work on the hands.
13.
Clean up the hands.
14.
I added a sweatpant seam line! Also, flowy leaves around her.
Maybe she jumped from a tree?
15.
Erase areas she is overlapping with the leaves and shade.
You are done!

THE LOLI

The loli is a character trope that involves a young girl who has a cute and innocent appearance. These characters are often designed to be small and petite, and may have a childlike or naive personality that makes them endearing to viewers.

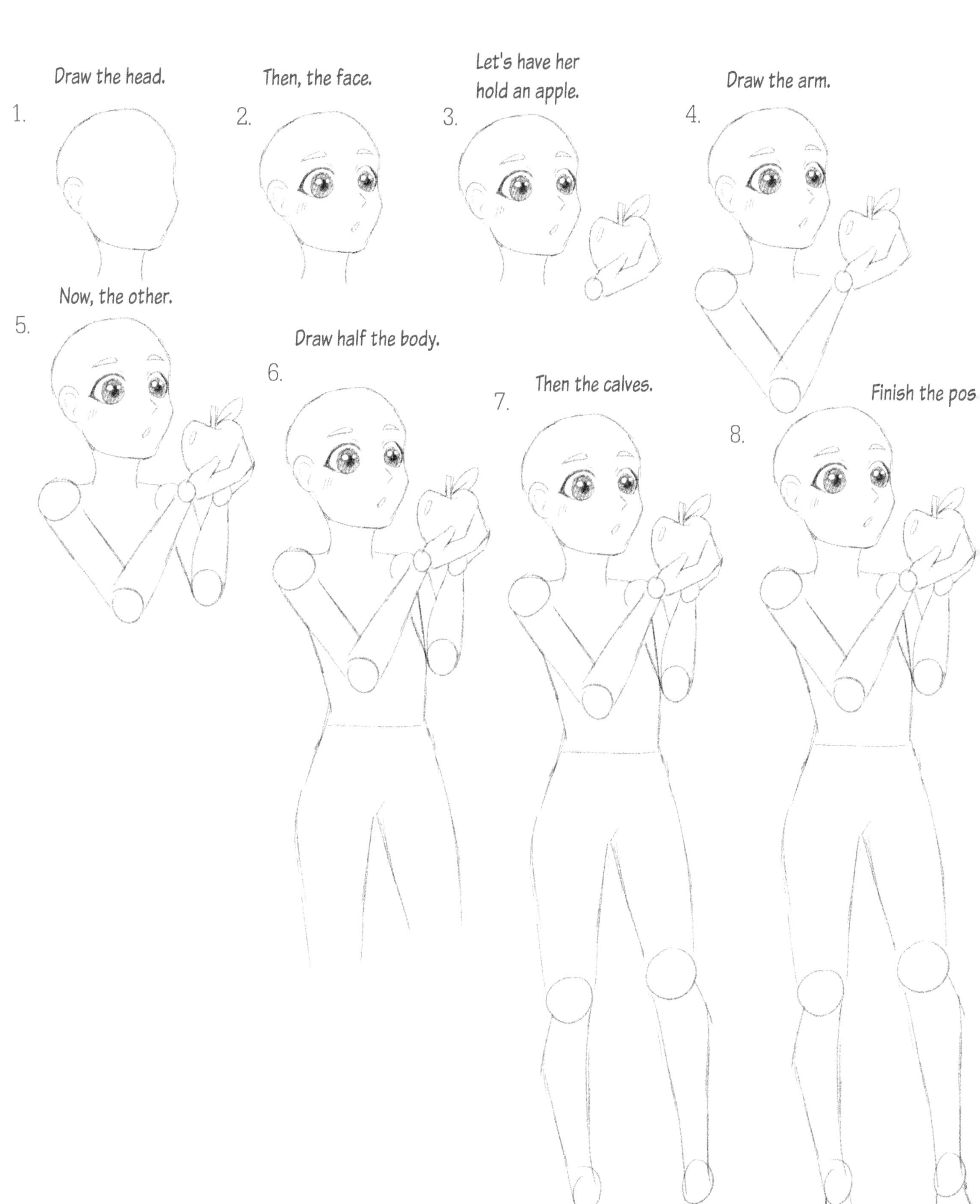

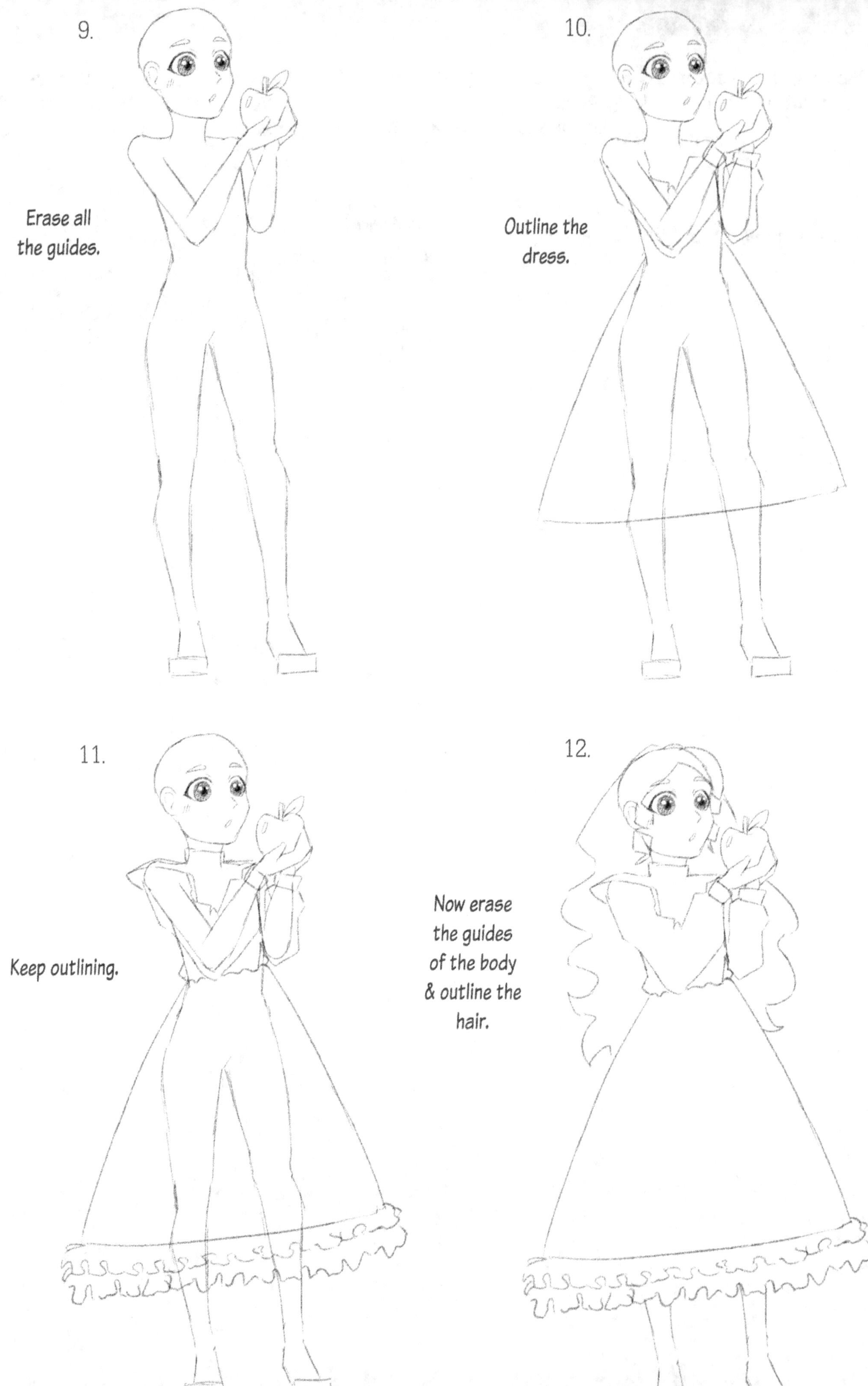

9.
Erase all
the guides.

10.
Outline the
dress.

11.
Keep outlining.

12.
Now erase
the guides
of the body
& outline the
hair.

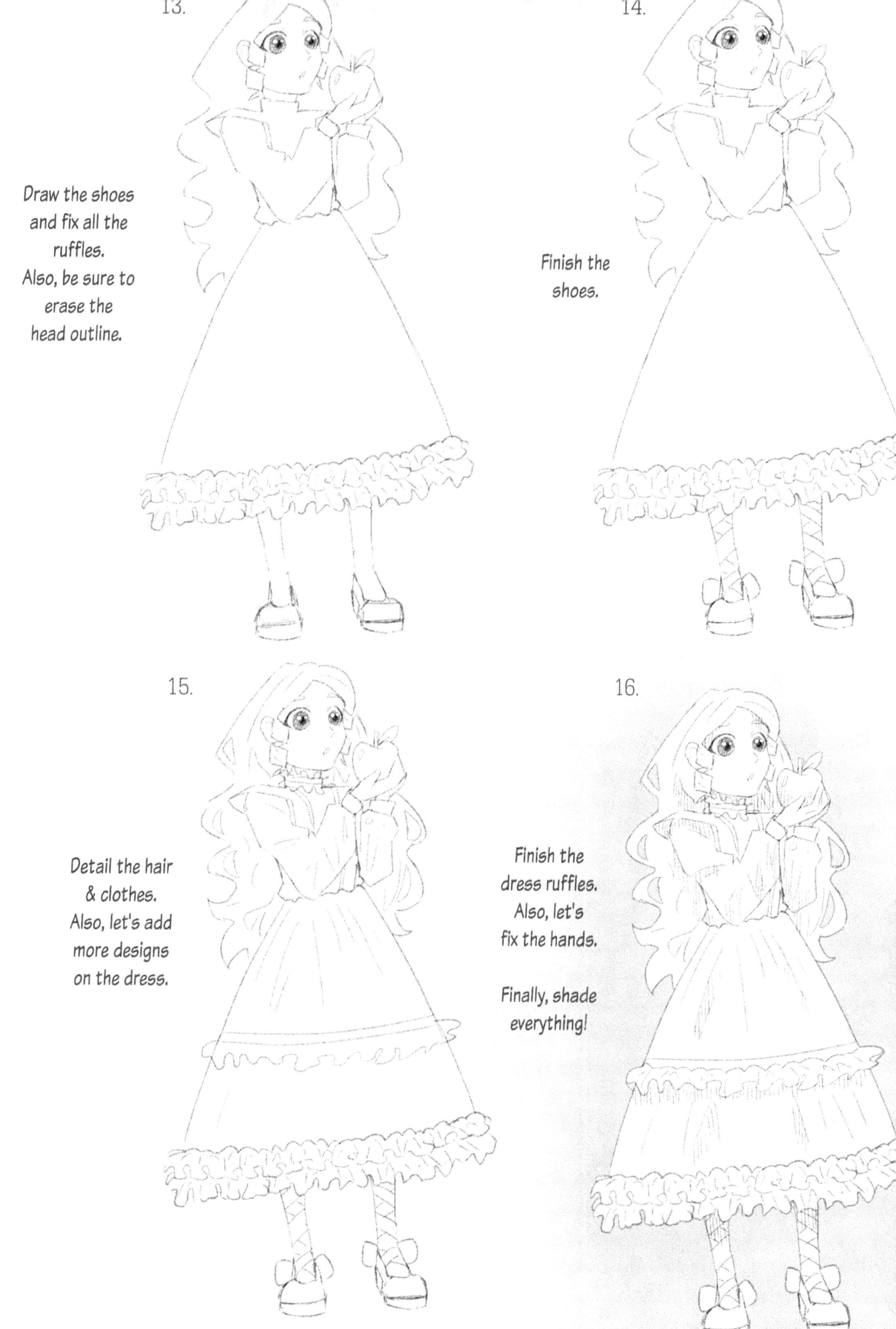

13.

Draw the shoes
and fix all the
ruffles.
Also, be sure to
erase the
head outline.

14.

Finish the
shoes.

15.

Detail the hair
& clothes.
Also, let's add
more designs
on the dress.

16.

Finish the
dress ruffles.
Also, let's
fix the hands.

Finally, shade
everything!

THE BISHOUNEN/BISHOUJO

The bishounen (for male characters) and bishoujo (for female characters) are character tropes that involve characters with a beautiful, almost androgynous appearance. These characters often have delicate features, such as long hair and slender limbs, and may be designed to be elegant, mysterious, or otherworldly.

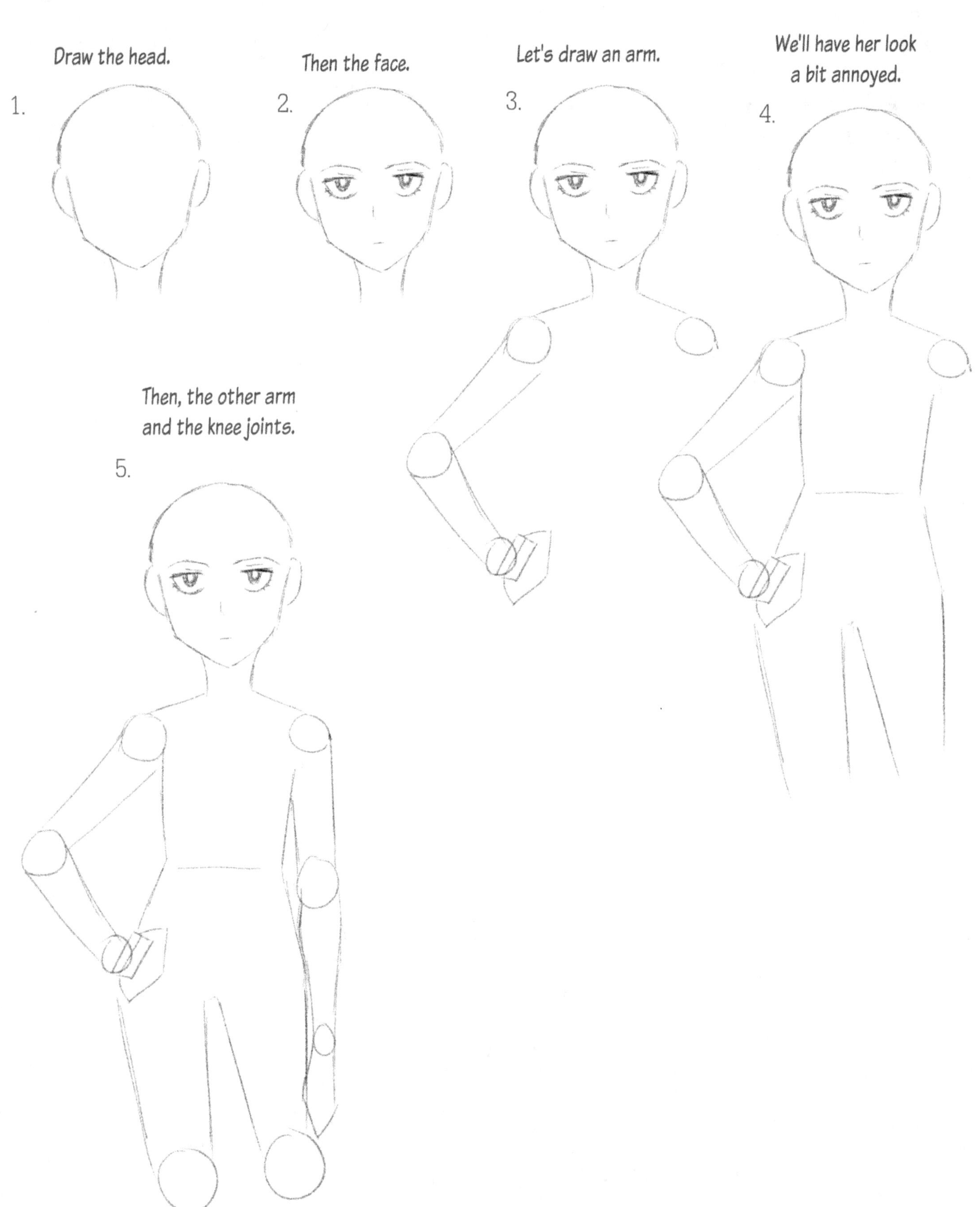

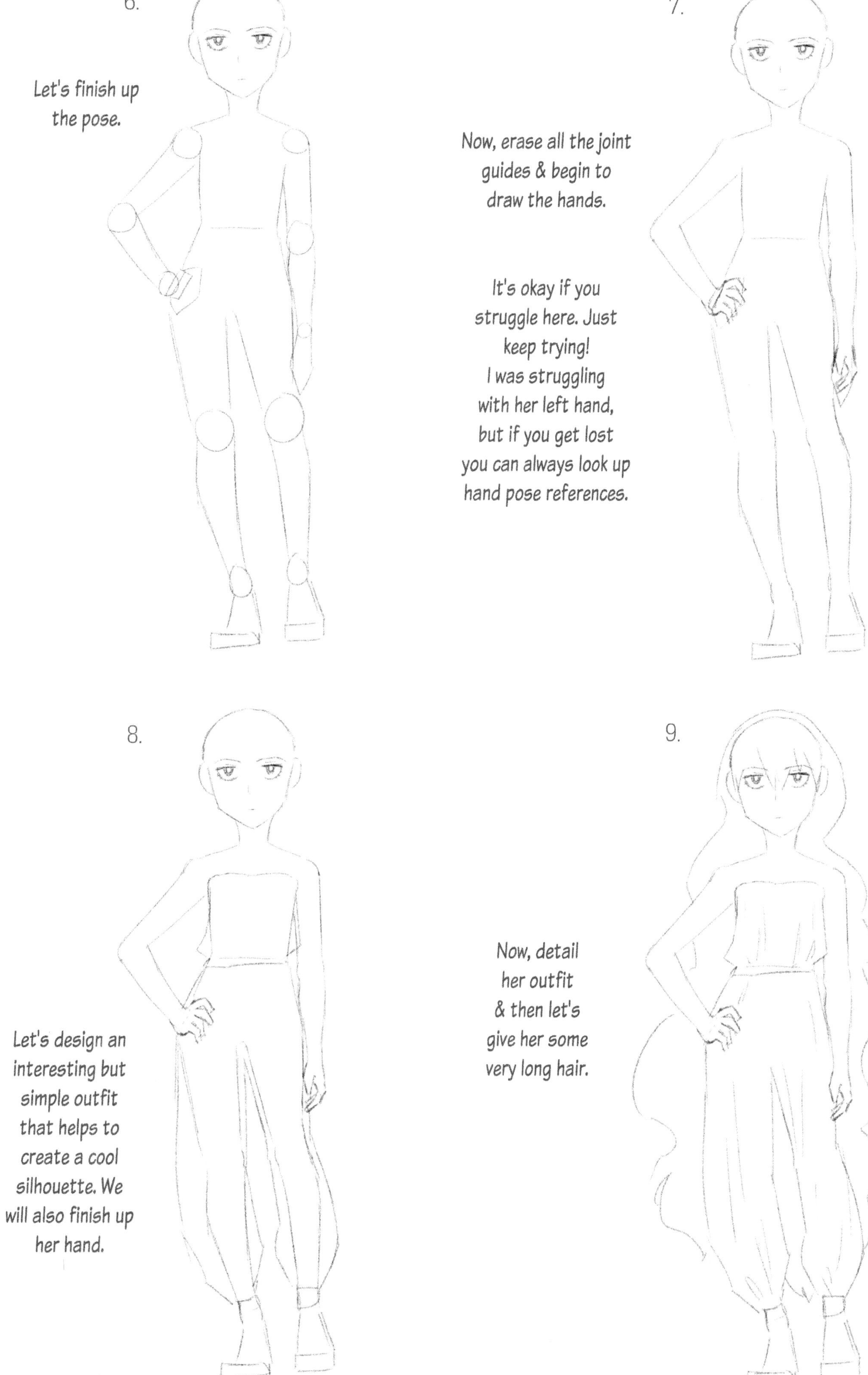

6.
Let's finish up the pose.

7.
Now, erase all the joint guides & begin to draw the hands.

It's okay if you struggle here. Just keep trying! I was struggling with her left hand, but if you get lost you can always look up hand pose references.

8.
Let's design an interesting but simple outfit that helps to create a cool silhouette. We will also finish up her hand.

9.
Now, detail her outfit & then let's give her some very long hair.

10.

The outfit can
still use some
more to it.
I added arm bands,
double seams,
and this lovely
extra hip fabric.

11.

Fix up the
hip fabric &
add detail to
her hair.

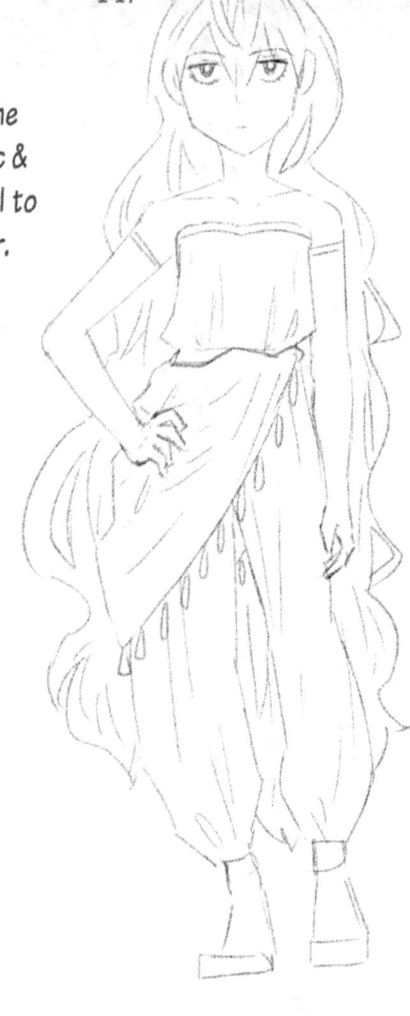

12.

I think she
shouldn't
wear shoes.
So let's just
make her barefoot.

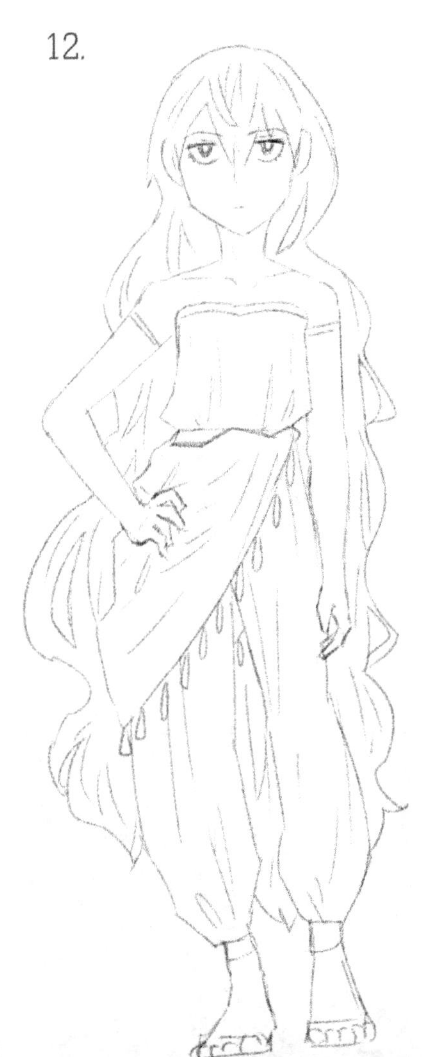

13.

Let's erase the
eye areas
that overlap the
hair.

Finish her
feet and
let's shade
everything!

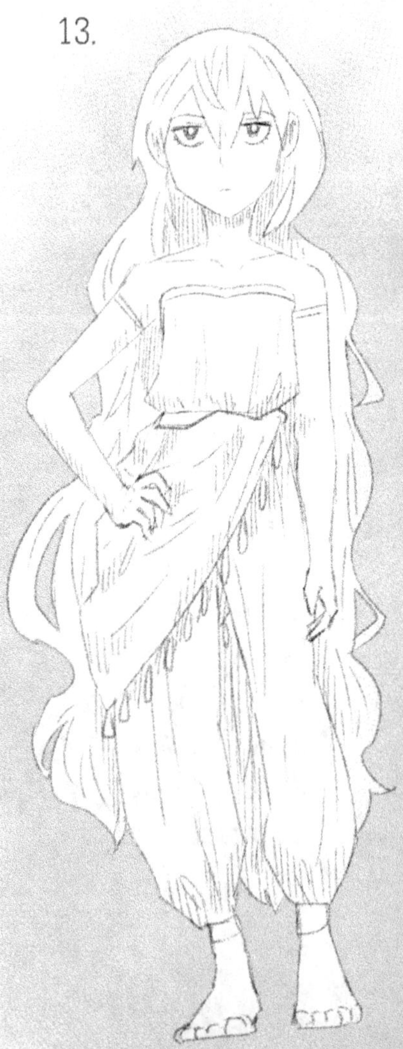

THE KEMONOMIMI

The kemonomimi is a charcter trope that involves characters with animal features, such as cat ears, dog tails, or even wings. These characters may be designed to be cute and playful, or may have a more serious or mystical appearance.

Draw the head.
Not the ears because
she'll have fox ears.

1.

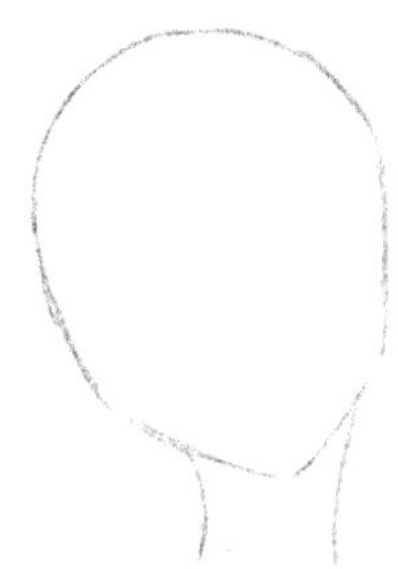

Then the face.

2.

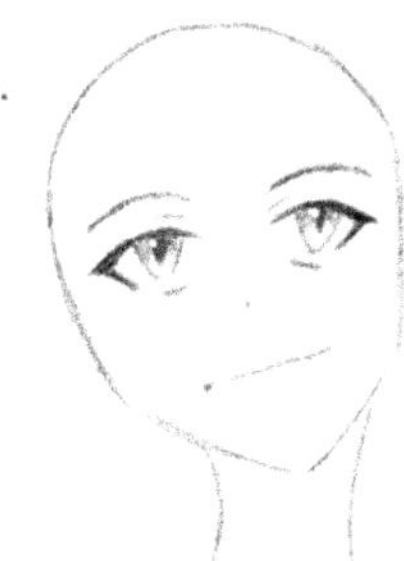

Then the shoulders.

3.

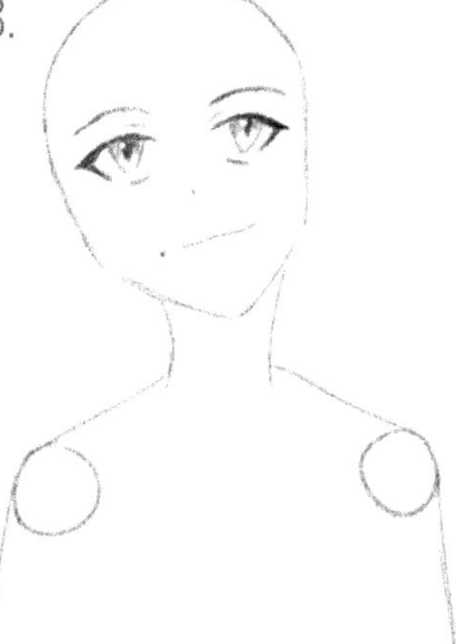

Let's have her cross
her arms.

4.

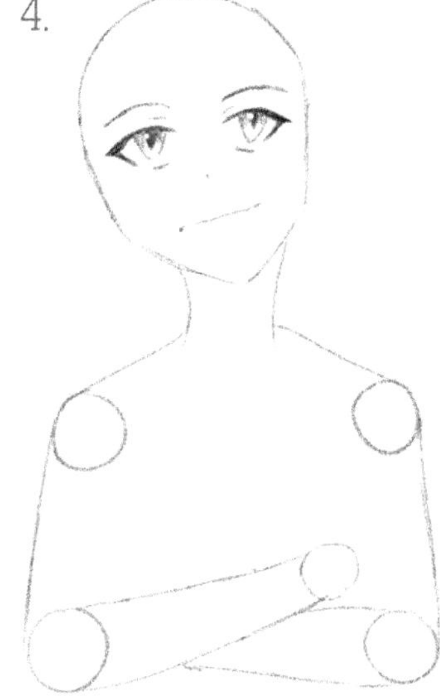

Finish her arms.

5.

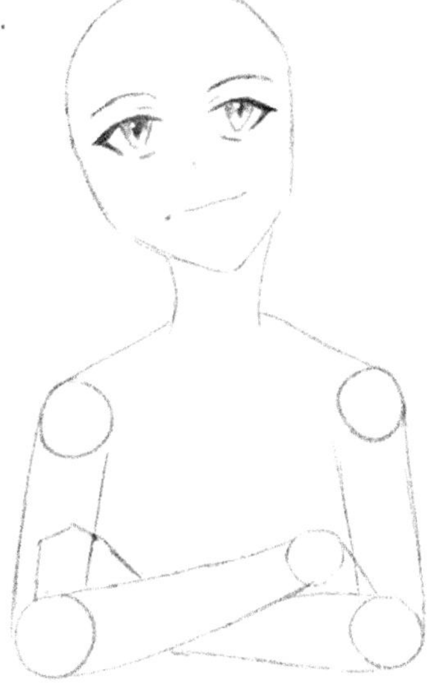

On to the hips.

6.

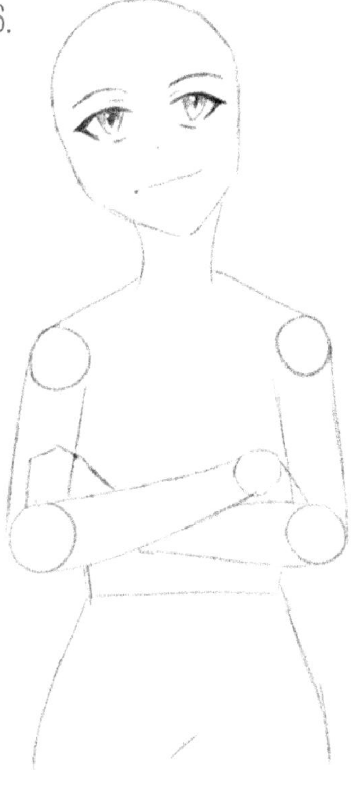

Let's draw the thighs.

7.

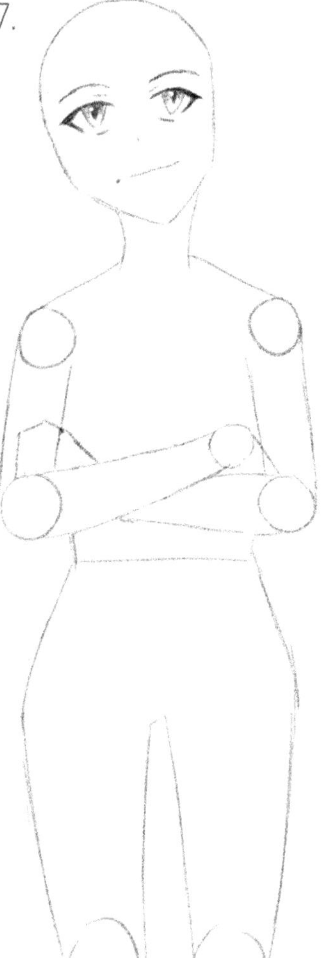

We've got to
finish the pose.

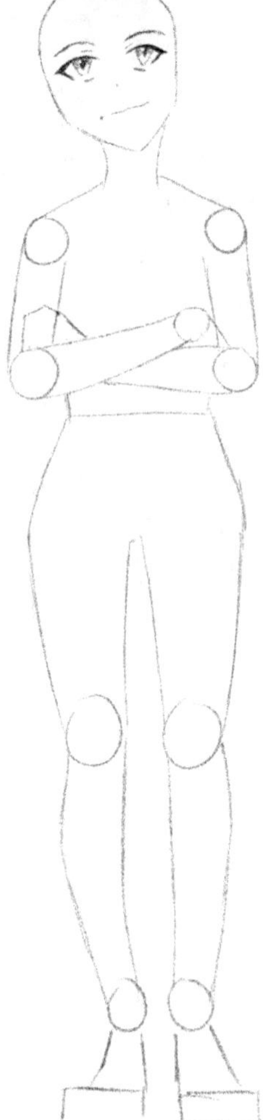

Now let's erase
all the joint guides.

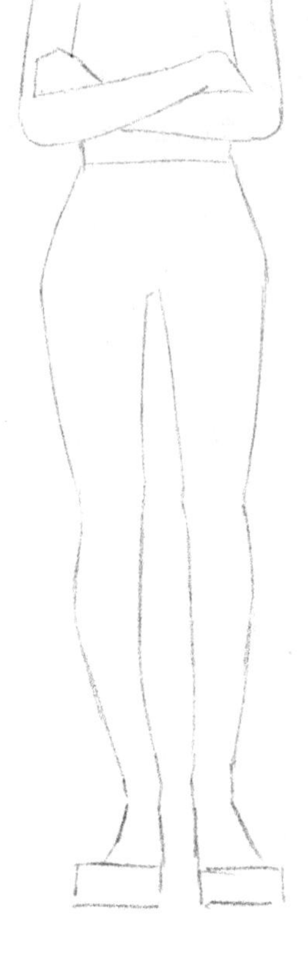

10.

When I think about
fox characters
I usually think
about fox shrines. So
let's put her
in a yukata (light kimono).
To match the atmosphere
of a shrine.

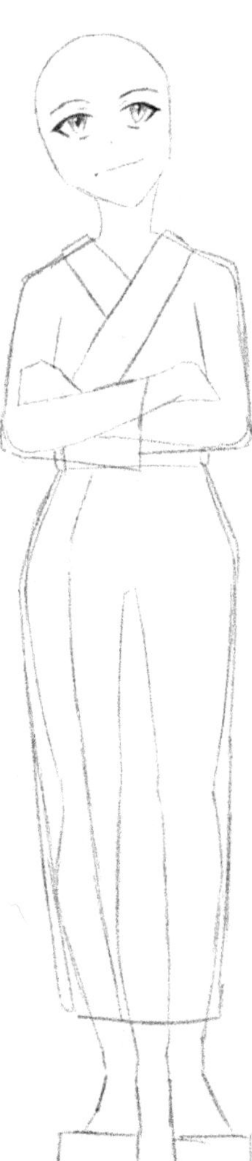

11.

First let's erase
what's under the
yukata. Then, draw the
bow in the
back of the yukata.
After that, the hair
outline, & finally
the ears!

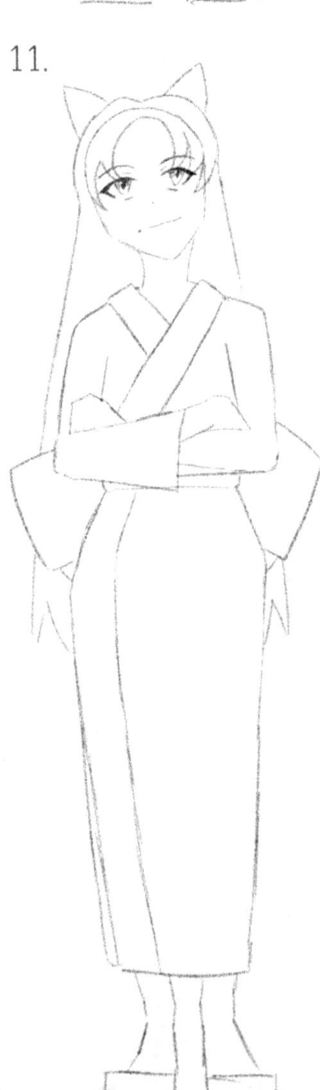

Now, let's
add details in
the ears & hair.

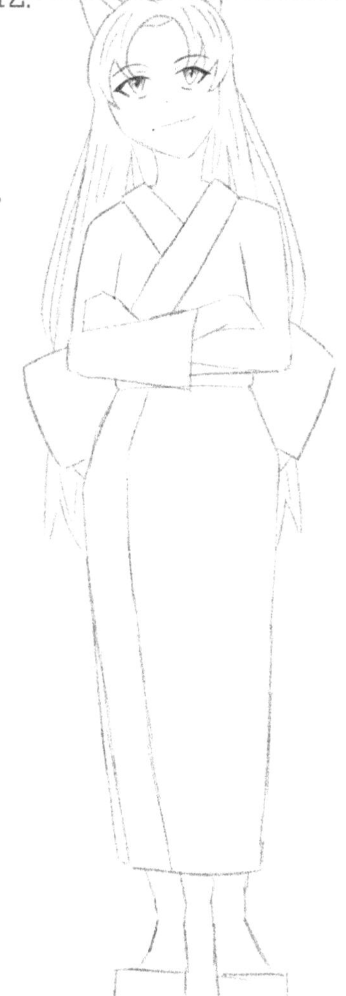

13

Draw some
wrinkles for
the yukata & bow.

I think she should
be in fancy
flip flops so
let's draw her
bare feet.

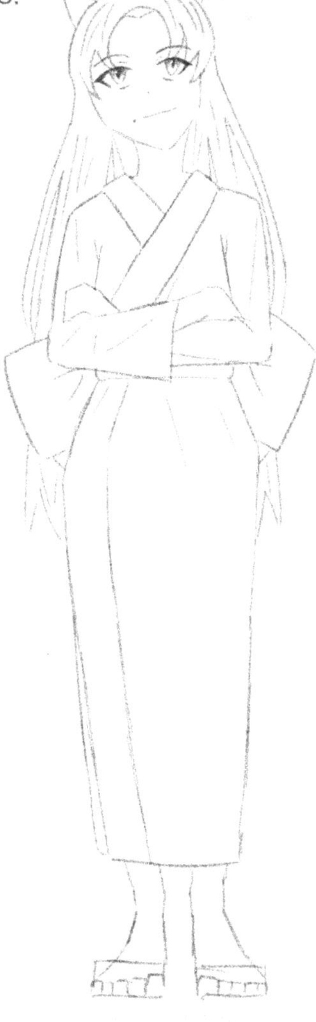

14.

I forgot to
erase the eye
areas that
overlapped the
hair. Let's do
that now.

Add in those
two lines in the
neck. It helps
give her a
slender look.

Let's add
in the flip
flops & I
also wanted
to add a little
extra for the
yukata. A simple
pattern.

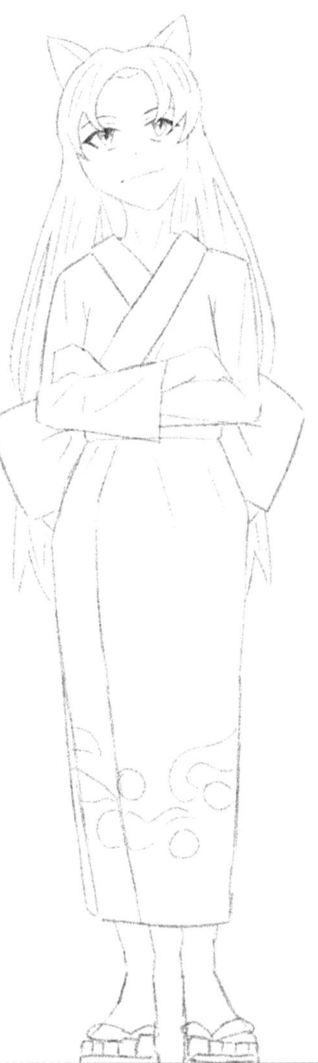

15.

Now erase
where the foot
overlaps the
flip flops.
Then, let's finish
drawing the hand.
Finally,
let's shade!

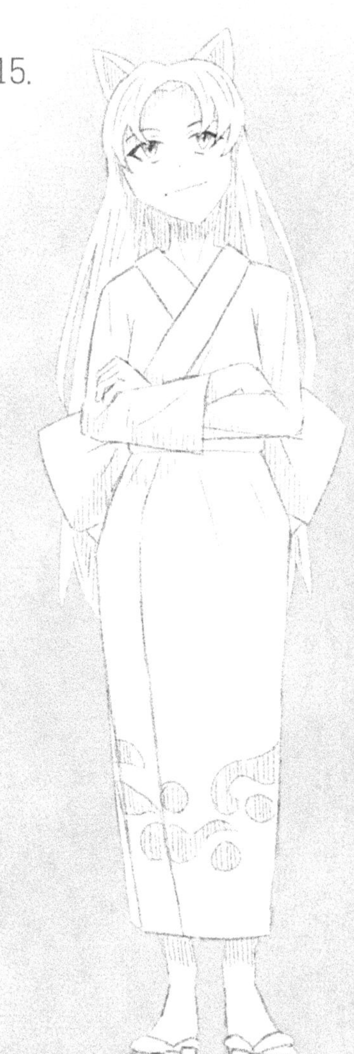

THE CHIBI-MOE

The chibi-moe is a character trope that involves characters that are simultaneously chibi and moe.
These characters may have exaggerated features, such as large eyes or oversized heads,
and may be designed to be ultra-cute and endearing.

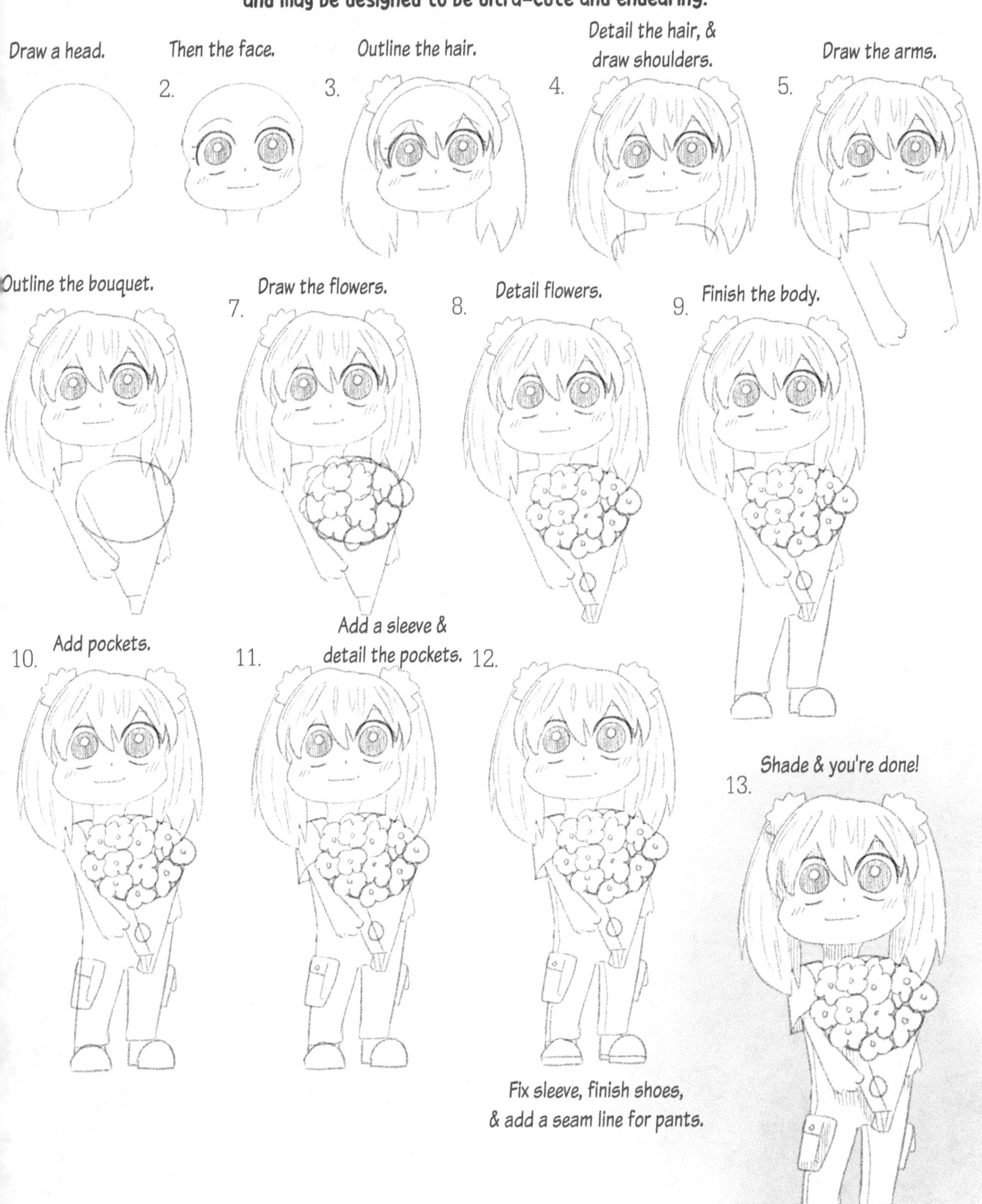

CONCLUSION:

WHAT YOU HAVE LEARNED:

-Drawing eyes like a champ!
-Heads, noses, & mouths: too easy For you!
-Hair: not even worth mentioning.
-Emotions...
-Bodies: please, step aside.
-Dynamic poses: we can all still use some help, including me!
-Accessories & clothing: pretty good but First we need to see what Fashion is popular.
-Chibi: not as bad as we thought it'd be.
-Kawaii characters & stuff: we're okay but can probably use more practice.
-Character tropes: you're so good at this. You're already making new tropes!

Any style is beautiful in its own way. IF you have a Favorite, definitly try and master it!
We've covered the anime style, kawaii style, and the chibi style.
Which was your Favorite?

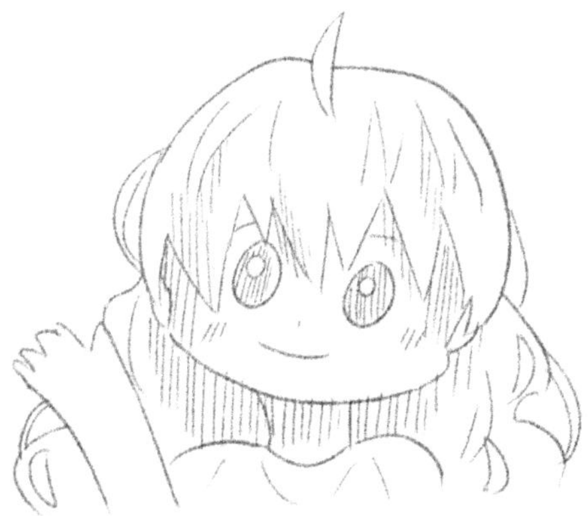

I encourage you to keep going and creating!
I know you have great and new ideas and the world would love to see them!
It may seem hard and scary with so many other people who might seem better, but
don't worry, your art journey has just started!
You will surpass them, trust me!
Keep moving forward and keep experimenting with styles!
But when you become famous, please give this book a shout for helping you. Hehe.

Anyway, good luck, artist!

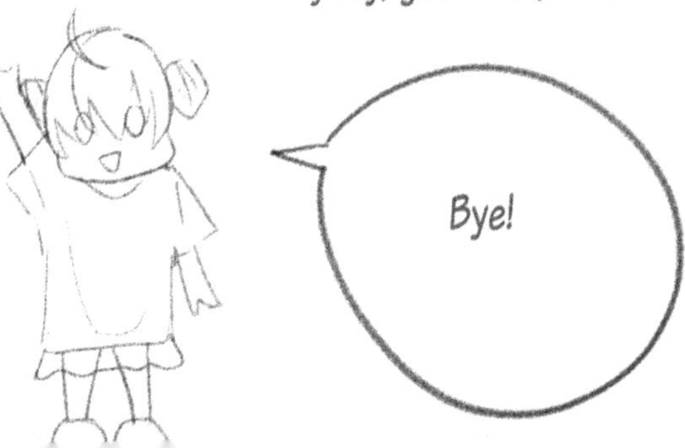

www.ingramcontent.com/pod-product-compliance
Lightning Source LLC
Chambersburg PA
CBHW080520030726
47592CB00012B/3417